D0669641

I AM THAT GIRL

ALEXIS JONES

I AM THAT GIRL

How to speak your truth, discover your purpose, and #bethatgirl

Copyright © 2014 by Alexis Jones

All rights reserved.

No part of this book may be reproduced, stored in a retrieval system, or transmitted by any means, electronic, mechanical, photocopying, recording, or otherwise, without written permission from the publisher.

The content of this book has been prepared for informational purposes only. Although anyone may find the ideas, concepts, practices, suggestions, recommendations, disciplines, and understandings presented in this book to be useful, the contents of this book are provided with the understanding that neither the author nor the publisher is engaged in providing any specific business advice to the reader. Nor is anything in this book intended to be a strategy or recommendation for any specific kind of business problem or business opportunity. Each person and business has unique needs, qualities, resources, abilities, and other attributes and this book cannot take these individual differences into account. Each person and business should engage a qualified professional to address his, her, or its unique situation.

Ten percent of the author's proceeds will go towards supporting I Am That Girl 501(c)(3).

I AM THAT GIRL: How to speak your truth, discover your purpose, and #bethatgirl

Published by Evolve Publishing, Inc.
www.evolvepublishing.com

Interior design by Ramsdell Design
Cover design by AVEC.US

978-0-9893222-8-7 paperback
978-0-9882245-7-5 ePUB
978-0-9893222-7-0 ePDF

Printed in the United States of America

10 9 8 7 6 5 4 3 2

For my mom, my dad, and Jane.

I am who I am because of you.
Thank you for giving me wings to fly.
I love you.

And to you my dear, reading this book,
and to all the girls I have met along this awesome journey.
I do what I do because of you.

CONTENTS

What do *you* want? What makes you happy? Write your own
constitution and start living by your own rules.

Are you compassionate with yourself? Practice making *you* a
priority in your own life.

How's your work ethic? Stop making excuses for not taking
steps toward your dreams and start making them come true.

CONTENTS

Do you dance to the beat of your own drum? Stop worrying so much about the naysayers and start surrounding yourself with people who support your dreams.

Dream big. Then even (especially!) when everyone else thinks it can't be done, put on your big girl boots and do it anyway.

Do you give up after the first sign of failure or rejection? Practice your rebounding skills and learn how to get up when you're knocked down.

Learn all you can from the awesome chicks (and dudes) who have come before you. Track down a mentor and soak up their knowledge.

Love yourself, live your purpose, and share your gifts.

FOREWORD

My dear friend, my soul sister, girl-who-can-finish-my-sentences-before-I-do Alexis Jones called me to ask me a question. Would I write the foreword to her book? I … uh … Would I what? What would I say? Where would I start? What was she possibly thinking? The swell of fear and self-doubt began almost instantly. I found myself saying "I'd be so honored" into the receiver while trying not to throw up all at the same time. She paid me some incredibly powerful compliments, telling me what a light I am in her life and in the lives of the girls I talk to every day. How much my passion and perspective mean to her and to my audience. What a fearless warrior for girls I am. I heard the words, but none of them could get past the force field of panic that had quickly enveloped me. Remember that movie *Bubble Boy*? I felt like that kid, trapped inside a plastic bubble. But my bubble was comprised of all of my innermost fears and deepest, secret insecurities. They were screaming things like, "I'm much better in the moment! How will I sit and write something without being inspired in the moment by a global issue, a twitter storm, or an injustice being done somewhere? I am terrible with a blank piece of paper. I need parameters. I need …" And in that moment I started laughing. It was slow, and then it got weird. Because

I was laughing hysterically, all alone in my house, with my dogs looking up at me like I was going crazy.

Want to know why I laughed? Because I realized I was smack in the middle of my own global issue. Girl-on-girl hate is a pandemic. And in this case, it was my inner critic hating on me. The screaming doubts. The shame spiral of inadequacy. Those things were all coming from inside myself. And I remembered something my friend Jo likes to say whenever any of her friends are criticizing themselves. "Hey. That's my best friend you're talking about like that." It's amazing to see girls react to that statement. Yeah, you're saying some truly negative things about my best friend. That friend just happens to be *you*. Why don't we love ourselves the way we love our friends, ladies? Because I know I'd die for my best friends. I'd run into a burning building, stand up to the most frightening opponent, and push myself harder and farther than I thought I could possibly go for any of you. So why not for me?

There are plenty of theories out there about why this happens. How we are taught to self-shame by society. How we are pitted against each other in some imaginary competition that becomes more and more real as we play it. How we are simultaneously hyper-sexualized and demonized for our sexuality. How we are criticized for being too fat, too thin, too girly, too butch. We get put down an awful lot. And we not only take it, we dish it out. Well, guess what? That is done. *Done*. One more time ... shout it out with me ... D-O-N-E. Let's go ahead, throw in the towel, and go have a meal together instead, shall we?

Now, to get to my point, I actually need to take you all back a bit. Way back. To college. A little over a decade ago—a decade which, by the way, has gone by in a flash yet also feels like it's taken

100 years to pass—I was a student at the University of Southern California. I'd arrived at USC from an incredible, and incredibly tough, all girls' prep school called Westridge. I arrived at college outspoken, highly educated, sheltered, utterly confused, and completely open-minded. But not without judgment. Sorority girls? Stupid. Party animals. Never going to be my friends. Until I found out one of my favorite girls from my hometown happened to be in one, and she was still a philanthropic wunderkind and academic superstar. She encouraged me to look beyond the stereotypes. Were there party girls in some sororities who were only in college to get what some girls call an "MRS" degree? Sure. But why did that affect me? There were also many brilliant, motivated, cultured, and culturally varied girls, pursuing academia as well as full social calendars. What was so wrong with that?

I was swayed by ideas of large-scale study groups and resources including senior students being able to help you out with work. I was also swayed by the way that the houses felt similar to the school I'd come from. Big groups of cool girls, hanging out on the front lawns of their Greek houses the way I'd hung out on the Westridge quad. And, low and behold, I was a Greek system girl. It was at USC that I first became the philanthropy chair of my sorority house—a title I held for two years—and learned to give my hyper-motivated-all to causes. It was there that I learned how to balance being an honors student on an academic scholarship with weekends spent cheering on our sports teams, going to formals, and learning who I was away from the safety net of home. I made mistakes. I had immense successes. I had my heart broken—utterly shattered—but I also broke a few hearts as well. It was glorious, silly, inspiring, messy, motivating, childish, and oh-so-grown-up. It was real life because it was gray and fluid and ever-changing. I learned to let go of my judgments. I learned to accept myself—ALL of myself. The good, the bad, and the in-between. And, somewhere in the blur of love and joy and growing up at college, I met Alexis Jones. You might not think of Lex as a "sorority girl" either. Well, we're sorority sisters all right. And best friends. In a place that seems like it could be a cauldron of girl-on-girl bullying and backstabbing, I made a friend for life. I knew she was special then. She was magnetic. Motivated. Excited about everything. A truly shining light. And she still is all of those things.

We parted ways for a time. Pulled to opposite ends of the country and put on opposite schedules, we lost touch in the shuffle of it all. She was working on creating a buzz for this idea that she couldn't stop thinking about: How to make a serious impact on girls. And I was off chasing my dreams on my first long-term television gig, *One Tree Hill*. She was building a movement on the west coast, and I was finding my voice outside of work on the east coast, beginning to champion causes ranging from the environment to education. Many of the conversations I found myself having were with young women. And then something exciting happened. Lex and I were looped into an email by a mutual friend who typed in her message to both of us, "I feel like you two should already be best friends by now." And how we laughed, because we were. Suddenly we were right back where we'd started, but now we were grown-ups. Now we were tackling the dreams and problems we'd sat up thinking about years prior in our twin beds after classes in college. Now we were truly living our dreams. We felt like fully formed adults. And we got to do it together. We still do. I am beyond lucky to have her in my life. I think we all are, ladies.

Lex has always been one of the girls who stood up for others. And she has hit the nail on the head by calling us all out about a major issue. We need to stand up for each other and for ourselves too. Ladies, we need to collaborate, not compete. We need to champion each other, send out high-fives across the World Wide Web, and give high-fives in person. We need to rally around one another in times of joy and times of sadness. This may be the age of faceless Internet monsters calling us names, but we can be the change. We can say no to all of that. And we can start a movement in our own backyards. We can be the ones who say "No thank you" to gossip and "Yes please" to friendships. When we start to praise girls around us, when they score the highest grade in class on a test, when they land incredible jobs, when they have beautiful families—whatever!—we start lifting up those girls and ourselves. When we reach out in tough times, when someone has lost in love, failed an exam, missed out on an opportunity they'd been dreaming of—any of it—we show that girls can be each other's backbones rather than the source of one another's pain.

That's what this book is all about—starting a movement with friends and strangers alike. Lex is setting a tone for us. She is reminding us that we can lay down the armor we wear and embrace rather than battle. We can each be THAT girl. The awesome one who lends an ear or a hand in times of need. The one who is so inspiring that she makes us want to be better. The one who is so vulnerable and honest about her feelings that she motivates us to look inward at who we really are, what we really want, and what we are afraid of. We ARE each that girl, if only we allow ourselves to be. Because, let's face it ladies, we are all afraid. We are all confident. We are all warriors on this road of life, and we're all a mess sometimes. Girls are multifaceted, complicated, layered, and emotional beings. So who better to understand us than other girls? Let's be the friends and sisters we deserve. That's what I wish for you. For me. For all of us. That we can be friends to the girls we know and the ones we don't. That we stop judging other girls. For everything. We should support the stay-at-home moms as much as we cheer the working moms.

We need to show support for the girls who are just like us and the ones who couldn't be more different from us. We have so much to learn from each other, so much to gain from one another's perspectives, and so much love to share. We should wish the best for each other—always. Let me say that again. Always, ladies, always! No more judging. No more gossiping. And no more looking in the mirror and being mean to that girl. Treat everyone, including yourself, like they could be your best friend. Yes, with that much kindness.

There is a term in Gaelic that seems to fit this wish. It's *Anam Cara*. It means "soul friend." In Celtic tradition, an Anam Cara is a teacher, companion, or spiritual guide. With the Anam Cara, you can share your innermost self to reveal the hidden intimacies of your life, your mind, and your heart. This friendship cuts across all convention to create an act of recognition and belonging that joins souls in an ancient and eternal way. What a term. What an *idea*! You hear that? A soul friend. Let's be soul friends, ladies. We deserve it. YOU deserve it.

Sophia Bush

INTRODUCTION

I am only one intro away from completing this book, and the blank cursor on my computer screen continues to mock me. I've typed and deleted more drafts than I care to admit, and in each one I find myself writing what I think you want to hear. The irony of that, right? I just wrote an entire book on how to find your own voice, how to not hang your confidence on the approval of others, and yet I find myself sitting here doing exactly that. But that's when it dawned on me; my intro is not going to be a fancy, pedantic pitch to impress you or persuade you to buy my book. And that's not what you want anyway, is it? I certainly am not a fan of fluff; I tend to be a "give it to me straight" kinda girl. So my intro, like me and like the rest of this book, is just going to be honest.

I wrote this book because I'm sick of it all. I'm tired of feeling inadequate, imperfect, desperate for approval, and chronically insecure. I'm exhausted from feeling like I'm always falling behind in some invisible race against the clock, against other women, and even against myself. It is a race I don't remember beginning, but one that I've decided to stop running. I decided, instead, to learn how to be who I am and to understand that that itself is more than enough, it's extraordinary. When I started on this journey I

quickly learned that I wasn't the only girl seeking external validation instead of authentic confidence and mere attention instead
of unconditional love.

So several years ago I decided to start a nonprofit whose sole
mission is to remind girls of their innate and immeasurable self-
worth. I named it I AM THAT GIRL and since then my best friend/
cofounder and I have traveled the world talking to, listening to,
and sharing our stories with girls from a stunning range of backgrounds and experiences. I was often shocked and always moved
by what I heard from these girls. But maybe most surprising of
all is that on my journey to ambitiously "change the world," it
was *my* world that needed the most changing. There's always an
ironic and humbling moment when the "teacher" realizes that
she has as much to learn from her students as they do from her.
I realized through this crazy adventure that we are all so much
more alike than we even know. Maybe our demons are different,
our challenges have different names, and our adversity wears different masks, but the fact that we ALL have them is the common
thread that ties us together and makes us human.

I decided to write this book to reach even more girls like us
and share what I've learned on my journey, what's worked for
me, what mistakes I've made, what fights are not worth fighting,
and which ones are worth your life. I'm here to tell you that none
of us have it all figured out; we are forever works in progress.
The moments of brilliance in your life will always be balanced by
moments of vulnerability, insecurity, and doubt. The sooner you
get around to being okay with that, the happier your life will be.

I know that's hard. I moved home a while ago to be with my
father who was battling cancer and during that heartbreaking
time my dad reminded me of one of life's most profound lessons.

He told me that it's important to learn how to accept and appreciate yourself for your shortcomings just as much as for your strengths because they will forever coexist. To invalidate part of who you are, to cast it out as "imperfect" and pretend it's not an integral part of you, means you will never fully know or love you. That's been my goal in writing this book—to help you, to release yourself from whatever is holding you back. To help you turn off the voice that convinces you that you're not enough and detach your mind and your actions from the part of you that wants to get it perfect instead of perfectly right *for you*.

That said, if you want a how-to guide on "fixing" you, I'm not your girl and this isn't your book. I don't think you need to be fixed. This isn't some self-help book where I'm going to promise that rainbows and puppies will replace your cloudy days or help you get your dream guy, dream body, or dream job. I'm not going to convince you that something is wrong with you, and then try to sell you "*my* patented formula" to cure it. And even if I could wave a magic wand and make all your problems go away, I wouldn't. Because living a "perfect" life is like watching television in black and white: you take out all the color. We need the adventure, all of the highs and lows, the unexpected heartbreaks, the ecstasy, the challenges, and the sweet, smooth sailing. Life is not about picking out the parts you like and leaving the rest, it's learning to coexist with it all and choosing to see the beauty, the grace, and the hilarity while also experiencing the inevitable disappointment and failure.

When I sat down to write this book I asked more than thirty girls, some of my favorite humans, to candidly contribute stories from their personal life experiences, and I wove them into these pages. I got advice on love, heartbreaks, failures, and successes. I asked them to share stories about discovering their passion, on reinvention, balancing work and play, and bouncing back. Then, I locked myself in a room for months, opened up my heart, and poured out my own thoughts and advice. This book, much like us, is an imperfect collage of tips sprinkled with wisdom, inspiration, and a little practical advice reminding you that you are awesome exactly as you are, that your dreams are possible, and when you shine the brightest you make the world and those around you better. I hope that within these pages, kernels of truth speak to your soul and add shimmer to your life. This book is a reminder that you matter, that what you think is important, what you say is powerful, and who you choose to be is sacred.

You already are *that girl*, my dear. Everything you're looking for exists right there, inside of you. Discovering and then reminding yourself exactly who you are is but one of many ways this book will help you kick off your cement shoes and fly. Somewhere along the way we girls forgot just how exquisite we are and how to help each other live our magnificent and unique lives. We forgot that we are on the same team and instead started being mean to each other and breaking each other down. Worse, we started being mean to ourselves. Fortunately, this is simply some bad programming, a virus per se, but I have seen in others and experienced for myself that we have the power to update our software.

If ever there were a time for our generation to step up to the plate, to carry the torch of the women who came before us, to wreak havoc, to ask ourselves, "Why not us?" it's now. Our generation is criticized for being the most entitled in history. I think that's the greatest problem we could possibly have because that means we are a generation of girls who actually think we can change the world. But before we get too big for our britches (as my Texas father would say), we have to humbly recognize Gandhi's powerful advice—we can't just talk about it, tweet about it, or post it on one of our many social media outlets, we have to *be* it. This book is my attempt to inspire *that girl* in you: the girl who has the potential to create magic, to ignite change, and to inspire the world.

I've dedicated my life to reminding *you*, the girl holding this book right now, that you are more than enough, that you are cherished beyond measure, and that your worth is, in fact, i-n-n-a-t-e and i-m-m-e-a-s-u-r-a-b-l-e. Don't forget it! While we're faced with some of the world's greatest challenges, I believe that we are also our world's greatest solutions. In fact, I think you and I are the secret weapon.

There will be a time in history when the world recalls this moment, the moment that a generation of girls stepped up to the plate, believed in themselves, took a leap of faith, and the world was never the same again. This is our chance, so in the midst of all the craziness in your own world, take the time to read on and then pass on what you've learned. Can you imagine what the world would look like with an entire army of girls who truly love themselves, and each other?! What would be possible then? Two words come to mind: *GAME ON*.

THAT GIRL MANIFESTO

I am enough. I have enough. I do enough.

I am me. Every day.
Not who I think others expect me to be,
But the real, unedited, beauty-full, perfectly flawed version.
I choose to think for myself.
I speak my truth
And wrestle with life's tough questions over and over again.
I daydream about a better world and strive to make it my reality.

My purpose drives me
And I give it the freedom to change and evolve.
I breathe life to my dreams and to the dreams of others.
I believe in magic. I look for it everywhere.
I make an adventure of ordinary things.
Create, imagine, reinvent, and get lost.

I do things that inspire me.
I defy the odds, raise my hand, sit at the table and lean in.
I refuse to give up.
I pursue my passion at all costs. I do things that terrify me.
My head dances among the stars, and my feet remain on mother
    earth.

I'm willing to ask the hard questions, to take chances, to love
with my whole heart.
My mistakes and failures make me stronger.
I do not ascribe my worth to external validation, but to my
character.

I surround myself with phenomenal people,
Especially ones who don't always agree with me.
I choose authenticity over perfection.
I appreciate the small details that tend to go unnoticed by
others.
My worth is innate and immeasurable. I try to remind myself of
that, daily.

I exercise patience as often as possible,
Stay vulnerable even when I want to close my heart
And practice coexisting with things that make me
uncomfortable.
I set boundaries, work to honor them,
And am willing to edit people out of my life who don't.

I walk more than a mile in other people's shoes,
And suspend judgment as long as humanly possible.
I remember to laugh more, stress less, forgive often, and inject
love everywhere I can.

I do my best to relinquish every ounce of control because it's
futile.
I throw my hands up, close my eyes, and
Revel in life's awesome and mysterious ride.
My emotions are fleeting, they do not define me.
My choices do, and I do my best to make good ones.

I feed my body good, whole foods,
But don't punish myself for the occasional indulgence.

I move my body every day. I stretch, challenge, and honor her.
I rest when I need to.

I don't accept every invitation that comes my way.
I practice saying "no."
Show myself kindness, compassion, and unconditional love.
I am my best friend, I'm proud of me.

I share my life's lessons with others, even the not so shiny ones.
I hold nothing back. Cry when I need to,
But also recognize when I need to buck up.
I remember to breathe and in that space, I find my calm among
the chaos.
I owe it to myself to be remarkable, so I am.

GEARING UP FOR TAKEOFF

Do you or do you not want an awesome life? Well before you can take the leap into authoring your awesome adventure, you're going to have to prepare yourself for the journey. In part I of this book we'll chat about the importance of grounding and listening to yourself in a world full of endless distractions. We'll talk about how establishing good habits and a personal constitution will provide a solid foundation you'll rely on in high times as well as when you're full-on freaking out, confused, conflicted, or generally untethered.

In chapter 1 we'll talk about how to find your soul's true passion and why that's step one to this awesome life you want so bad. In chapter 2 I'll introduce you to the good kind of selfish and how to put your needs first in a way that allows you to be even more effective in helping others without slighting your dreams and goals. Chapter 3 is all about avoiding the excuses we all make that, whether we know it or not, hold us back from living a powerful life built on a foundation of honesty and integrity. Last, in chapter 4 we'll talk all about the inevitable challenges you'll face on your dream-seeking journey, how to live the life that is right for *you*, and why you need to surround yourself with an awesome crew of people who will support and love you through it all.

Basically, part I is about gearing up, getting ready, and preparing for battle. This is where the important, hard work happens, where you find out all the things you'll need to live the kind of life you want and give your best day in and day out. So, put your game face on, my dear, because the next few chapters are not for the faint of heart.

In short, GAME ON.

CHAPTER 1

BE A PASSIONISTA

*"Every great dream begins with a dreamer.
Always remember, you have within you the
strength, the patience, and the passion to
reach for the stars to change the world."*

—Harriet Tubman

I was a sophomore in college, living in sunny Los Angeles, attending my dream school. I had everything the world taught me to value and yet I still hungered for something more, something I couldn't put my finger on. I heard other people talk about their lives and their passions with such conviction, and I knew I didn't have that "thing" that lit me up from within. I didn't have a purpose that ignited my soul and got me out of bed *before* my alarm clock because I was bursting with ideas. I desperately wanted to feel more alive.

Then one day, my roommate (who was deeply passionate about acting) came home raving about a new play by Eve Ensler called *The Vagina Monologues*. She had the script and was practicing for her big audition. When she told me the play was about women's rights and highlighted the atrocities going on with women around the world, my ears perked up; I'm still not sure why. This play was about the farthest thing from what I would normally be interested in.

Two days later I saw posters on campus for *The Vagina Monologues*. The next day I was randomly introduced to the director on my way to class. You know those times in life where it feels like something is banging at your door and it becomes so loud that you can't drown it out any longer? This was that moment. As I sat there talking to the director, I said, "So I've heard a lot about your play" (kind of jokingly because little did she know this play was flat-out stalking me). She responded, "Oh lovely, so are you coming to the audition tonight?"

Naturally with no acting experience, I laughed and quickly replied, "Oh, um … I'm not an actor." As though she were prepared for this, she quickly responded, "I didn't ask if you could act, I asked if you were going to audition for my play?"

As luck would have it, my night class that would have interfered was canceled, so technically I *was* available to audition. However, the idea of stepping outside my comfort zone made me instantly nauseous.

Looking back, I realize the only reason I showed up to the audition was because I was too much of a pansy to say no to her face. Call it peer pressure, or intimidation, but either way, a few hours later, I found myself in a room, holding a piece of paper with several monologues on it, wondering how the hell this conservative, Texas tomboy was going to audition for a freakin' feminist play with the word *vagina* in the title?

Before I knew it (and before my insecurity had a chance to bustle me out the door) they called my name. As soon as the director spotted me, I knew there was no way I was getting out of it. I had only a few moments to nervously glance at the monologues—I had spent the last fifteen minutes trying to come up with a good reason to leave. But it wasn't until I starting walking toward the front of the room that I could hear my heartbeat coming out of my chest. Pure panic.

At that moment I asked myself, "What the hell have you gotten yourself into Lex? And *now* what are you going to do?"

I sat down in front of the few people whose job it was to critique my every move. Resigned to the fact that I might as well get this torture over with as quickly as possible, I began reading the monologue entitled, "My Only Daughter."

I had no idea how to deliver a monologue, so I just began to read. I couldn't hear the words coming out of my mouth, and when I finished I simply stood up to leave. That's when I heard the director say, "Can you do it again, Alexis?" Are you kidding me? At this point I was in agony. Every second I stayed in this room, competing with girls who had years of experience and actually knew what they were doing, was causing me physical pain. "But this time, when you're reading," she continued, "envision what is going on. It's an Iranian father talking about his only daughter. She has been brutally burned with acid and she and he both know that life, as they know it, is over. You have a father, so imagine what that would be like in a culture that has not only shamed you, but your entire family as well. Now, please, read it again."

No pressure. I take a deep breath and begin again, only this time, I envision my father, how much he loves me, and how his whole world would simply come crashing down if anything ever happened to me. In seconds, my voice is cracking as I try my best to get through the text. I look up moments later, horrified that I now have streams of tears rolling down my cheeks, which apparently invited my mascara to take a ride with them.

I wiped the black streaks with the back of my hands and rubbed the mess on my jeans. If I thought I was embarrassed before, nothing compared to this—sitting in silence staring down at my sneakers, wishing I could crawl in a hole. With four older brothers, I grew up learning that "crying is for girls," a weakness that would earn you the dreaded label, "cry *baby*." I'm the girl who doesn't cry. I'm the girl who, even when she falls or gets teased on the playground, does not cry.

And worse, it was a drive-by cry attack. You ever been there? When a cry sneaks up on you altogether? The thirty seconds that I sat fiddling with my nails, feeling like my tough girl mask had been torn off, still unwilling to look up, felt like a hundred years. I finally stood up and began to walk out because that's what embarrassed people do. We just awkwardly bolt for the door because, since sticking our head in the ground isn't an actual option, fleeing the scene is a good second.

Three feet from the door I heard my name again, "Alexis." I stopped, closed my eyes, and prayed to God that this whole thing would just end already. Without turning around, I heard, "You're cast. We'll see you next Monday for rehearsals."

On the walk home that day I had one of the most confusing internal conversations I have ever had. To this day I can't fully explain how, but my life, on that Tuesday night in a plain old theater classroom on campus, changed forever.

TAKING THE FIRST STEP TOWARD YOUR PASSION

Despite my stage fright, I went on to perform *The Vagina Monologues* in front of not only an entire audience, but also my parents and my four older brothers who had all flown in for the occasion. My father cried as I recited the monologue I read during my audition. My brothers' faces were frozen with shock and emotion.

These five men sitting side by side in the front row were white as ghosts as they took in the reality that so many fathers and brothers have experienced, the horror I was simply recounting on stage. My mother, though similarly affected, had a powerful and regal expression that indicated her pride and the importance of my sharing this girl's story. They all could see that something had changed in me, that a bonfire had ignited in my soul and my passion-filled eyes were foreshadowing my adventure to come.

I took a Polaroid picture of my passion that day. I realized as I stood on stage that my passion for storytelling, for entertaining, and for public speaking would become my destiny. I knew that I had a gift, a raw talent that was God given. I knew I could spend the rest of my life developing and using my voice to inspire people, to educate them, to entertain them, and to love them back to life. I didn't know exactly how I was going to go about doing that, but I knew that more would be revealed.

Clues to your passion are always around you. The sequence of events that led me to that stage began when I least expected it, but I was on the lookout for something more, something meaningful in my life. And even then I had to battle my natural instincts to experience it. You'll only find your passion if you search and fight to discover it.

For most people you have to get out there in the world, do things that scare you (whether it's auditioning for a play, taking a new class, or tagging along on a friend's adventure). You have to trust that if you try enough things that something will hit home, and like a fire truck siren in your heart, you'll know.

Right about now you might be thinking what I hear frequently, "Good for you. You found yours. But I don't know what I'm passionate about." So, how *do* you find your passion? First I'll ask you the simple (and according to my mother, inappropriate and unladylike) question, "What pisses you off?" I mean it. What really gets you riled up, so angry you could punch a wall, or so upset you cry right there on the spot? Because somewhere in all that emotion can often be a clue as to what makes you tick.

However, passion is not always associated with an injustice that infuriates you. For many, discovering their passion is what brings them the most amount of bliss and serenity, and often it even seems effortless. For me, writing and speaking are my super powers, the things that light me up from within, and how I choose to exercise and share them is my choice. Whether it's opening up your lungs and singing your head off or sharing *your* unique gifts with the world, our passions come in all shapes and sizes, but it's impossible to live at the brink of your greatness if you do not take the time to discover it.

Finding your passion is surely not as simple as making a list of possibilities and picking one. As you can see, I stumbled very unwittingly into finding my passion. But I would never have found it if I hadn't been on the lookout and open to trying something new. The journey to finding your passion begins with some simple changes. Think about what makes you angry or blissful or what you do that makes you lose track of time. Scribble words, phrases, or even doodles on a piece of paper and see what jumps out at you. Then start there. This is a process, not a single act. Curiosity or even peer pressure might get you to try something new, and who knows where that will take you.

One of the greatest life lessons I learned along my humble journey was that I had as much to learn from people as I had to teach them. Throughout the book, I've sprinkled some stories from my wisdom-teachers, my dearest friends, and my favorite people. Jackie is the best way to kick off the stories because she might be the best entertainer and funniest human I've ever met.

JACKIE TOHN (Singer, Songwriter, Actor, Comedian): I started acting professionally when I was nine. Not because anyone made me, but because I wanted to. I had to, really. There was nothing else that could keep my busy little ADD mind occupied other than singing, dancing, and making up voices and characters. I would put on shows for anyone who wanted to listen and some who didn't. At that age, I wasn't often impressive, but my parents heard and supported me just the same. When one day I switched gears and said I wanted to be a painter, the next minute we were at the art store buying an easel, paint, brushes, canvas, and making it happen.

Years later, at eighteen, with love in my heart and support all around me, I moved from New York to California to pursue my dreams of entertainment. Los Angeles is a big competitive city. Where I was once the big fish in a small pond, I was now a moderately sized fish in an enormous body of water filled with so many hot, funny, and talented people. This place was riddled with hotness.

Support from home only goes so far when you find out all the roles you're reading for are the "quirky friend" or the "weird one." Casting people would say, "We know Jackie. She's not model pretty and her voice is very … um … specific." Uh, thank you? I was beyond grateful to have had these opportunities, but I'm still a girl. I still look in the mirror and wonder why she looks like that and I look like this. I still have days where the bags under my eyes are seemingly packable. But because I was blessed with such a strong foundation, I try not to let what gets me down *keep* me down.

Eventually, after spending the past fourteen years of my life acting, I wanted to take a stab at my other passion: being a guitar- and ukulele-toting singer/songwriter. Enter: Top 24, *American Idol* Season 8. This was an absolute game changer. What a dream. Then I was eliminated. Not as much of a dream. I didn't make the tour because I wasn't in the top ten, but I held my head high and capitalized on this amazing opportunity in any way I could.

A few short weeks after my elimination, I did, in fact, go on tour. By myself. I booked it. I planned it. I figured it out. I wasn't about to let the fact that I didn't make the official tour keep me from *my own* tour. I had songs to sing and stories to tell. And the stage in my mind and living room wasn't cutting it.

Something happens as you get a little older (and maybe a teeny tiny bit wiser) and you realize that you have to do it on your own. No one will work as hard for you as *you* will. It's scary to admit to yourself. But if inside your guts and bones, you feel you have something to offer, don't let self-doubt keep your magic from the rest of us. We want in.

It wasn't easy, but I took my own advice. It was thirteen years in the making but I finally wrote, produced, and starred, Off-Broadway, in my one-woman show entitled *There's a Show in Here*. It was one of the most exciting and validating experiences of my entire life. I did it.

In the same way that some people are born with an innate sense of math or science, I am wired to entertain. And there is something mighty inside me that yearns for the stage. The amazing part is that everywhere and everything *is* a stage. And I don't believe in hiding my mighty.

Now you show me yours.

I know that asking yourself the hard questions isn't easy, and putting yourself out there is not always a natural impulse. As Jackie's story shows, it takes energy and courage to get back up when you fall. It's far easier to sail along on the peaceful waters of life, never facing any storms, never rocking the boat. Sorry ladies, but that's not living! Please don't spend your days finding the least disruptive way to go through life. That may bring you comfort at first, but I promise you'll eventually get bored and begin to feel stuck or even purposeless.

MAGGIE HA (Creative Director): Passion. It's certainly something that I feel has changed many times over in my life. But in some way I always knew I was going to do something creative. As each year went by, I started to really define what that was. And I started making a bucket list of things I wanted to do. Not just for my career but things I wanted to accomplish in life. Things like: work for a magazine, write a children's book, live in New York, travel to every continent, make a movie, bungee jump, always keep painting, learn to play the guitar, learn French, etc. Being a designer was a career goal that solidified at some point in high school. I wanted to work in music, so I did. I wanted to work in advertising, so I did. I wanted to create online experiences, so I did. Every time I come across something I want to do, I set my eye on the prize and I go for it. But I seem to keep wanting more.

For the past few years, this goal has been harder to chase. Mostly because it keeps changing, shifting, and evolving before I can even get there. Recently, when I decided to focus on working in food, something stopped me from wanting to quit my job as a designer to go to culinary school. I didn't want to quit my job, I loved my job. So I started a food blog as a passion project and continued with my design career. Then I decided that fashion is my passion. But then what happens to food? What about my other passions like music and technology and all the other things I want to do?

It really didn't dawn on me until recently. I was invited to speak at an event for an in-house design team. I was told to talk about what I do and how I am inspired. In the process of writing the speech, I found myself frustrated that I have all these different passions and I can't seem to find a way to incorporate all of them. Do I have to? Maybe it's just not meant to be?

And then it hit me. What I do is simply create. My passion isn't so specific as designing branding for a website or experimenting on a dish or baking an elaborate cake or telling a story with imagery and music; it's the process of making it. I have always been so ambitious and determined, and I found that I have had blinders on for a while. Sometimes all you need is to take a step back.

My passion is to create things and share them with people. That's how I find joy in waking up every day to do what I do. It's because I surround myself with many different channels to create. I am constantly surprised by things around me, whether it's an object, an image, a song, or a person. What I love most about what I do is that I can draw inspiration from everything. It fuels my creativity.

My name is Maggie Ha. I am a creative consultant—I've been called a designer, a foodie, a storyteller, a techie, a branding girl, a fashion enthusiast, and a daydreamer. My passion is creating things, so for now I'll call myself a creator.

Like Maggie, your passion may not be easy to spot and wrapped in a neat bow. That's okay. There is no rule that says you can't have more than one passion or the kind of passion that brings you many different interests and takes you on many different adventures. It's not necessary to have a narrow focus in order to live a meaningful and passion-driven life. Don't be afraid to try new things—it is only important that you do something that fuels you.

Discovering how you can contribute to the world in a unique way makes you feel useful, inspired, and alive. It doesn't have to come in some pretty package or make sense to anyone else, just you. How many stories have you heard about people who "had it all," and before you know it they are checking into rehab for the third time? Having the trappings of success—fame, wealth, beauty—doesn't necessarily bring us true happiness or a sense of self-worth. Our life's mission is not to achieve the appearance of success or whatever version of success your parents, friends, or teachers want for you. Nor should you sit around and wait for someone to drop something wonderful into your lap. It is to discover that thing that makes you tick and then to spend a lifetime doing it. So fight to find it, to figure it out, to stumble upon it, and chase it down. When you do, your passion will shine so brightly through you that it's contagious.

TIME OUT! WHAT'S MY PASSION?

Agreed, finding your passion isn't simple. It's a journey. But there are a couple of things you can do right now to start on your path.

Step 1: Turn off everything. Your phone, your iPad, computer, music, and go sit somewhere quiet where you won't get interrupted. Our passion exists within us, but more often than not we are so distracted that we have a hard time hearing our heart's whisper when it's competing with the deafening distraction of our busy lives.

Step 2: Now, whether you like to journal or just close your eyes and pray or meditate, spend five uninterrupted minutes in complete, intentional silence. The hardest thing for most of us is to just *be*. It may feel awkward at first, but in this precious space you grant your soul permission to be heard and to really listen.

My greatest moments of inspiration, my life-changing epiphanies, always seem to occur in this place of quiet. Remember that your passion lies within, so take the time to be quiet enough to let your truth speak up.

Now let's back up for a second. I said that before I walked on stage that fateful day, I was on the lookout for my passion and that I felt that something was missing from my life. These feelings sprung from the one thing that you must, must, must have before you can hope to recognize your passion. And that's your own personal constitution.

WHAT ARE THE RULES OF *YOU*?

The other day I found myself transfixed by an old *Cinderella* movie poster I saw hanging in my childhood bedroom. This beloved story teaches little girls that if we wait long enough, if we are good and do our chores, that maybe, just maybe, a fairy godmother will swoop in and make all our dreams come true. With the swish of a wand (and the help of a few singing mice), our tattered clothes transform into a magnificent white ball gown, and in no time we're engaged to the ultimate prize, none other than Prince Charming.

No effort, no searching, just some waiting around, and then poof! We've fulfilled our destiny without lifting a finger and get to spend the rest of our lives as the Mrs. in a kingdom far, far away.

Okay, so I can see how this is tempting. Dream guy handed over on a silver platter, check. Enemies bowing at your feet, check. And you get a princess tiara to boot? Check, check. I'm not going to argue that a fairy godmother would not come in handy every once in a while. It sounds nice, but of course the reality is that few things in life come so easily. And even more importantly, have you noticed what's missing from this story? *You!*

Reading fairy tales and learning how to dream big and expect magic in your life is an awesome and important part of growing up. But when you're living a dream that isn't yours, it can turn into a nightmare. Maybe Cinderella would have preferred to move from the fireplace to a sweet apartment downtown? Maybe her life's ambition didn't involve marrying a stranger—maybe her Prince Charming isn't a prince at all!

Anything is possible for your life, that part is true. But whether we realize it or not, all those fairy tales we were raised on have made us a little lazy. Stop accepting the dreams of your parents, friends, and teachers as your own and start thinking about what it is *you* really want out of life. You may discover that you've had the same dream since you were a little kid—you do want to save the whales—but you may surprise yourself by discovering that a passion has been brewing inside of you that you simply hadn't made the time to notice.

"To live is to choose. But to choose well, you must know who you are and what you stand for, where you want to go, and why you want to get there."

—KOFI ANNAN

All I'm saying is maybe if you were asked, you didn't need saving after all, and even if you did, maybe you wanted to save yourself. This is your life, your dreams, your love story, and your greatest adventure. So what do *you* really want? Most of us don't ever get asked the question, much less take the time to ask ourselves. That's the real problem with so many fairy tales; you don't know what your Prince Charming is coming to save you from because you haven't taken the time to figure out what you want in the first place.

When you don't know what you want, all the options look good: whether it's college, a significant other, a career, or what you're going to order for dinner. Before you look at all the mind-numbing options, you have to ask yourself, what do *you* really want?

So the next step to discovering your passion is to think about what qualities and actions are important to you. What defines you and what will you and won't you tolerate in the people in your life. Use the manifesto on page xv for inspiration or come up with something completely different; it's up to you. Of course nothing is set in stone, and you may find that after a few months of thinking about it you need to adjust your manifesto. And naturally over the years your priorities and needs will surely change. That's great. What I'm suggesting is that you begin a practice of checking in with yourself, understanding what you value, and creating a personal compass that you can use to sail the rough waters ahead.

TIME OUT! MY PERSONAL CHECK-IN

No wonder Cinderella married the first guy she laid eyes on. It's much easier to take what's in front of you than to decide what you want and then go out and find it. As you move along your life's journey, every once in a while take the time to stop and ask yourself the hard questions so you can figure out what you actually want and what will make you happy. Get into the practice of getting to know yourself.

A few times a year, I sit down and examine my life. I ask where I've been, where I'm at, and where I want to be. I write down these questions in my journal and answer them as honestly as possible. While the questions are always being tweaked, my last check-in went something like this:

- What are you most proud of recently? What are you least proud of? What did you learn from your least proud moment, and what can you do to inspire more of what you were most proud of?

- Rate yourself from one to ten on the following attributes: humility, selflessness, kindness, compassion, patience, creativity, forgiveness, and passion. What areas need the most improvement? How can you put them into action? Schedule them into your calendar.

- List out your top priorities (ideally) in order.

- Where are you spending most of your time (I'll list what a typical week looks like)? Where are you spending most of your money (I'll print out three months of bank statements)? Do your priorities match your actions (because where you spend your time and money is a direct correlation to your *actual* priorities)?

- How do you feel in general? Physically, mentally, emotionally, spiritually? Do you feel deprived in any area, too focused on any area, or in need of serious attention in any area?

- What are your current personal and professional goals? Write them down, steps to accomplishing them, and schedule them into your calendar.

- What was the last kind act you did? Think of a new one and schedule it.

START STEERING YOUR OWN SHIP

When you were a baby, chances are your parents would never have guessed that you would turn out as you have today. Your personality, your favorite things, your quirks, talents, and even your smile is unique to you and you alone. And precisely because you have a combination of talents given only to you, your destiny will look like no one else's. Yet, if I asked you, what do you want out of life? I wouldn't be surprised if you said you really had no clue. That's understandable but now it's time to think about it.

From the beginning, most of us are trained to follow the rules, to learn and succeed in very specific ways, and not question how or what we're learning. But just because you may have grown up with your individuality on autopilot, it doesn't mean you can't take control of your own thoughts, your own feelings, and your own destiny. In fact, you'll find out (if you haven't already) that real life, the life you'll lead after you graduate high school or college, requires you to choose your own path and figure out how to travel on it. The magnificent, and sometimes scary, part about it is that this life is yours, not anyone else's.

So maybe you did or are doing great in school, and the chaos of real life is daunting. Maybe you aren't or didn't do so well in school, you love the freedom of the world outside, but don't have the tools to make it work. Maybe you weren't gifted with encouraging parents, friends, or mentors growing up. You're not alone. But regardless of your circumstances or the hand you were dealt, we have *no* excuse to not rock and roll in this lifetime.

No matter how you got here, what challenges you've had to overcome or are still dealing with, I promise that you can find your true heart and learn how to trust yourself. Now is the time to start steering your own ship, regardless of where other people think you should sail. Throughout this book we'll talk about lots of ways you can get the help you need to realize your dreams, from inside and outside of you. You'll learn how to gather a great team of cheerleaders, get back on your feet after a disappointment, and believe in yourself even when others don't.

MAHSHAD VAKILI ("The Cadillac of Gypsies"): I am a living, breathing, walking embodiment of the American Dream, and it is my right and my duty to fearlessly pursue my life's unique journey. You see, in their mid-thirties my parents picked up their lives and three children and fled a war-ravaged, revolution-torn country with nothing more than some clothes and a carryall of courage on their backs. They bled, sweat, and wept into the soil of this country for over twenty years, sacrificing their own comforts so that their children would have the opportunity to be and do something spectacular. And now, here I am, a lawyer, a music industry consultant, a makeup artist, a mixologist, and a continental bon vivant. The Cadillac of Gypsies, a bona fide bohème. Some people think I lack focus. I think they lack imagination. What drives me? Love and compassion.

Even as a little kid, people thought I was "different," and, by the way, I've always hated that word. I prefer *weird*, or *eccentric*, or even *freakish*. It's so much more interesting than *different.* Anyhow, I was always rifling through people's closets for costumes and theatrical props, speaking to my brothers (or sometimes no one) in a bricolage of foreign accents, etching masterpieces into the shiny new paint jobs of neighbors' cars (I got into a lot of trouble for that one), getting "pretty good" at seven different instruments, but never really mastering one. I've always marched to the beat of my own mercurial drum, and while my family didn't always know how to handle my idiosyncrasies, or even approve of my choices, I always knew that I was loved. Sometimes it was tough love from my dad, who also gave me a stubborn tenacity and penchant for rambling parley. Other times, it was the benevolent love of my mother, whose beatific kindness instilled in me a compassion that I proudly display toward even the most obnoxious driver ("What if he just lost his job/spouse/child?" I often think to myself, when confronted with inconsiderate road behavior). I've been surrounded by love for as long as I can remember, and I've learned that it is the most valuable currency of all, especially when you save up a personal reserve in a shatterproof piggybank.

Love helped me develop the confidence and the bravery to take some crazy serious chances—to shake the tree and try my hand at really *living.* Why stay in an objectively perfect marriage when you can have a precarious rock star fling? Why use the $100K and 3.5 years you spent on law school to actually practice law when you can build furniture in your backyard? We all trip and fall. We all have moments when we give more than we get. We all grieve and ache and lose. But there are a couple of lessons I always come back to, based on my unshakable belief in love and compassion, that help me to regain focus and follow my muse.

First, never forget how utterly unoriginal your suffering is. I know that sounds harsh, but it's a great way to remember that we're all in this together, and somewhere, someone else has already won this battle for me. In a way, acknowledging the banality of my trials and tribulations allows me to stay unique and true to my purpose and my passion. Second, find the silver lining. Always. There is one, I promise. There's a lesson to be learned, a joy to be derived, from every moment in our lives. Whenever I forget this, I dishonor the amazing sacrifice my family made to get here, wherever "here" may be at the time. Suffering is the path of least resistance, but it is so cliché. Happiness is the harder choice, trust me. But love and compassion, toward yourself above all, and in spades toward others, makes it effortless.

You can certainly get by in life—most people do—without a single original thought. But then you are left living out someone else's dream, someone else's destiny—chosen not by you but *for* you. Would you rather not live the life that Mahshad describes? One that she devised and lives with abandon, but also humility and gratitude. The problem is this kind of life takes work, and many of us choose the path of least resistance instead.

I see it all the time. I just flew home to Austin for the weekend to see my family and ran into some of my old friends. I immediately asked what they were up to and one of them really surprised me by saying, "Yeah I'm working for my dad now, you know, same old, same old."

What?! This is the guy who swore he would never conform, who was the life of the party, energetic, adventurous, and passionate to do something unique with his life. Sadly, only a few years out of college, he had already given up on all but his father's dreams for him. The more I asked about his old dreams, the more he shrugged his shoulders and said, "Well, what are you going to do about it? We all have to grow up sometime and that's life."

If that's what it means to grow up, then I prefer to be Peter Pan, because I'm not interested in that version of the story. I believe life is riveting and it only gets better with time. Life can be whatever we make of it. And while that certainly doesn't mean you have to travel the world or become rich and famous, you are selling yourself short if you think growing up means doing something that bores you. You are so much more valuable to everyone around you and to the world if you begin every day knowing exactly who you are and try to be the best, brightest version of yourself.

> **"You can only become truly accomplished at something you love. Don't make money your goal. Instead, pursue the things you love doing, and then do them so well that people can't take their eyes off you."**
>
> **—MAYA ANGELOU**

Destiny is synonymous with dreaming. And you truly can author your own life's adventure story. When you discover your passion, it's as though the world all of a sudden makes sense, colors get brighter, a part of you awakens, and quite frankly you'll never be the same again. If you don't know what you want, it's hard to know what you're passionate about. And never discovering your passion is a dull and hollow way to spend the gift of your life. As a friend's father liked to say about life, "This ain't no f-ing dress rehearsal." Maybe it was the shock of a parent cursing, but combined with a knowing smile, it resonated deep within me because Mr. Lack spoke the truth. This is, after all, *your* life, and you only get one shot, so it matters what you choose to do with it.

BUT, WHAT DO I SAY? WHEN SOMETHING COMES BETWEEN ME AND MY PASSION.

Sometimes discovering your passion isn't the biggest hurdle, it's living it. When you're faced with a roadblock on the way to your passion, take a step back and think about just why you want to do what you do and what it means to you. I first put this into action with my parents. During college I wanted to study abroad in Spain. It was a lifelong dream of mine, but my parents were not supportive. My pitch went something like this:

"Mom, I know that when I first brought up moving to Spain for the summer, it wasn't a big hit with you, and I want to bring it up again because it's a dream of mine and you didn't raise me to let obstacles or "no" get in the way of authoring my own life. Now I've thought a lot about it and I can understand that you've spent the past twenty years of my life doing everything in your power to protect me, that you've showered me with unconditional love and poured your heart and soul into me. I can imagine how scary it would be, the thought of me, on my own, halfway across the world where you can't protect me from every possible danger. But I'm also here to say, you've done an amazing job and you've taught me to make good, wise decisions with my life. I know I may seem young to you, but fortunately you raised a daughter to dream big, to stretch her wings, and to sign up for an extraordinary life. I know it's expensive, and scary, but I also know that I'm ready for this and I'm capable of taking really good care of myself. Traveling abroad may not make sense to you, but it makes sense to me. I don't expect you to understand every life decision I make or to agree with all my choices, but I do hope that you can be supportive of the things that are important to me, and this is one of them. I love you and I would never be reckless with my life or jeopardize the

lifetime you've spent protecting me. My wings are strong and I'm ready to use them. Please reconsider your original response to my summer immersion adventure. It would really mean the world to me."

You can imagine. With tears in her eyes, the only thing she could say was yes (even though to this day my dad wasn't necessarily happy with it). Our parents' job is to protect us, but sometimes they want to protect us so much that they prevent us from really living. I refer to that summer in Seville as, "the summer I left a little girl and returned a woman." I saw the world, I made new, international friends, I had my heart broken, I picked myself back up, and I laughed and cried, and yes, came home safe and sound.

You have to fight for the things that are important to you, and that discussion with my mom was the first time I stood my ground and she respected me for it. We have to teach people how to treat us, negotiate and renegotiate our boundaries, especially with the ones we love the most. Be bold. Be brave. Chase your passion and stop at nothing.

BE, DON'T JUST DO

Too often we are taught that our self-worth and our identity is wrapped up in what we do. But I challenge you to focus on who you are being, not what you are doing. It's a slight distinction, but a vital one. You can have a job as a lawyer, but are you being a kind and compassionate lawyer. Maybe you pick up garbage for a living, but are you doing it with a sense of pride and commitment. When your days are over, you won't be taking your fancy car, job title, or famous face with you. What you will leave behind, however, is a legacy. You can leave the love you invested in your work and close family and friends. Those people will carry on your memory, they'll remember what you taught them, and so your impact lives on.

It really doesn't matter what job you have or what kind of house you live in, but that's easier said than done. I understand that. But discover a passion, a fight worthy of your time, and the rest does matter less.

I had a conversation with my grandmother months before she passed away. She was ninety-four years old, a five-foot-tall pistol of a woman, and the wife of a well-respected Texas judge. Somewhat unusual for her generation, she was a woman determined to have a college degree. She was smart, opinionated, and stubborn as hell. Her second child was born severely crippled at a time when handicapped people were harshly discriminated against and families were taught to be ashamed.

However, my grandmother would not back down. She fought for the rights of handicapped children, fought to change legislation to provide them equal rights, and fought to change how handicapped people (especially her son) were viewed and treated. My grandmother achieved social change, and is responsible for securing the Austin State School, a place where mentally disabled persons could live on their own with dignity. But she did not do this for the prestigious accolades or lifetime achievement awards. She did it because she believed that all people should be treated with respect. She did it because she believed that her voice mattered and that real change was possible.

As she sat on what would become her deathbed, I sat next to her holding her tiny arthritic hands, painting her nails a soft pink. She asked me to look around her room. It was lovely—one of the nicest suites in an expensive retirement home in Austin. She said, "This is all I have to my name." There was a desk, a television, a dresser, and a few other small pieces of furniture. "But dear, I can't take any of this where I'm going, and nobody will remember the immaculate house I kept, the car I drove, or the public awards I received. What people will remember is that I didn't give up. I fought for the disadvantaged, and while it isn't over yet, I gave it one hell of a fight."

She was right. I wasn't able to attend my grandmother's funeral. She passed away when I was on an island during my stint on the reality show *Survivor*. But when people talk to me about my grandmother they talk about the woman she was, the tenacity and resilience she embodied, and the courage it took for her to speak out against something she felt was unjust. People talk about her compassion, her unwavering dedication to leave this world better than she found it, and her ability to never, never, never give up.

"For what it's worth: it's never too late or, in my case, too early to be whoever you want to be. There's no time limit, stop whenever you want. You can change or stay the same, there are no rules to this thing. We can make the best or the worst of it. I hope you make the best of it. And I hope you see things that startle you. I hope you feel things you never felt before. I hope you meet people with a different point of view. I hope you live a life you're proud of. If you find that you're not, I hope you have the strength to start all over again."

—F. SCOTT FITZGERALD

After realizing my passion for storytelling, for entertaining, and for girl empowerment, I had so many temptations that could easily have taken me off course. Whether it was other professions offering more money, security, prestige, or flat-out presented an easier path, I had to choose to not give up on my passion. It's not easy to be driven by passion, it's exhausting and at times feels hopeless. There are days I wonder why I didn't take the easy road, why I'm fighting so hard to make a difference in the world while others just get to clock in and collect a paycheck.

Sure it's easy to check out. It's easy to do what you're told, no more no less, to never get too angry or too sad, to never be disappointed or let down. Autopilot is perfect for feeling numb rather than the pain of failure, injustice, or disappointment. But that numbness also kills your chance to experience immense joy and the fullness that comes from knowing you've touched someone else's life.

People will judge you and your dreams. They'll tell you you're crazy and try to convince you that mediocrity is the smarter choice. And that's because it's easier if you buy into the same lie they have, that no one person can really make a difference and that life is about "growing up" instead of working toward your personally authored, happily ever after. If you want to live a life driven by passion, if you want to make a difference in the world, to fight for something bigger than yourself and prove to others that yes, one person can make a difference, you're in for one of the hardest battles you'll ever fight. But it's also the most rewarding.

e.e. cummings once said, "To be nobody-but-yourself—in a world which is doing its best, night and day, to make you everybody else—means to fight the hardest battle which any human being can fight; and never stop fighting." He was right. So what do you want? What are you willing to fight for in this lifetime? If you don't know, I'm going to help you find it.

It is important to tune out what everyone else thinks—the world, your friends, your parents, teachers, coworkers, and the strangers who also have their opinions. It's easy to get lost in the game of living for everyone else but you. It's easy for all the noise to complicate, confuse, and distract you. Part of knowing what you want is sitting in silence long enough to hear your own thoughts. I've discovered that only in that space of quiet are you able to think for yourself. When you have the courage to silence the world, you can start by asking yourself, "What's worthy of waking up for every day?" It's the most important question you'll ever ask yourself, and if you don't take the time to figure it out, you'll walk around your entire life with a hole, trying to fill it with everything else but what you really need. Discovering your passion is a journey and for some, a lifelong one, I just want to remind you that it's there inside you. I promise. You find it by learning to listen for it.

Sometimes it seems as if our passion chooses us. Had my grandmother never had a handicapped son maybe it wouldn't have been her fight. Had I never auditioned for that play, maybe I wouldn't have stumbled upon my life's passion. But I know that both of us had a choice to make when we saw these opportunities out in front of us. We could go for it, strap on our armor, and spend the rest of our lives fighting for something we believed in. Just as we all can follow a path of someone else's choosing, so could my grandmother and I have put on blinders, ignored these opportunities, and sunk back into autopilot. She could have been a gracious hostess and housewife, and I could have taken a job that would bring me fortune and regular office hours. I can't say that either of us wouldn't have been happy with another life. But I do know for sure that what I saw in my grandmother's eyes in her final days—the look of satisfaction and peace—is what I want for my life. And no matter what kind of life you lead, I wish that you are the one to make that choice for yourself.

SURRENDER IS NOT THE ENEMY
OF CHOICE

For some of us our destiny is loud and clear, for others it's a faint squeak. Either way, we are all called to something specific. Don't be afraid that you only have a single calling that you might miss if you aren't paying close enough attention. Doors that open to your dreams are everywhere, and when you're ready, you'll see them. But if you're waiting for someone else to find your dream for you or hand it to you, good luck with that.

I'm sure you've heard your friends describe their significant others as "the last thing I was looking for, the last thing I expected." The saying "You'll find love when you least expect it" is a cliché for a reason; it's usually true. The same goes for discovering your passion. It might seem contradictory, but while I've been encouraging you to take control of your life choices and steer your own ship, I'll also tell you that surrendering to what life has in store for you is the other side of the same coin. Being able to do both is something I still struggle with in many parts of my life, and I will talk about this throughout the book. But, having a strong knowledge of yourself and what you want will help you in this. The same foundation that allows you to discover your passion will also make it easier for you to let go and let it come to you. When you're living your own best life and enjoying the ride, it's easy to take your hands off the wheel every now and again and let the world take you where it wants.

As I've said, the passion that I discovered in college was far from what I expected, but that's the best part about stumbling upon something that moves you. Suddenly I was acting in a play, which led to pursuing broadcasting and eventually to my career as a public persona speaking all around the world. My bewilderment in discovering my passion didn't last long because nothing had ever moved me like using media and storytelling to make a difference and inspire people.

I promise that your heart won't mislead you. Listen to it, believe and trust in yourself, and accept that you have an awesome purpose. Then you have to be courageous enough to accept the challenge before you, to discover your passion (no matter if it's the one you expected or not), and accept the destiny that calls to you.

CHAPTER 2

BE FIRST

"Don't compromise yourself.
You are all you've got."
—**Janis Joplin**

From the time that we're toddlers, ankle deep in the sandbox, we are taught to share. At first we learn that if we share our new toys with our little buddies, mommy and daddy will reward us with ice cream after dinner. A few years later we realize that knowing how to share or "play nice" wins us friends, popularity at school, and maybe even more attention from our teachers. And while there are certainly good motives behind teaching children to share, as adults we sometimes take this directive too far, at the expense of ourselves. As women, we seem to be particularly vulnerable to the appeal of sharing, putting our needs aside and bending over backward to help a colleague finish a late report or fill in for a classmate who didn't complete her part of a group project. When we do this reflexively, focusing on sharing our time and resources without considering our own needs, it is detrimental to both health and happiness.

Sure, selflessness often feels good, and it *is* good to help the people in your life. But have you, more than once, said yes to something and then regretted it afterward? Have you ever resented or lashed out at the person you agreed to help, angry that they "made" you change your plans? Maybe you do think about what else you have to do, but decide that skipping the gym or canceling dinner plans with an old friend is easier than saying no to your boss or disappointing your significant other. When being selfless becomes so automatic that your first instinct is to think of others first and you second, you've lost grasp of who you are and what you need.

When I was dating my first long-term boyfriend, like many girls in the throes of puppy love, I had a full-blown breakdown when he told me he was leaving to travel through Europe for the summer. Not only was I going to miss him for the several months he would be away, but naturally I imagined all the beautiful women he was sure to encounter, the exotic wines he'd sample each night, and the awesome adventures he'd have—none of which would include me.

I will never forget the question he asked me that day. In the midst of my breakdown it only upset me more, but in retrospect, it drastically impacted the rest of my life. He asked me, "Lex, what makes *you* happy?" At the time, I didn't have the courage to be honest because, if I were, my response would have been "you" and I felt immediately ashamed that that was the beginning and end of the list. I realized I didn't have a life outside of him and his dreams. After college he wanted to travel around the world snowboarding, and I figured I'd tag along and work in a coffee shop. I was basing my life and my future on his dreams and lost track of my own budding interests. That moment forced me to see that I had never taken the time to find or nurture my own passions. I realized that in my efforts to be selfless, to please, and to be a good girlfriend, I had no clue who Alexis Jones was without this guy. I'd lost myself, turned down the volume of my voice, and hung up my jersey so I could sit in the stands and root for him. Sadly, the person I saw in the mirror was clingy and one-dimensional, insecure and willing to jump through hoops to be what I thought he wanted.

The reality was that at seventeen, my boyfriend had become the sun in my universe, and it wasn't until he decided to travel that I realized just how much I depended on him for my identity. So him traveling around Europe (which was, of course, an unbelievable opportunity), couldn't have been more threatening to me. Not only was I jealous that he was pursuing his passion without me, but I was left behind with only the reminder that I didn't have my own passion to pursue.

Okay, I'm not trying to be too hard on myself here. When you're young, head over heels in puppy love, especially in your first serious relationship, it's hard *not* to want to be with that person all the time. We get the message loud and clear from the time we're little girls that it's romantic to swoon, especially over our crushes. And it is, okay I admit it! It's kind of fun to play that princess role … for a little while. But what we aren't taught is that when we never come back to reality or incorporate our new love into our real life, we lose our glow and we lose our sense of self. My friend Julie learned this firsthand when she discovered just how much she had sacrificed at the altar of couplehood.

JULIE SHANNAN (Nonprofit Consultant): If life with your boyfriend isn't better than life without him, then it's time to say good-bye. It's not worth losing yourself to gain a "couple" status. I learned this the hard way.

I took this advice my whole life, until my early twenties, when I married my college crush. I was in love with everything about him, and so happy to have a "plus one." Life seems to cater

---

to couples, and I finally had a partner. I was part of something that I loved! But after we got married, I slowly lost myself. Not purposefully, and I wasn't even aware of it at the time, but little by little I sacrificed my own desires to be the person I thought he wanted me to be in the relationship. Not because he was asking me to do this, but because I wasn't tuned in to what really made me happy. I didn't take time to discover that personal happiness makes you a much better partner.

So little by little I traded my wants and desires for what I thought he wanted. I wanted to please everyone around me, including him, and slowly lost my voice. It wasn't without a fight though. I realize now that I was fighting an internal battle between my own life calling and my idea of "perfect." I wanted him to love me so badly that I gave up my personal style, my decorating style, and eventually parts of my outgoing personality. I was miserable, but had no idea why.

It's probably no surprise the relationship didn't last, but what I didn't expect is that it would be a blessing. The loss of couplehood was devastating to me, but somehow through that loss, I regained my self. My voice. My dreams. I realized I *am* good at decorating. I'm a great cook. I'm a great businesswoman. I gained my confidence back and also regained my sense of belonging and feeling comfortable in my own skin, which is way more important than belonging to a couple. Feeling confident, happy, and content in your own skin will make you a better partner to someone else. I also learned that trying to change someone, or even yourself to fit their idea of perfect, is the biggest recipe for unhappiness in a relationship. No one is perfect, but the last thing the world needs is *two* of the same person. Our perspective, style, and passion make us unique, and our uniqueness is what makes us ideal for our calling. The calling we each have to somehow impact this world and leave it a better place.

Don't be afraid to be yourself—the best version of yourself you can be. And don't be afraid to walk this path alone. Because whether or not you have a significant other, you are walking your own path and responsible for your own impact on this life. Your uniqueness is a gift, and you will find someone who will embrace it instead of want to change it. Don't change who you are to get someone to love you or stay in love with you. Because *true* love means they will love your unique personality and cheer you on in your life journey.

THE GOOD KIND OF SELFISH

I'll be forever grateful to have dated a guy who unknowingly taught me one of the most important lessons in my life: the value of being (the good kind of) selfish. I learned that if I don't nourish and take care of myself, I can't begin to take care of someone else. And while it's easy to do it in relationships, we can just as easily lose ourselves to our job, our family, and our friends.

So start being selfish. It's tempting to begin your day by checking your inbox for emails from your boss, classmates, friends, and family. But that's another way that putting others first immediately puts you in a reactionary state, prioritizing their needs above your own. The real question here is, when you wake up in the morning do you know what you need to do to fuel yourself? If not, find out! Whether it's getting some exercise, eating a healthy breakfast or packing a great lunch, meditating, journaling, talking to a friend, getting outdoors, or something else that keeps you sane, do it. Paying yourself first will help you build or maintain your foundation, it will remind you who's your first priority (hint: it's you!), and will put a spring in your step. Much better than racing to the office in a panic over who needs you or what you haven't done yet.

If you don't learn how to be selfish in the good kind of way, it is a matter of time until you combust. Because here's a news flash: *No one* is going to make you happy or create a fulfilling life for you. If you're looking for someone else to do that, it's a doomed relationship with an expiration date on it. It may be your boyfriend or girlfriend, or even a sibling, parent, or mentor that you're relying on. But if you don't have the guts to take care of yourself, then you're mooching off of someone else, and that process is dangerous for both of you and for the relationship.

I don't regret one day I spent with my first love or all my now ex-boyfriends after that; they were all perfect trial runs, love guinea pigs. In each relationship, I made a lot of mistakes, but I also learned so much and hopefully we were both made better and stronger because of it. I'm especially grateful that through my crazy relationship journey, I realized that I had to find *me*. As for my first relationship, when we inevitably broke up, it was terrifying to walk away from something I allowed to define me for so many years. It was scary to start from what seemed like scratch, but it was how I discovered who I really am. I'm so proud of who I am now, despite the battle wounds I endured along love's awesome warpath.

Whether it's your passion, your career path, the way you like your eggs (think Julia Roberts in *The Runaway Bride*), or the kind of person you like to date, it's easy to fall into the trap of playing a role written for someone else's life. However, doing this leaves you with a false version of yourself. Don't wait until your midlife crisis to wake up and start living the life you've always dreamed of. Do it now. Get into the habit of listening to your own changing needs and wants and learning how to deliver them.

Start by dedicating a little time every day or week to doing exactly what you want, alone. We talk about needing more quality time with friends or family to catch up or just be together and share a new experience. Well, the same is true for your relationship with yourself. Even if you have a great group of friends that you love being with every day, make time to hang out alone, with just you. And when you're dating someone, continue dating yourself also. This may sound silly, but it's so important that you take care of *you* first, and blocking off alone time is a great way to do it. Go for a drive along a pretty road and blast your favorite tunes. Catch a movie you've been dying to see. Sit in your favorite coffee shop and watch the world go by for an hour. Or you can simply lie on your bed and let your mind wander, look through old photo albums, and let your creativity have free rein. If you become inspired, start writing, drawing, singing, filming, or capturing your thoughts in a way that works for you.

> **"Power can be taken, but not given. The process of the taking is empowerment in itself."**
> **—GLORIA STEINEM**

Recently when I was home, a guy I had grown up with and was re-introduced to after several years asked me out to dinner. It sounded like fun, but I had just hosted company in town for a week and was exhausted. Rather than give in to what was convenient for him, I told him that I was busy and already had plans with myself. He chuckled and sounded a bit confused, so I explained that I needed a night to myself, that I was going to order in food, take a bath, watch a movie, or maybe read a book. I followed up by saying that I was excited to go out with him and really looked forward to it, but I just needed a night to recharge. At first, I was concerned that setting those kinds of boundaries might have scared him away. However, he had quite the opposite reaction. I'll never forget him saying, "That's awesome, I love that you take 'me' time."

Maybe you do this already. That's great! Maybe you have a different hurdle—you know exactly what you need and feel very strongly about how to get it, but just can't seem to do it. The good news is you're halfway there. But putting yourself first does take courage and a level of confidence that we sometimes lack. And what about your image? Do you spend a lot of time and energy striving to be someone else's image of perfection instead of focusing on your unique needs? I have certainly been caught in this trap of wanting to be "perfect" to past boyfriends and friends at school. But while molding myself into what I *thought* was perfection, I stopped being the person that they were attracted to in the first place. It took me a while and some broken relationships, but I eventually navigated my way out of that minefield. I made a pact with myself to never, never again lose myself in a relationship or ignore my own thoughts and feelings. Add to your personal manifesto a reminder to be true to *you* each and every day.

Learning to listen to yourself and knowing what you need and when you need it is step one to becoming the good kind of selfish. Asking for it is the next step. Tell your parents' friend (without guilt or excessively repeating how sorry you are) that you can't babysit on a night when you're too exhausted to even think. Calmly tell your boss that you can't make the twenty-four-hour turnaround she requested, but will be happy to have it back to her in seventy-two hours. The goal for all of us is to learn how to best take care of ourselves, to set achievable goals, to have realistic expectations and boundaries that you honor and that those in your life are expected to honor as well.

BUT, WHAT DO I SAY?

WHEN MY GIRLFRIEND INVITES ME OUT BUT I'M JUST TOO TIRED.

Friend: Hey, I'm headed downtown tonight and I seriously need a wingwoman, you gotta come!

You: I'd love to be your wingwoman and it sounds like so much fun, but realistically, I'm just exhausted. I need a night to recoup and just relax. Sorry I can't make it this time, but would love to hang out next week.

WHEN MY SIGNIFICANT OTHER MAKES UNEXPECTED PLANS FOR US TO ATTEND A PLAY, CONCERT, SPORTING EVENT, OR DINNER.

SO: Babe, I totally forgot to ask you, but I told (blank) that we'd join them at the game tonight so can you meet me there at seven p.m.?

You: Honey, I wasn't expecting to have plans tonight and honestly, I've actually made plans to stay in and cook myself dinner and watch my favorite guilty pleasure on TV. I love you but I'm going to stay in tonight. Please tell (blank) that I look forward to seeing them soon.

WHEN MY BOSS ASKS ME TO DO SOMETHING, AND I'M AFRAID TO SAY NO.

Boss: Hey, I'm going to need that report by the end of tomorrow.

You: The amount of work I need to do to make that report as good as it needs to be while maintaining the integrity and expectation that our company is known for will require at least two days. I'm incredibly passionate about this job, and I know that pulling an all-nighter to complete that document would leave me depleted and worthless for the rest of the week. I don't want to sacrifice my health, productivity, or the standard of my work. In two days I can hand deliver a phenomenal report that I know will knock your socks off. Does that work for you?

When you put your needs last, you're like a plant without water that's worried about providing enough shade for others. But if that plant doesn't have water to grow, it will shrivel up and die, providing no shade or comfort for others anyway. I was the queen of "yes" and have to practice saying "no" every day. Because when I stretch myself so thin that I end up crawling in a hole and disappearing for a week or getting sick, no one wins. Feed your soul, get enough rest, emotionally protect yourself from people who drain you, be selective about who gets access to you, and learn to say no. "No, I can't go to the party with you tonight, but thanks for the invite." "No I'm not able to serve on the board of your non-profit, though I'm flattered to be considered, and I will continue to support your organization." "No, I'm not interested in going out with you, but thanks so much for having the courage to ask me." No, no, no. You have every right in the world to say no and you'll be a better woman because of it.

GINA RUDAN (Author, Thought Leader, and President of Genuine Insights Inc): Ladies, here's a funny truth: Time management is a hoax. Billions of dollars a year are spent by well-meaning women who have an idea that they're not getting enough out of their days and will go to great lengths (and expense) to organize their lives, to be more productive, and to figure out the secret to checking off every item on their over-the-top daily to-do lists.

Think about the routines and patterns of your typical day. Are you one of those Type As who approach each day with a plan of attack, feeling delicious pangs of gratification with each accomplishment? Is your schedule like a carefully planned military campaign, with every objective supported by a strategy and clever tactics for getting it all done? Or are you more relaxed about how your day unfolds? A little of this, a little of that, but without much to show for your twenty-four hours. Well, as different as these two approaches seem to be, they have one mistake in common—they assume that time is a tool you can wield like an axe.

I know this because I've been there. I *was* that person celebrating every task ticked off my many lists, thinking that they represented the important work I needed to accomplish every day if I could only organize myself and manage my time properly. In my mind, ticking off the tasks proved my market value; the more I could do, the more I was worth to the people I worked with, my friends, my family.

Do you see why this is not a viable or even humane way to look at your time? Attempting to "manage" your time in order to increase output misses the point of time entirely. It's the time itself that has the value, not the millions of tasks and chores and to-dos we try to pull off within the time. Time is precious, limited, and the single most important resource supporting your genius. You don't *manage* time, you *spend* it.

TIME MATTERS

Instead of attempting to manage your time by focusing on output, think about how to *spend* your time feeding your genius. Consider for a moment the act of spending—making a choice to acquire something you believe has value, taking out your wallet, carefully counting out your hard-earned cash, handing it over in a permanent transaction, and finally extracting the value out of the purchase itself. Thinking about time that way changes things, doesn't it? And thinking about it pointed inward instead of outward ups the ante, no?

Somehow, we have gotten into the bad habit of assigning value to the time we manage (our working hours) and looking at the time we spend (after-work hours, vacations, Sunday mornings) as *free*. The fact is every minute of the day, awake or asleep, is valuable and free, strictly optional and ready currency. Here's the crux of it: Managing time is an organizational pursuit. Spending time is an expression of your purpose.

Why do you think vacations are so good at recharging your batteries and reengaging you with your more authentic self? Because you *pick* everything you do on vacation to indulge your passions, your physical desires, your intellectual curiosities. You're much more inclined to say, "What the heck," and try a new food or activity or pass an hour doing something you would never do at home. You're more relaxed and open, you're feeling risk-frisky (Hang-gliding? Hovering over a volcano in a helicopter? Taking a tango class? Why not!), and everything feels like a little treat you're giving yourself.

This is because you are 100 percent in input mode. On vacation, it's all about feeding and indulging and replenishing. You're turning your energy inward, pursuing pleasure, wellness, contemplation, and a little mindful stillness. You're exposing yourself to sights and sounds and experiences that stretch and enrich you. You go home feeling more than just refreshed; you are expanded.

Back at home in your time-managed life, you're in the output mode, turning your energy toward what you think you must produce or accomplish, which tends to sap, deplete, and expend your resources rather than increasing them. Routine replaces enrichment; your schedule puts you back to work on tasks, chores, and obligations. Your to-do lists do not include items like "seek adventure" or "ride bikes at twilight." You see why the genius is not having any of this, right?

A few years ago, I realized I had become a slave to the output-oriented way of life and I made the conscious decision to build my days around what I love first and foremost, and to look at the input—the content I consume—as the prioritizing force in my life. I made a commitment to use my natural resources to make this shift and the outcome was more dramatic than I even imagined. Here's what I learned along the way:

FEED YOUR GENIUS FIRST

You know when you're on a plane, about to take off, and the flight attendants are explaining the emergency procedures? I love the part where they tell you to put your own oxygen mask on first before helping someone else. From an emergency procedures standpoint, this is necessary because you're not going to be much help to that child who needs assistance with his mask if you're gasping for air yourself. So it goes with genius. Your primary obligation—to yourself, your colleagues, your friends, and your family—is to take care of your own needs first in order to be most useful and valuable to others.

From a strictly practical perspective, the best way to do this is to feed your genius first. That means spending time on your own edification and growth before you do a single other thing in your day. So in other words, you don't reach for your smartphone first or dive into email before you focus on yourself. Instead, get up an hour early with the express purpose of investing in your genius assets—stimulating your curiosities, stretching your intellectual or creative reach, taking a brisk walk around the block to fill your lungs with the fresh air of a new day, listening to music that inspires you, thinking about color or light or anything that interests you that is outside of the "what you do" scope of your day.

This is not just to encourage you to use your energy and best resources early in the day, when you have them, rather than later in the day when they are depleted. This actually will cause you to *generate* energy and fresh resources that will sustain you throughout the day. Instead of being beat when you turn your attention to your family and friends after classes or work, your engines will be running on a store of genius energy that will make the end of your day as rewarding and engaging as the start of it.

One trick to this is being careful to address the transactional stuff you need to do *after* you have invested the time you need to in the genius stuff. Email, returning calls, side projects, anything that falls in the category I call the "housekeeping" of work and life should happen in the later part of your day. Making this shift sounds radical, and you may have trouble justifying it to the people you work with. But trust me—you make this change in the way your day unfolds and everyone in your life will fall into line. You will be profoundly more productive and the quality of your work will improve. People will be begging to get to work and play with the "new you" and won't even notice that the price for this privilege is that you don't answer their dumb emails until after 3 p.m.

These are choices, people! Every day is filled with dozens of exciting choices most of us simply don't make. Or to be precise, we make choices, it's just that they're often likely to be the choices that will de-genius us (ahem, *NCIS*). Things to read, see, listen to, taste, do—they're out there, and they *will* grow your genius.

> What I propose is nearly as dramatic in its transformative potential as the "feed your genius first" morning ritual: Do one thing every day that represents a conscious effort to expose yourself to the extraordinary instead of the ordinary, the profound instead of the pedestrian, the breathtaking instead of the mind-numbing. This is *so* easy to do, and the rewards of this simple effort are monumental.

Chicks like Gina fuel their genius first and put on their own oxygen masks before attempting to help others. So tomorrow, before you do one thing, remember your time is precious, as are you, so start acting like it. Your time is important, your energy is finite, and your attention is precious, so value who and where you spend it accordingly. You are the only one who can set those kinds of expectations and teach people how to treat you. Be selfish, and I promise everyone will benefit.

LOST IN MY PASSION: A CAUTIONARY TALE

When you live each day catering to your loved ones before yourself, it's easy to see how you can lose track of your own needs. But it's also surprisingly easy to lose yourself to your passion, your profession, and to society's expectations. For me, my success came at the expense of my happiness, my relationships with loved ones, and ultimately my health.

I was in graduate school, doing a two-year degree in a single year. I had been accepted and, due to the outrageous tuition bill, I discovered the only way I could afford the program was to take on twice the workload and cram two years of school into one. I then convinced a girlfriend's mom to let me live in her garage to lower my overhead and got a job working at Fox Sports to help pay my bills. I bittersweetly remember that year as both one of the best and one of the most humbling of my life.

To get through each grueling day, I set up a system where I would wake up at 4 a.m., pack my meals for the day, load three different outfits in my car, and head to the gym. After my workout I would get dressed for work, eat in the car as I drove to Fox in downtown LA, and put in a full day at the office. I'd munch on a sandwich (I couldn't afford much else) as I worked through lunch, and around 5 p.m. I'd run to the bathroom to change into my third outfit of the day, hop in the car, and drive to grad school. After sitting through classes from 6 to 10 p.m., I arrived home at around 10:30 p.m. and did my homework until 2 a.m. I would then wake up a mere two hours later and do it all over again. Brutal.

In order to cope with getting (on a good night) two to three hours of sleep, I would come home Friday night and sleep for a full twenty-four hours and then spend all Sunday doing home-work and preparing for the next week. Sadly, from the outside, it was a wildly impressive lifestyle. I was getting accolades from everyone who thought what I was doing was incredible. Yet no one saw the toll it was taking on my body, my mind, and my spirit.

I remember falling asleep driving, skipping meals because I "didn't have time" to eat, and forgetting entire classes because I was such a sleep-deprived zombie. I became a total hermit, not seeing my friends for weeks at a time or returning my family's phone calls because I couldn't fit them into my schedule. I was so worried about maintaining this façade of perfection and achiev-ing my goals that I wasn't taking care of myself, and I wasn't mak-ing time for the people in my life who really mattered.

Within two months I was hospitalized for exhaustion. It started with a killer migraine, the kind where you lose all vision, can barely breathe, think you're going to throw up, and at the same time want to cut your head off. I was given a shot of Demerol and sent home. What's horrible is that at the time, I remember sitting in the hospital, withering in pain, thinking just how "inconvenient" this was for my life and how much it was going to set me back.

"And above all, watch with glittering eyes the whole world around you because the greatest secrets are always hidden in the most unlikely places. Those who don't believe in magic will never find it."

—ROALD DAHL

Obviously the life lesson hadn't sunk in, so the second chance came when I was admitted to the hospital a month later. I had all the same symptoms, only this time I also spiked a fever of 104 degrees. The same doctor who had been the doctor on call the first time I came in looked far more concerned this time. The added fever made me a perfect candidate for bacterial meningitis so I was given a spinal tap and kept overnight for close monitoring. I walked out of the ER a few days later, groggy, doped up, but still eager to get back to my studies and make the appropriate apologies to my professors and coworkers. Still in a productivity haze, I couldn't help but wonder how I was going to make up all the lost time, unable to see that my need to "achieve" was coming at an extraordinarily high price. I had been hospitalized twice in less than a few months, and still I was unable to slow down and hear my body begging me to give it a break.

I'll never forget the look of disbelief on the doctor's face when I was carried into the ER a third time. Despite his warnings, I hadn't slowed down. If anything I had sped up to make up for the lost time. The doctors couldn't figure out exactly what was wrong with me so they ran every test in the book and all of them came back positive: positive for bronchitis, positive for pneumonia, positive for mono. I had a headache that left me feeling paralyzed and a fever just under 105. I was hospitalized for almost a week, and (found out later that) the friend who had admitted me was pulled into the hallway by a hospital staffer who suggested he, "Tell her good-bye." I was so sick that they weren't sure if my body could recover and whether I'd *survive*. Are you kidding me?! By the grace of God that wasn't the case, and after sleeping for almost a week straight, what my body apparently had been begging and pleading for, it finally hit me.

A few days later the same doctor came in and sat by my bed. He asked, "What will it take, Alexis?" He had already warned me twice that if I didn't change my lifestyle, I'd only get sicker and sicker. This time he said that my body began systematically shutting down because I wouldn't stop. "You're not Superwoman, Alexis. Nobody expects you to be. But as a physician, I have to warn you that if you keep this up, it will kill you. Our bodies are fragile, this life is precious, and you my dear are taking that for granted."

Those powerful words never left me. I seemed to be incredibly successful that year. I was working at a prestigious TV network, had completed my master's degree by twenty-two, founded and ran a legendary sports blog following the USC football team called insideusc.com, and had even taken the initiative to complete a triathlon. In the eyes of the world, I was perfect. But the reality is, it nearly cost me my life. What's so impressive about that? Like the man behind the thick velvet curtain in the *Wizard of Oz*, I was unable to keep up the façade any longer.

I wasn't being the good kind of selfish, I was being the *really* bad kind. The kind of selfish that put my life at risk to impress people. Not once did I take into consideration how achieving my wildly inappropriate and dangerous goals would affect my loved ones if something really had happened to me that day in the hospital. Yes this is an extreme case, but we do it in smaller ways all the time, and I don't want you making choices at your health's expense, at the expense of your happiness or your sanity.

REBEKAH ILIFF (Writer and Entrepreneur): *Perfection is:* you, as you are, with all of your mistakes, failures, freckles in weird places, and beliefs you had that simply didn't work out the way you thought they would. *Perfection is not:* others' ideas and perceptions of you, so clearly unattainable by any human being as to almost be ridiculous.

I remember, over a decade ago at a ballet audition somewhere on the West Coast, standing in front of mirror after mirror with a slew of other girls vying for the same validation: Whoever had the power to "make the call" would see something in us that was special. As we anxiously waited for our numbers to be called—some would be sent to their fate in the waiting room, while yet others would be pulled for another round of grand jetés across the floor—I had a moment of enlightenment that still drives nearly every major decision I make in my life today.

Through my mind went a little thought like this: "I'm tired of waiting. I work hard, I know I'm good, why do I have to wait for someone else to tell me or decide for me? What am I doing? I deserve better. *No.* I deserve the best."

Then I got mad and thought: "This is b*#&s^%t." And that was it. The insults, the criticism, the incessant need for perfection suddenly seemed unappealing. What had once been a form of beautiful expression for my soul had been ruined by a culture that didn't recognize my true value.

I was pissed. I'm not sure about what exactly, but all I knew is that I was tired of playing a role that didn't fit. Somewhere, from almost nowhere, came a fire that was unstoppable. I wasn't sure in which direction it would go or how far it would spread, but I knew to deny it would betray a universal plan for me that didn't involve tiptoeing around to the beat of someone else's drum.

The seeds of doubt that plague your mind after a lifetime of criticism are not easily rooted out. I've had to revisit the "enlightenment" lesson several times over. From finally deciding to pursue a graduate degree to leaving a long-term relationship that ultimately wasn't working, I've been humbled time and time again with just how insidious these stories can be if not continually kept in check with rigorous self-reflection and introspection. Furthermore, I've had to let go of this idea of "perfection" and accept that perfection is a ludicrous pursuit only leaving us lonely, exhausted, and depleted.

You see, to be loved is to be hated. To be good is to be bad. To be selfish is to be unselfish, because with every decision we make, someone else may choose to see or do it differently. So perfection is just that: a perception. And it's our job to decide what side of perfect we want to be on. Ours or someone else's.

Become what you dream, and dream as big as you deserve. Be your own perfect, and reserve a level of love, trust, and compassion for everything you do and everyone you encounter. The rest falls into place.

I can't say that I've mastered a perfect work/life balance (or that one even exists), but what I have learned is that if I don't make me a priority and make sure my needs are met, then I am not much good to anyone else. As Rebekah's story reiterates, it's so easy to want to impress people and look to them to tell you you're worthy, successful, talented, whatever adjective you crave. Without knowing it you may spend enormous amounts of time and energy to keep up the façade that you do more than you really can and to try and make everyone happy. People pleasing may be instantly gratifying, but the long-term effect of living for others at the expense of yourself is too high of a price to pay. I know that you are worth more than that.

When you're feeling overwhelmed or your body is giving you signs that you're overdoing it, stop, breathe, and remember one thing: Everyone else can wait. Fall in love with you. Love, support, validate, and nourish a relationship with yourself. Give yourself what so many of us are trying to get from others and just watch how much the world steps up to support you.

THE FOUR STEPS TO BEING "THE GOOD KIND OF" SELFISH

Making a practice of being alone and centering yourself isn't just some woo woo idea I picked up from my favorite yoga instructor (although she does agree, of course). There's evidence that the time you spend with yourself has a positive ripple effect on certain areas of your life. Leon Neyfakh reported in the *Boston Globe* that, "An emerging body of research is suggesting that spending time alone, if done right, can be good for us … and that even the most socially motivated among us should regularly be taking time to ourselves if we want to have fully developed personalities, and be capable of focus and creative thinking." Research has even suggested that alone time is good for our social lives and that, "If we want to get the most out of the time we spend with people, we should make sure we're spending enough of it away from them."

So you get the point, you gotta do you! But how exactly you make time for you in an already hectic life may seem like a daunting if not impossible task. Over the years, I've found that focusing on being selfish in four main areas helps me stay focused on my needs and fueled and inspired in the rest of my life. When I check these items off my to-do list on a daily basis, everyone benefits:

1. Morning journaling or meditating
2. Hitting the gym or another form of exercise
3. Eating healthy meals
4. Making time for the most meaningful people in my life

JOURNAL POWER

I devote some of each morning to prayer or meditation. I have a journal that I keep by my bed, and I start each day by checking in with myself. This is the most important key to my sanity. Sometimes I vent, sometimes I write love letters to myself (it's so important to acknowledge things you're proud of), and sometimes I write down my hopes, dreams, or really anything that comes to mind. But either way, it is my personal time, every morning, just for me to sit and think and write.

I find that the physical act of writing down what I'm feeling helps me unlock ideas, dreams, and preferences that are lurking in the back of my mind. How do you know if you're taking good care of yourself if you don't check in and see how you're doing? And there is something beautiful about recording the good, the bad, and the ugly because your journal becomes both a time capsule of where you have been and a way of measuring how much you have grown. I frequently look back on an entry a few months later, and laugh at what became of that problem that felt like the end of the world when it was happening. Journaling can give you a massive amount of perspective.

The key to making any kind of strategy a regular practice that focuses your mind is to discover what works best for you and to create a daily habit of it. If writing isn't your thing, try meditation or prayer. I tend to be too energetic to sit still for too long, so writing it all down gives me something

> "Your own words are the bricks and mortar of the dreams you want to realize. Your words are the greatest power you have. The words you choose and their use establish the life you experience."
>
> —SONIA CROQUETTE

to do. Consider it a written meditation. But no matter what strategy you choose, find something that feels right for you because it's those precious minutes each day that will bring clarity and peace to your daily life.

In addition to journaling, each day before I leave the house, I look at myself in the mirror, straight into my eyes, and I say, "Alexis, I'm going to take excellent care of you today. You're in good hands and I love you." And I go on with my day. I know it may seem strange or feel awkward at first to talk out loud to yourself or to write yourself love letters, but the power of that support can't be denied. When your parents or your partner tells you how much they care about you, how special you are to the world, or just a simple "Go get 'em," don't you feel better, encouraged, and loved? Well, you don't have to wait for someone else to motivate you or give you a gold star! Becoming your own best friend requires willingness to nurture and work on your relationship with yourself just as you tend to the other important relationships in your life. Whether you spend five minutes during a busy day or take forty-five minutes to revel in your own thoughts, you must show yourself that you are worth the time.

It took my friend Noa many years to discover the positive effects of slowing down long enough to hear what her body and soul needed. But when she learned how to make that practice part of her daily life, many of the demons she battled vanished into thin air.

NOA TISHBY (Actress, Producer, Activist): When I was asked to write this piece and give advice to a young-ish woman, I knew I wanted to write about weight. This topic is extremely close to my heart, and it is possibly one of the top three issues girls in our day and age deal with alongside love and career. So let me cut to the chase.

I was an average looking baby. Average looking child. Not ugly by any means, but certainly not one of those girls who hears how pretty she is every now and then. I had a buzz cut. Wore shorts and sandals. Climbed trees in my neighborhood and was mostly confused for a boy. Somewhere around fifth grade something happened. I grew up. My hair grew out. My dad remarried a lovely woman who took me shopping and put me in cute dresses. And suddenly people around me started to change. As far as I was concerned, I stayed the same, but people looked at me differently. Out of the blue, I was kinda pretty. I got into acting, got a drama scholarship, and started booking small roles and commercial gigs here and there. Life was great... until puberty hit.

I was always an athletic child, swimming and doing gymnastics and never thinking about weight. But with puberty came the hormones and with the hormones came the additional pounds.

It kinda snuck up on me and by fifteen, I was, well, a chubby girl. Pretty, but chubby. The entertainment world is especially cruel when it comes to your weight, and I started hearing, "You are so pretty, if you only drop a few pounds." Over and over and ooooover again. When I was sixteen, I was cast in a musical, surrounded by waif-thin dancers. The more pressure was put on me, the more I wanted to eat. By the age of seventeen, I started throwing up, binging and purging on a daily basis. The musical became a hit and I was becoming a bit of a star in my country (Israel). I appeared on talk shows and magazine covers and had screaming fans wherever I went.

And I hated myself.

Everything I did was experienced through the prism of "Do I look fat?" The years passed and I became even more successful. I was the lead on the highest rated prime-time drama, a bona fide star in Israel—and I was miserable. I seemed extremely confident and became overly aggressive and loud in order to compensate for feeling so powerless. I mean, how hard can it be for me to drop a few pounds? Well, it was hard. It was actually impossible for me at the time.

In my mid- to late twenties I went through a major life and career transformation. I moved to the United States and started a long and exhausting process of self-searching and understanding, going to therapy and studying everything from Kabbalah to Landmark Education, with the intention of understanding who I am and what drives me. As a part of that amazing self-search, my body image issues came up. And it was beyond liberating.

I realized that what was making me powerless was not the additional pounds, but the conversation I had in my head about those pounds. I was listening very carefully to my thoughts. And they were pretty harsh. It sounded something like this: "You look awful! You're a weak girl! You're never going to make it!

Everyone is judging you!" We are always so nasty to ourselves. We would never let anyone talk to us the way we talk to ourselves when no one can hear us!

Throughout that process, slowly and gently I started shifting my mental attention. I wasn't thinking about the weight or the food anymore. I just focused on quieting down those conversations in my head. I decided to let go of all the disempowering stories I have attached to both weight and food.

It took a bit of retraining for me to transform how I think, but if you're committed to something, you'll eventually get there. A few things happened as a result. First, instead of listening to the conversations in my head, I started listening to my body. What do I really want? What does my body need right now? Do I really feel like chocolate or am I afraid of something and eating out of panic or boredom? I realized that when I listen to what my body wants, it actually speaks to me very clearly. Sometimes my body needs a salad and sometimes it needs a cookie. But it really only needs one cookie, never the whole box. Eventually, the bulimia went away. I didn't have a need for it anymore.

The second thing I found out was that actually this is me. I am healthy, I work out and eat right, and that's the only thing that matters. I am not a size two and I never will be a size two. I am naturally a curvy girl, and you know what? Some people think that's kinda hot.

I realized something profound. No one can be a better version of Noa Tishby than me. No one. I may not be everyone's cup of tea and I will probably never be a swimsuit model, but 'f' it. That's me.

And this is you as well.

So instead of trying to fit a mold, any mold—size, color, boyfriend, or career path—find out who you are and what is your true voice in this world. There is no point in trying to become something you are not. There is a reason for you being who you are, and it is your job to find out what that is, because no one, and I mean no one on the planet, can be a better version of (your name here) than you can.

And if they don't like what they see, they can simply look away.

EXERCISE HEAVEN

I grew up an athlete, so working out has always been more of a lifestyle than just an item on my to-do list. However, if I go more than two or three days without getting some form of exercise, my whole body is out of whack and my mind is the next to go. I feel better, I have more energy, and I am more disciplined in other areas of my life when I make exercise a priority.

As soon as I toss out my workout and reach for a huge bag of potato chips, I know I'm out of sync. That's my signal that "mama is stressed out" because I've stopped taking care of myself. My day is best when I wake up early, write in my journal, and hit the gym. If you're groaning about how hard working out is or if you think it's just "not your thing," hold up a second. If working out were easy, we would all be running around with six-pack abs and marathon-like endurance. Amen?! Living your best life requires frequent and vigorous physical activity—there's no way around it. And getting the activity you need requires commitment, especially on those mornings when you want to hit "snooze" and sleep in.

Feeling good takes serious effort. Don't listen to people who offer you cheap, fast, and easy ways to be fit. They're lying. For the record—get this—98 percent of "diets" don't work. There are no shortcuts to getting and staying healthy. However, there are ways to make the "work" more fun, it just takes some creativity.

If you're using the "I hate to work out" excuse to avoid getting exercise, it just means you haven't taken the time to find things you actually like doing. Whether you head to an actual gym, join a sports league, or do yoga, Pilates, or other workout classes, there are so many things you can do to get your heart pumping and your mind calmed. Some days, when I am feeling the most stressed and crunched for time, I like to strap on my tennies, grab my cell phone, and start returning phone calls while walking around the block. It's insane how easily I can walk for over an hour while also getting work done. Despite what you might be telling yourself, you always have the time to be physically active. The trick is to make it a priority and actually schedule it in your calendar.

The benefits are out of this world. Exercising can't be your only source of confidence, of course, but when you feel fit you feel better about everything, including how you look. And that kind of confidence can, at least, start your day off right. Looking good can be an awesome motivator, but so can the benefits that you don't necessarily see. Consistent exercise gives you more endurance, more energy, and more strength. Plus, getting your heart pumping helps it deliver more oxygen to your brain, which makes your whole system work better.

A fit body also says a lot about who you are and what you value. It reflects the intangibles of work ethic, determination, resilience, commitment, and self-discipline. Obviously there are medical reasons preventing a myriad of people from being as fit as they would like, but for the average, healthy person, your body can be a strong indication of how you feel about yourself. If you care about yourself and feel empowered, you want to eat well, work out, and look great. But the opposite is also true. If you don't treat yourself well, make good decisions, or take care of yourself, that also speaks volumes about how much you value yourself. You deserve to be the best version of you, and it can't happen when you're not filling your tank with the right fuel or exercising your body the way it needs.

If you don't make exercise a priority, it's the easiest thing to throw out of your routine. One of my friends told me that whether it was sneaking a bag of grapes into the movie theater, munching on raw almonds from her purse, or stashing protein bars in her car glove box, she was never caught without something healthy when she got hungry. She also kept a gym bag in her trunk at all times so she could never use the excuse that she was unprepared to exercise. I took a page from her playbook, because now I keep a treasure chest of workout gear in my trunk. I have a bathing suit, goggles/swim cap, cycling shoes, a sports bra, shorts, a tank top, a yoga mat, tennis shoes, hiking shoes, a volleyball, and even a baseball and glove. My philosophy is that being active is my daily adventure so I'm always prepared for the opportunity to move my body. I do my best to set myself up to win because I'm determined to take good care of myself.

It's important to find your own rhythm and the bag of tricks that works for you. But whatever activities you choose, set a daily routine that gets your body moving and challenges you. Fight your snooze button and make the choice to give yourself the gift of health, every single day.

EAT WELL

Eating well goes hand in hand with exercising. In the past, it was one of the most troubled places for me; it is for the majority of women I know as well. My true love (and nemesis) was sweets. I could easily eat chocolate-chip cookies for breakfast, lunch, and dinner. Admittedly I perpetuate the stereotype of women's obsession with chocolate. In fact when I was on *Survivor*, I had a reward of eating as much chocolate cake in sixty seconds as physically possible. I thought I had died and gone to heaven, that is, until I got sick like a ten-year-old who'd eaten too much Halloween candy.

Unfortunately, I used to have a hard time eating chocolate (or any sweet, really) in moderation. I'd eat when I was tired, bored, hungry, not hungry, stressed, celebrating, depressed, mourning, happy, sad, mad, for my birthday, for other people's birthdays, every major holiday, a random Tuesday night, a random Sunday night. Some people call it emotional eating, I called it living! You get the point. I could come up with almost any excuse to justify a huge piece of chocolate sin, lava cake with two scoops of vanilla bean ice cream.

The problem is that when I reach for the sweet stuff it usually means that something else is going on with me. When I'm stressed out, I turn to the fridge or the cupboard, and into the zone I go. You see, I have self-control when I'm centered and focused, confident and driven. But when I'm disappointed, overwhelmed, irritated, and feeling that I'm drowning beneath my responsibilities, I turn to the greatest distraction of all: Reese's Peanut Butter Cups.

So I've learned that I have to work extra hard here. My favorite food is pizza. I'm a Tex-Mex connoisseur, and few things make me as happy as a burger, a milk shake, and fries. But if I ate this stuff all the time, I'd be a dull, lethargic, and unhealthy version of myself, unable to have enough energy to sprint in the direction of my dreams.

Of course, I make room in my diet for the occasional delectable delight. But the majority of the time I make healthier food choices because I'm determined to take good care of my body. The reason why parents don't let their kid eat Halloween candy for every meal is they want them to be healthy. So I try to be as loving and protective of myself as a mom is to her child. I deserve to eat healthy and to fill my body with the right kind of fuel.

It's the little wins in life that build your confidence. Every time I choose to eat healthy, I honor myself. Through action, I show myself that I am worthy of being taken care of and that given the choice I will prove it. For instance, when I get tempted, I tell myself, "Nothing tastes better than fit feels." It's a little mantra that I learned from Tony Robbins. I imagine myself strong, lean, and with endless physical endurance and suddenly I am willing to make a choice that supports that vision as opposed to the girl curled up on the couch munching on fast food tired as a slug on a Sunday. It also helps imagining a healthy body and lifestyle before I show up at the restaurant where I know I want to order deep dish, Chicago pizza because the instant gratification can be too tempting. However, if I decide in advance that I'm going to order the spinach salad loaded with veggies and steal one slice of pizza (not eight) from my brother, I can relax and enjoy the company instead of focusing on battling my cravings.

I also keep my goals taped up around my house because when I'm hungry and stressed out, I need all the reminders I can get not to dive into a tub of cookies. Another key I've learned is that sometimes when I think I'm hungry I'm really just thirsty. I read in some health magazine that a body can send a similar message to say it needs more water, and we often interpret it as hunger. I put this advice to the test when I was on *Survivor*, and it held true. My body reacts to thirst the same way it does to hunger. So now when I'm feeling a bit hungry, I'll dump a ton of water in and often, that's exactly what my body needed.

KEEPING UP WITH MY PEOPLE

The fourth key to leading a healthy life is to make time for your favorite people. I often find that when I'm feeling disconnected, out of balance, or just down in the dumps, I need a little quality time with a friend or family member. Nothing takes my mind off a problem or helps me let go of some stress like sitting on the couch with one of my favorite people. Something about intimately sharing my life with someone helps me make sense of it, and in turn I get to do the same for them.

Only recently did I really stumble on the life lesson of quality over quantity, and it has drastically changed my relationships. Not that I don't have time for acquaintances, it's just that now I take intentional time for the most important people in my life. I'll never forget my grandmother saying, "At the end of a very long life, if you have your family and a handful of dear friends, it's all you could have asked for." I really took that to heart and for the first time am really exercising that bit of advice. I'm more conscious of where I spend my time and with whom because I want relationships that edify, encourage, and strengthen who I am and who I want to be.

So rather than just catching up with people over a big group dinner with several friends (though that's still fun), I make an effort to schedule quality one-on-one dates for coffee, snagging lunch or any other excuse I can make with a friend to really dig into each other's lives. Something about the intimacy of two people sharing their life experiences makes them more inclined to be real and vulnerable. My relationships are stronger because of it, but selfishly I am also a better human and more fulfilled for having richer interactions and deeper relationships.

TIME OUT! A LITTLE SELF-LOVE CHECK-IN

I know we all have our quirky habits that help us avoid life's challenges and alleviate the often unbearable stress we're under on a regular basis. As I've mentioned, I tended to eat when I wanted to avoid and ignore how I was feeling. Whatever your tendency is, when you notice yourself doing it, take these steps to break the cycle:

Step 1: Of course, before you can do anything to stop this behavior, you have to (without judgment) realize that you're doing it. Whether it's nail biting, reckless eating, reaching for that extra glass (or four) of wine, smoking, popping a pill, mindlessly turning on the television, or whatever you lean on to medicate yourself out of stress, take a minute to notice what you're doing and calmly tell yourself, "You're doing it." For me it was always, "Lex, you're doing *it*, you're opening a large box of donuts and I know you want to down every last one of them." (obviously insert whatever your "thing" is for my "donuts")

Step 2: This sounds super simple, but it's so easy to skip. After you realize you're headed there, close your eyes, take several deep breaths, and sit in silence a few minutes. You will ground yourself and find your strength and composure. The benefits of deep breathing have been documented for decades now, the overflow of oxygen into your system (what cells need to thrive) literally gives your body a boost, it clears your mind, it relaxes your muscles, and it gives you a chance to connect with yourself.

Step 3: Once you're in a place of calm, surrender, and peace, you can make a smarter, more compassionate choice. You turn off the frantic monster inside you (or at least calm her down) and give yourself a chance to make a loving, thoughtful, and respectful decision that has your best interest in mind.

When I breathe, close my eyes, and silently ask my body what she really wants, rarely does she say, "Now that I think about it, yes, please fill me up to my eyeballs with a box of sugar-frosted donuts and continue to ignore the fact that you're heart is sick over your dad being ill because I'd much rather be focused on feeling guilty for eating crap food than face the fact that my dad is battling cancer and it's absolutely terrifying. So, *please* eat on, sister!!"

Instead, when I'm being honest, present, and empathetic, really listening to myself, she responds to my box of donut inquiry with something that sounds more like, "Of course I don't want to eat my week's caloric intake in a single sitting that leaves me belly-ached with the same problems. What I really want is to cry my eyes out, to acknowledge what a scared little girl I am, and to talk about my fear of my favorite person in the world potentially not surviving a life-threatening disease. I want you (self) to listen to my insecurities and fears about who will take care of me if my daddy is gone. So yes, I am hungry, but not for food, I'm starving for you to let me be heard and to share my feelings without you stuffing them down and pretending that I'm fine, because I'm *not* fine. I'm absolutely freaking out!"

LOVE YOURSELF FIRST

Last summer I moved home to be with my family as my dad battled cancer. Falling in love was the absolute last thing I ever imagined happening while I was there. But it must be true, "you really do fall in love when you're least expecting it" because one night I ran into an old friend from middle school, and within weeks we were hurtling toward a serious relationship. I was officially head over heels, a smitten kitten, and "didn't know love could be like this." While I could write ten pages about it, about him, about us, I'll spare you the smoochy details and skip directly to an important epiphany. Soon after we reconnected and spent a summer completely inseparable, my boyfriend had to leave the country for work. Being a professional basketball player in Europe, him leaving didn't come as a surprise, but the day after he left, it felt like there was a hole in my heart. I'd spent every waking minute with him for two and a half months and then just like that, a steel-bellied bird stole my best friend and the best kisser I've ever met. So I did what any girl would do; I cried my eyes out because I already missed him a disgusting amount and knew that six weeks apart was going to be brutal.

But then the tears stopped, and I sat in wonderful silence, the kind that you only get when you're completely alone. In that moment I realized I hadn't been alone with my own thoughts in a long time, and I had actually missed it. I also knew that I would be okay because distance would only strengthen us. And I was right. As we got back to our individual passions and had the time to take care of ourselves, we had so much to share, and our daily Skype sessions were full of excitement, new insights, and details about other important relationships in our lives and our latest revelations.

This was the first relationship I'd ever had where I was determined to take care of me too, because not only did I deserve it, but so did he. So, if you're blessed to meet someone really specially, your life partner or soul mate, remember to make it your priority to fall in love with yourself at the same time and nourish a relationship that creates an unshakable confidence along with a strong individual self-worth. Nobody wants to be responsible for your happiness, and nobody can do it as well as you.

I don't know what your recipe is for taking care of yourself. I don't know the things you need to be the most awesome version of yourself. The important thing is that you do, and it's up to you to do them each and every day.

I was recently talking to a woman who is incredibly successful in her line of work. She speaks all over the world and was telling me about a time she was recounting a long story to her husband about a recent trip she had gone on when suddenly he interrupted her (about the only way he could get a word in) and said, "Honey, I hope that one day, far down the road that I can learn to love you…" (There was a long pause as he gazed into her beautiful eyes, her heart melting at the sentimental moment.) He dramatically dragged it out, "I do," he proceeded. "I hope to love you one day, almost as much as you love yourself." She was shocked at his loving jab, and they both started cracking up. Her fantastic and truthful response to him, "Honey, it is in your best interest I love me as much as I do."

And just to piggy on her back, it *is* in everyone's best interest that you love yourself that much. Because when we are healthy, happy, vibrant, fit, complete, then, and only then, do we have everything to offer those around us. When we are full to the brim with unconditional love for ourselves, then we can pour out love, support, inspiration, and focus on the other people in our life. But if you're not charged up (or when you're broken down on the side of the road), how in the world are you going to give another car a jump-start? You can't.

There is nothing more beautiful than a confident woman who knows what she wants. There is nothing like a woman driven by passion, selfish in that she takes good care of herself, and believes she's worth it.

You are worth making yourself a priority, to love yourself, to shower yourself with compliments, to treat yourself with rewards for being fabulous, to make time in your schedule for the things you love doing and that make you happy, no matter how big or how small. Start making a list of what makes *you* happy. I started mine a few months back. Currently on my top ten list (in no particular order):

> "You alone are the judge of your worth, and your goal is to discover infinite worth in yourself, no matter what anyone else thinks."
>
> —DEEPAK CHOPRA

1. My best friend driving us down Sunset Boulevard all the way to the beach, blasting music, singing at the top of my lungs, windows down, my hand out the window, flirting with the wind.

2. Lying in a hammock. Anywhere, any place, any time.

3. DANCING!!

4. Spending time with my family brings me more joy than just about anything.

5. Watching superhero movies. Any and all.

6. Sitting on my couch with my best girlfriends, giggling way past our bedtimes.

7. Traveling around the world. I don't care where. A new country, a new city, a new language, new scents and sounds, food and colors, new languages, and unique fashion statements.

8. Flowers for no reason. When I show up at my house or office and there are flowers sitting there I can't stop smiling for the entire week.

9. Making other people smile (especially strangers). I refer to myself as a "day-maker" and I mean it, I love making someone's day!

10. Reading a really good book followed by a daytime nap.

Everyone has a different fuel for what makes their car go, so put your list together and make sure you're getting exactly what you need. The beauty of it is the better you learn to take care of yourself, the better you can take care of others, and they know how to take care of you in return.

I met with a life coach recently who told me, "There is a symbiotic relationship with yourself and others because the way in which you treat yourself is practice for how you treat others, and the way in which you treat others is practice for how you treat yourself." I panicked when I heard this because I tend to be so critical with myself, and I don't want to be that way with others. It also made me focus on how much compassion I show others. If the way I treat others is in fact practice for how much compassion I show myself, I could use as much as possible.

Practicing gratitude and good self-care can sometimes seem strange. After a recent workout at the gym, forgetting my headphones were on, I said out loud to myself, "Thank you Alexis for getting me to the gym today." Chuckling, I responded, "Well, you're welcome." That got me a few looks from my fellow exercisers. But that's okay. It also spurred an interesting conversation with two women who started laughing and asked me who I was talking to. I said I was talking to myself and proceeded to tell them that I was working on being better to myself and wanted to give myself some credit because I didn't want to go to the gym that day, but got myself out of bed anyway, and because of my initiative, I felt amazing and was grateful that I did something that proved to myself that I could walk the talk. They were so inspired by our conversation and said they too really needed to be kinder to themselves and wanted to practice giving themselves the same encouragement. It's pretty awesome that in moments when we need encouragement the most, we can actually inspire those around us.

So make your list. Revel in being you. Date yourself. You have one life to live and one chance at manifesting your unique dreams, so focus on *you* and watch just how many people will benefit from it.

CHAPTER 3

BE HARD-CORE

"Real integrity is doing the right thing, knowing that nobody's going to know whether you did it or not."

—Oprah Winfrey

Why, why, *why*, is it so easy for us to put off things until the last minute, especially the things that are the most important to us? I've never understood how I mastered the art of procrastination at such a young age. If you're anything like me, it seems like the least important things are the ones you get done, and the things you actually care about keep getting pushed off until the next day. Fortunately, we're not in this boat alone, that's for sure. But while that's comforting, it doesn't mean that we don't have to make some changes. There's a difference between thriving under pressure and dropping the ball. If you find that you're chronically late, ignore urgent matters for weeks or months, or avoid responding to the important people in your life, it's possible that more than your sanity is at stake. When you don't follow through on your promises or meet your commitments, your good name and your integrity as a friend, partner, or colleague is on the line. So why do we do this? What's so hard about showing up? And what toll is it really taking on our lives, relationships, and reputations?

ARA KATZ (Designer, Storyteller, Director, Entrepreneur): I've now missed two deadlines to turn in these six hundred words for Alexis. And ironically, I'm supposed to write about *showing up*. I immediately started to call myself a hypocrite and considered asking Alexis for another topic. But then I realized what an amazing opportunity this is—a real gift actually. So I've canceled a meeting and shut my office door to write this—not just for you, but also for me.

I too often put off the things that I know I want to do and have the intention of doing. But somehow I can't get there. I essentially don't show up. Now, if it's something for work it gets done well ahead of time and meticulously. So I've spent the past year figuring this out, and I'm still trying. But in doing so, I've realized that showing up doesn't always mean coming through on something you said you'd do or always attending an event to support a friend or always being there for someone going through something in the way you would like to be.

Sometimes, showing up is about what you do when you feel like you didn't. It's about the way you go back to a friend and say, "I just didn't write this on time. I don't know why, but I'm working on it," or it's texting someone fifteen minutes before an event and saying, "Hey—so sorry, I just don't have it in me tonight. I was really looking forward to it." So showing up for me has become awareness and acceptance; awareness of how I am and how I want to be and acceptance that I'm just not always going to get it right. And that's okay.

Surround yourself with people who also are accepting and compassionate so that when you don't get it right, it's a softer landing and maybe even an opportunity to become closer with someone as a result. What about the people who aren't as accepting and compassionate and aware? What about the people you're just getting to know, the guy you just started dating, or the boss you just started working for? What does showing up mean then?

One of the best ways to understand this is to hear a girlfriend read aloud a text or email from a guy she's dating. Afterward she might say, "Can you believe he was so short with me?" or "Can you believe he didn't write back to that?" What this guy is doing is a gift. He's showing you how he shows up. We want him to do all the right things and say all the right things. We want him to text right back right away. We want the flirty comment. We want him to be good at making plans because it will mean he wants to spend time with us. Wow, that's a big story from a little text, huh? And what power to give someone who may just be having a busy workweek, untangling a family situation, or, I hate to say it, *may not be that into you.* Either way, he's saying (without saying), "Hey, this is kind of what you can expect from me right now, and this is how I'm going to show up at this moment," and then you have the power to decide if that's okay for you. And then it's about how you show up for yourself that really matters.

Once I accepted this—that showing up isn't just about what people do or don't do, but *how* they do it—I started deciding what works for me. I started to learn about how that could help me adjust expectations, and in return, how much less I am disappointed, how much more accepting I am, how much happier I feel, and how much closer to people I am.

Ara is readjusting to the new reality that she can be honest about her limits, and what she didn't accomplish during her crazy busy day or cross off her personal to-do list doesn't have to be the measuring stick to her happiness. That expectation is part of the reason that we put things off—we just can't face knowing that we've failed so we ignore it all together. Well, we all know what happens next. It makes matters worse, and it holds you back. The reality is that our excuses, our justifications for not doing something, whether it's returning that phone call, writing that email, confronting that person, getting to the gym, dropping off your resume, auditioning for that part, telling a dear friend you have a crush on them, or whatever else you've been putting off for the past day, week, or years keeps us exactly where we are and prevents us from getting to where we want to be. It's like we're sitting in our car, but refusing to drive to wherever it is we want to go. In this case, the idleness prevents us from reaching our potential and that is the very real and expensive cost of procrastination.

We all have excuses, and they are as independent as each of us. What is it that you want but haven't done, haven't accomplished? We all have one, that "thing" we didn't do, an opportunity missed, that haunts us. Regret is the worst, but it's important to focus less on the things you haven't done in life, and more on *why* you haven't done them.

Procrastination is usually one of many symptoms of a deeper issue. Perhaps you don't truly believe you're worthy of your dreams, hopes, and desires. You have to feel that they are an actual possibility before you can imagine accomplishing them. And maybe without even realizing it, instead of encouraging yourself, you've been listening to that discouraging voice in your head saying that you're going to fail anyway, you're not good enough, smart enough, savvy enough, or pretty enough. That's enough to justify anyone's list of excuses.

Making excuses instead of putting yourself and your dreams first only leads to a life of mediocrity and regret. And you don't deserve that, nobody does. But to stop the excuses it's going to take getting hard-core and figuring out exactly what you want. So push yourself to ignore all those excuses that pop into your head, and accept the truth that you are the master of your ship, the author of your life, and that your adventure is only as awesome as you can imagine it. Once you stop talking yourself out of doing what you really want, you'll find the shiniest version of you and experience a sense of accomplishment that rivals any accolades.

TIME OUT! ARE YOU AN EXCUSE-AHOLIC?

How often do you make excuses? The moment we decide we don't want to do something a comforting menu of excuses drops into our head with viable reasons why we are in fact not going to attend X, or why we forgot to do Y. Follow the steps below and see my own experiences observing my behavior.

Step One: Spend a week scribbling down your "excuse menu," then take some time to look through the most common ones and think about the real reasons you made them. I did this recently and every time I had an excuse to do or not do something, I wrote it down in a little notebook along with a few details about what I was doing at the time. At the end of the week, here is what I noticed.

1. I'm exhausted: I mostly used this excuse to get out of exercising or when I wanted to skip an after-work commitment, telling myself that it was better to get some rest than "push myself" to do more.

2. I don't have all the information I need: Shifting the blame for not completing a task on time onto others simply whisked away the guilt!

3. I'll do it tomorrow: This was my blanket excuse for all kinds of large and small tasks that I just didn't want to deal with.

4. I don't have enough time: Similar to number three, I seemed to use this one when a project or task seemed too unwieldy.

Really, I think I felt intimidated and didn't want to admit I needed help or look stupid getting it wrong.

5. I'm just really stressed out or overwhelmed: My personal favorite, I caught myself saying this more times a day than I care to admit. I used it to avoid or lay the groundwork for getting out of a task or event without having to say "no." Many people seemed to take my cue and avoided me altogether.

This is the short list, but I can tell you it was humbling to see just how many times I made (sometimes pretty pathetic) excuses to avoid people and difficult conversations and shirk responsibilities.

Step Two: Go on an excuse diet. The following week, every time something came up, I had a responsibility, or was asked to do something, if my first response was one of my top five or ten excuses I couldn't use it. I'll tell you what, I've never been so productive in all my life. Try it for yourself!

THE FOUR STEPS TO GETTING HARD-CORE

Like any change, becoming hard-core about your dreams and what it takes to achieve them is a process. It starts by doing what we discussed in the first two chapters of this book: identify your passion and then begin a practice of putting yourself and your basic needs first. Next you'll need to do four things: let go of your past hurts and let them fuel your fire, trust that you can achieve your dreams, be honest about your time and precious personal resources, and ditch your need for approval.

The importance of developing a fierce will for getting things done hit home for me recently when I faced one of the most tedious, arduous, and yet crucial tasks of my career: applying for nonprofit status for my organization, I AM THAT GIRL. For those of you not familiar with the nonprofit world, there's an obscene amount of paperwork required to establish a nonprofit status. We're talking a ridiculously long application printed in size 10 font, legal jargon that reads like a foreign language, bylaws, articles of incorporation, proof of everything, and the list goes on. For months this application stared at me from my dining room table. Every morning I said, "Yeah, I need to get that done," and every single afternoon, I creatively came up with an excuse for why "tomorrow" would be a better day. Of course, tomorrow never came and my anxiety rose to a heart-racing speed.

Then, after six months of superficially attempting to crack open a book the size of the Bible to learn how to become an official nonprofit, I finally woke up one morning, and made my mind up to just do it. Conveniently my brother, a recent law school grad, was easily bribed with breakfast-in-bed to help me. And so day after day I patiently sat for countless hours, tossing back shots of espresso to keep my eyelids open. A week later (and with the diligent help of my amazing brother!), I had an enormous, bound, and completed packet in hand, ready to be sent off.

Was it brutal? Absolutely. It was time consuming, patience testing, difficult to understand, tedious, frustrating, and boring to boot. But it needed to be done, a step in the long-term goal for the vision I had for the organization. As much as it added to my stress as it hung over my head for months, avoiding the task hurt my dream's potential even more. I used it not being done to prevent me from making progress in other areas of the organization, which was thwarting its overall progress and jeopardizing our impact.

In the end I discovered that, even though filing the paperwork was difficult and time-consuming, I felt empowered by the hard work and wonderfully relieved and proud when it was done. I try my best to remember this feeling whenever I catch myself putting off a difficult task or trying to back out of a sticky situation. Staying accountable and checking in with myself helps clarify what it is I really want and gives me the strength to get the job done. Now, before I get myself into a situation like that again, I keep in mind the following steps to becoming and staying hard-core.

STEP ONE: LET THE PAST FUEL YOUR FIRE

I'll never forget when I got the phone call. I was twenty years old and working at a summer camp. One afternoon I went to check my phone messages. I had sixteen. They were all from my mom, and with each message she left I could hear the panic growing in her voice, the urgency. She kept repeating, "Just please call me when you have a second." I immediately hung up the pay phone (we had no cell service at the camp) and called my mom.

She picked up instantly and even though I had a feeling something was going on, I began recounting my campers' latest antics just as I would on any call home. I told her about the food fight the night before and the latest camp counselor I had a crush on. After a few minutes, she finally interrupted and said, "Alexis, there's something I have to tell you." The pause that came after felt like an eternity. One of those pauses where your guts send a direct tweet to your brain, telling you that something is seriously wrong.

Her next words changed my life forever. "Sweetheart, Ashleigh was in a bad car accident." Ashleigh was one of my dearest childhood friends. And I had just seen her the week before—we chatted about her big move back to Austin and reminisced about our seventh grade slumber parties at Jackie Rado's house.

I felt my heart sink into my stomach and I began stammering, "Okay, okay, everything is going to be all right, I just need to tell my boss I have a family emergency and I'll drive straight to the hospital…" She cut me off. "No honey, that's not what I'm saying. What I mean is she didn't make it. Ashleigh died." The last two words cut straight to my heart. I dropped the phone. My stomach clenched and my head screamed with disbelief. I left the phone off the hook and like a zombie walked out of the phone booth toward my cabin.

A few campers ran up to me with huge smiles begging me to go swimming. I didn't even look at them, or respond. I just kept walking. I informed my boss in a robotic tone that I had a family emergency and needed to leave. Without waiting for his reply, I walked out of the office, got into my car, and drove four hours home. When I got there I walked through the door, past my mom, into my room, and shut the door. I barely remember the next week. I didn't leave my room. I didn't change out of my camp clothes. I barely ate. I had never been that angry, I had never experienced firsthand how unfair life could be. It felt like those two little words, "Ashleigh died," had sucked all the happiness and enthusiasm out of me. All I wanted to do was sleep because somewhere in that dreamy state Ashleigh was still alive. It was the only way I knew how to cope, to literally close my eyes and trade in dreams for my tragic reality.

On the sixth day, after ignoring all phone calls and too angry and catatonic to attend the funeral, my mom walked in and sat on the edge of my bed. Undoubtedly she was concerned. Despite my staring off in space she said, "It's not fair, Alexis. It's not fair that she was taken and you're still here. And you can absolutely push the pause button on life, you can sit in your dark room for as long as you want and the world will justify it because you just lost one of your best friends. But it doesn't serve you, and it certainly doesn't serve her. And this is neither the first nor the last time you will have an opportunity to excuse yourself from living, but don't. The world needs you and so does Ashleigh because her hopes and dreams are now riding alongside yours and you get to carry her with you. You get to live two lives, one for you and one for her." With that she got up, walked out, and snugly shut the door behind her.

There was no lightning or loud crack of thunder, no voice of God or angels visiting me that night. But I woke up that next morning and got out of bed. I peeled off the camp clothes I'd been wearing for a week, took a shower, put on clean clothes, and came downstairs for breakfast. My family hugged me, smiling awkwardly, and said, "It's good to have you back."

That day was a turning point for me, but I didn't suddenly become my happy-go-lucky self immediately. It took months to fully rejoin the land of the living, and to this day, years later, I still think about Ashleigh, all the time. Old pictures of us immediately bring tears to my eyes, and it's hard to talk about the memories without breaking down; I miss her immensely. However, despite the pain, the one certainty I have is that she has never left me, she never left any of us, and I refuse to let her death be my excuse not to live. It can't be the reason to live a dimmer life. If anything she would want exactly the opposite; she would want me to live bigger and brighter because I had the privilege of having her in my life for that short amount of time. Ashleigh is now my shooting star, a reminder of the brilliance that can exist in this world and a reason to feel electric, not mad that it didn't last long enough, but blessed to have witnessed its resplendence. Ashleigh is the wind in my sails and my invisible confidant when I struggle, when I doubt, when I wonder whether I'm good enough; she's my guardian angel who blessed me in human form for many years and now watches over me.

We all have our stories, our baggage, our person who hurt us deeply. But you know the life challenges you encounter along the way, the broken hearts, and all the things that *could* hold you back? Let those things be the fuel for your fire. Those things that you're holding on to, those constant reminders that life is unfair, aren't making your life better or helping you live your dreams. They might even be drawing so much of your focus and energy that they're blocking you from discovering or living out your passion in the first place. Whatever you're using as ammunition to blame others, to blame the world, whoever betrayed you, disappointed you, let you down, left you, cheated, lied, or messed with your head, you *have* to let it go. I'm not asking you to forget, you can't erase the past, but I am asking you to find a way to move on and forgive them, especially if it's you who needs to be forgiven.

Moving on or forgiving those who hurt you doesn't discount what you went through or make it "better." You have every reason to be angry or discouraged. But don't let that be all you are. The past is just that, and you are the only one in charge of which memories you take with you and which you haul overboard as your boat sails on. As for forgiveness, it's for you, my dear. When you get caught in the past it's like you're walking through concrete. Free yourself. You're the only one who can. I know it's easy to say, and just about the hardest thing to do, but the grace you bestow on them is really the gift you give yourself.

I spent a lot of years harboring anger about past relationships, and I mean *years* of my life replaying scenes in my head, making myself right and them wrong. Then one day it dawned on me, this has nothing to do with them. This has to do with me. That moment presented me with the opportunity to ask forgiveness from *myself*, for being prideful and self-righteous. People are brought into our lives to teach us things, to help us grow and stretch. My resentment immediately evaporated when I humbly admitted my wrongs and my shortcomings. My forgiveness for others' past iniquities came easily when I was willing to recognize and forgive my own. My reward for that life lesson is the compassion I'm now able to extend to myself and others. Rather than vilify people in your life, you can *choose* a radical kind of forgiveness that actually allows you to appreciate the people who hurt you the most because in those moments we tend to learn our greatest lessons.

If you haven't yet been served a huge slice of "life's not fair" pie, I'm sorry to report that you will. It's a natural part of life. And when you face this challenge, like me, you will have to choose how you are going to handle it. You can fold your cards, push the pause button on life, or flat-out give up. If it's bad enough, your friends, family, and colleagues will probably excuse your behavior, for a while anyway. And you can begin to put up walls to keep them away even longer. You can use your experience to justify not trusting people or not accomplish all the goals and dreams you once had. Or you can be one of the few who uses it as fuel to light your fire. The choice is yours. Sometimes we forget this and fall victim to our emotions; we forget choices exist and we slip into a reactionary state. Just remember that your emotions and feelings are fleeting and certainly don't define you. Empowerment is recognizing that in any situation, no matter how small or lost or scared you feel, you have a choice in how you choose to react to your life circumstances. Exercising that choice is freedom and it's also the warehouse of your power.

So the bad news is you will be hurt and hurt again and again. And you will be the cause of that pain for someone else. So stop suffering. Scream at the top of your lungs, punch a pillow, confront it, face your dragons, whatever you have to do. But make it stop, this second. Make a commitment that whatever happened in the past does not define you, it doesn't get to dictate your future, and it says nothing about what you are capable of or who you choose to be.

I have learned to appreciate the adversity, challenges, disappointments, and failures that have led me to who I am today. I've also come to expect more obstacles in the future, and while I'm not excited to crash into them, I am grateful for what I know they will teach me.

So for the people in your life who have not known your worth, who have been reckless with your heart or fallen painfully short of your expectations, sincerely wish them well, forgive yourself for holding on to it and preventing yourself from really living, forgive them for their shortcomings (as well as your own), scoop up that huge beautiful life lesson and all the pieces of your heart, and sail on. You have mountains to move, dreams to dream, and a world to change, even if the only world is your own.

STEP TWO: TRUST YOURSELF

Trusting yourself is the second essential step in climbing through your self-made spider web of excuses. Sometimes we make excuses for not doing or trying something because we lack the confidence. If you don't believe you can do it—ace the test, get through a cocktail party with a room full of strangers, move to a new city for the job of your dreams, go to night school while you work full time, meet a person who loves and values you—if you never have the guts to try in the first place, excuses will justify you settling for what you have and prevent you from chasing down what you really want. You have to believe you can do it before you can drown out all the convenient reasons for why you think you can't.

SUMMER RAYNE OAKES (Model-activist, Cofounder of Source-4Style): Get on the bus. Sounds like an easy thing to do, right? It takes at least five hours to travel by bus from Cornell University to New York City. I know the route well because I took it every week for three years during college. Tuesday, Wednesday, Thursday I'd be at school and then Thursday night or early Friday morning I'd wait for the bus to rumble into the parking lot and take me away.

On a good day Anthony would drive the first leg of the journey from Ithaca to Binghamton. He was a tall, jaunty Jamaican who worked as a DJ on weekends at a local Ithaca nightclub, but his day job was bus driver. We became friends of sorts. Anthony always told me, only half-jokingly, that he'd be my bodyguard and driver when I became famous. Most days he would cut me a break and take me to the city for free. This was a very big deal: a round-trip ticket with my student discount ran around $86, a serious amount of cash for me at the time. I was accustomed to scraping by. A small act of kindness such as a free bus ticket could have enormous repercussions. Anthony's largesse would mean $43 extra in my pocket for food and subway fare when I got to New York.

Those days were both difficult and exciting for me: difficult because I had struggled most of my teenage years with finances; exciting because I was setting out for uncharted territory armed with a vocabulary that lacked the word *impossible*. In college I studied entomology and environmental science. By my second semester I had convinced myself that I should use my knowledge of the environment and my outgoing disposition to reach a wider audience. I balked at the notion that my research would be restricted to science journals. I needed to get my message to the world. I just had to find the right way to do it.

The right way, I decided, was fashion. I happened to know absolutely no one in the fashion industry, but that wasn't going to stop me. I wanted to see if I could bridge those two unlikely worlds, fashion and ecology. So there I was, taking the long ride to the big city on nothing more than a whim (though I'd like to think that my gut instincts have never steered me wrong). Like a million other girls before me I set my sights on becoming a fashion model—but my motivation, I believed, set me apart. I was on a mission, and I never forgot that as the modeling jobs rolled in. I have managed to align my image, my passion, and my expertise with environmentally and socially relevant projects. I work only with brands that share my vision or that want to tap into that knowledge and passion. They don't have to be perfect, but they have to work in the spirit of positive progress if they want my support.

Since that time, my world has opened. A number of possible paths—some that I surely would have never foreseen—lay before me now. It's all because I chose to get on the bus—to take a sensible risk on myself. The experience, the act of getting on the bus, both figuratively and literally, was a monumental moment in my life. It taught me that if you don't believe in yourself enough to take a risk, then no one else is going to either.

Be daring. Be bold. Be inventive. But most importantly: Believe in yourself. Society has a way of coaxing you into a corner. It's not necessarily a bad thing. It is what shapes us, gives us form, and makes us into who we are today. The key is to always remain pliable. That gives us the ability to be shaped and re-shaped so that we continue to learn and grow. It's when we've been baked too long that we become brittle and break.

I don't know if I was ever taught to want something different than what my passion has willed me. For me—as for many of us—it stems from the initial notion that one person can make a difference. We have the power to change the way people think and act, beginning with ourselves. And maybe by showing that one person has the power to take a sensible risk, others will do the same. In doing so we can change the fabric of society. It's the same belief that moved me to take the bus. In the end, it doesn't matter what we dreamed up or how we got there; what truly matters is what we do once we arrive.

Summer may have had an innate belief that she could make a difference, and as she says, it likely helped that she didn't yet know the word "*impossible*." But she also worked hard to achieve her goals while facing the many challenges in her path. She got on the bus and believed in her vision and herself enough to remain true to it even as the culture and the status quo exerted its pressure. Like Summer, not only do we all have to take that first scary step to realizing our dreams, but we have to stick with it when the going gets rough. That's all but impossible if you're not confident in yourself or your abilities. And insecurity is fertile ground for excuse making to thrive.

So when you begin to feel intimidated, question your goals, or find yourself avoiding a task or project, get quiet and think about what you want and if you still want it. Reread your manifesto and ask if what you're doing and how you're doing it aligns with your values. If it does, this will give you confirmation that you're on the right track and perhaps the boost you need to get moving again.

And if you find that your path does need some adjusting, you can do that with the clarity and confidence that your decision came from a place of careful consideration and not solely due to outside pressures or expectations.

TIME OUT! TO TACKLE A BIG PROJECT, "SUFFER FOR FIFTEEN MINUTES"

When you're facing an intimidating assignment or a project you really want to accomplish but can't seem to prioritize, often just getting started can make the difference between success and leaving it to collect cobwebs on your desk. But that's the problem isn't it? Either you don't know how or where to begin or how much time it will take to complete so it's easier to ignore and hope it goes away.

Gretchin Rubin, bestselling author of *The Happiness Project* and *Happier at Home*, has a great solution for building up the confidence to tackle that big project that's hanging over your head. She calls the strategy "suffer for fifteen minutes." It's simple. For just fifteen minutes every day, you sit down and work on the task. During the first few days you might take stock of what needs to be done and make a schedule. Chipping away at the task will become easier by the day, and working on it in bite-sized pieces will keep you motivated to return to the project day after day rather than abandon it when something urgent comes up. Even at your busiest, who can't find fifteen minutes to spend on something that matters to you?

Once the first project is done, don't stop there! Now that you're used to blocking off those fifteen minutes, begin another project. Before long you'll have created a habit of getting things done without putting yourself through all of that fear and anxiety.

STEP THREE: BE HONEST

Being honest with yourself and other people about what's going on in your life can dramatically cut your excuse making in half. Early on in my career, instead of simply apologizing for forgetting an appointment or losing track of time, I learned to make excuses when I thought I was in trouble or hurt someone's feelings. But frequently this exacerbated the problem, making me seem either flaky, untrustworthy, or both, and it even drove a wedge in some important relationships. My choice to not be honest with myself and others or set clear limits on my time was causing even more stress in my already hectic world.

It took me years to kick the habit of not being honest about my time and resources. And now, when I do overextend myself, I try to readjust as soon as possible, communicating my needs and any change of plans clearly and honestly. Don't make your life more difficult or convoluted than it needs to be. Eliminating the first excuse prevents you from having to scramble to come up with more or remember the arbitrary details of the excuse you came up with on the fly. You may be surprised at how understanding the people in your life will be when you tell them what's really going on or even fessing up to a mistake.

As I said in chapter 2, putting yourself and your needs first benefits everyone in your life starting with you. When your priorities are clear, life will become clearer as well and making decisions about how to spend your time won't cause the angst it once did. As with step two, making excuses to cover up how you really feel often comes from a lack of confidence. When you believe that putting your health and well-being first makes you the girl you want to be, it will become easier to make the right choice for you while remaining sensitive to the needs of others.

I know this may sound easier said than done. I'm the queen of not wanting to hurt people's feelings and for years incorrectly thought that making excuses after the fact would cover up my mistakes or oversights. I was wrong. You hurt the people in your life even more by not being up front, and your integrity takes a hit as well. There are only so many times someone will accept that you simply forgot or wrote it in your calendar on the wrong day. It's so easy to think you're avoiding conflict, but you're really just pushing off the inevitable: having to be honest and accountable for your decisions and actions and how they affect others. Once you make honesty and integrity a top priority in your life, it becomes easier to walk the walk. I decided I wanted to build powerful relationships based on honesty, trust, and reliability and to be known for being as good as my word. More importantly, I wanted to be honest with myself. That is where I found the root of my integrity. Once I could look at my reflection in the mirror and trust myself to do what was right in spite of circumstances, temptation, and potentially hurting people's feelings I could be honest with those around me.

> **"Honesty is the cornerstone of all success, without which confidence and ability to perform shall cease to exist."**
> —MARY KAY ASH

Sometimes getting hard-core about your passions and your priorities means saying no to activities that sap your time or energy. But if you're anything like me, you may have a hard time saying no. My schedule is often filled to the brim with to-do's and obligations. When I say yes to these events—anything from dinner with a friend to being the headline speaker at a major event—most of the time, I truly do want to be there. But often I realize I've double-booked myself or overestimated my stamina or the number of hours in a day. When this happens I am tempted to grasp for some lame excuse for why I can't, didn't, or won't attend. I may think making excuses like these will help me save face, but experience has taught me that these attempts to hold on to my integrity and good name only achieve the opposite effect, and I end up disappointing and disrespecting the time and efforts of others.

If you can do a better job of scheduling your life, realistically instead of optimistically, you will decrease the number of excuses (necessary or not) that you need to make as well as the amount of stress in your own life.

SARA BORDO (Entrepreneur): I've been fortunate to have a very eventful career: eight internships in college, the youngest hire at the time at The Estée Lauder Companies in New York, supervising the Aveeno account at DDB Chicago, marketing the GRAMMY Awards in Los Angeles, brokering the early deals between eBay and the film studios in Hollywood, followed by executive positions at Paramount Pictures, MGM Studios, and now founder and CEO of a start-up called NowLive.

Every writer and blogger around the world is trying to solve the work/life balance, and ironically most are geared toward women. I am in no way the expert on that, as I believe I need to start my own twelve-step program on overcoming an addiction to productivity. But I do know that life naturally demands balance— for every action there is an equal reaction. It's not a cliché that life has its ups and downs, it's a rhythm that simply is. Once I was educated on this, it allowed me to gain a better sense of where I am now and that what I'm feeling now will shift to something new, and I have the ability to get there faster if I pay attention.

I am proud of being able to have the above career, maintaining friends and family relationships, and doing my best to tend to my overall emotional health. But as we all know, there are some moments when we just break down in tears. Here are three tricks of my trade that I hope will help you secure a place within that serves both your internal self and external productivity.

- *Know yourself.* What are the things that bring you some calm? Not the shopping excursions that might bring you "retail therapy" (which by the way I feel was a term created by a department store chain) but the true moments of serenity. Being out in a breeze for thirty minutes with no talking, a run listening to your favorite song on repeat, talking to your best friend, a long bath with a concoction of your favorite hotel body gels. Know what it is for you and give yourself a "(your name here) Appreciation Day." Every week.

- *Breathe in times of stress.* There's a difference between taking a deep breath, and knowing how to breathe your way out of a stressful situation. Here's the trick I learned: Silently count for how long you can inhale and exhale—it should be the same number for both. I count one, two, three, four, five and then I exhale one, two, three, four, five. I do it five times. This is my breathing ritual—it has saved me many times, taking my mind off the frustration or impatience and placing it in a productive process of calm.

- *Give yourself small treats.* When you're building your career and your stress is high, but your bank balance is low, make sure you're not blowing the money you do have on things that may not last. Spending money on short-term gratification is only going to make you more frustrated. When I was working at The Estée Lauder Companies, I learned an insider fact that when the economy was about to be struggling or already struggling, lipstick sales always went up. That is the smart woman saying, "I need something for me, but I'm only going to give myself a $20 treat." Balance your need to treat with small things that get the job done.

As Sara learned, taking the time to breathe, refuel, and even giving yourself little lasting treats is a great way to get to the top and stay there. And your needs are nothing to hide or feel embarrassed about. In fact, being honest about what you do to maintain your good health sets a great example for the women around you and can help create a healthier work or school environment. You may not need to go into detail, but declining invitations or scheduling "me time" in your calendar is more than okay, it's your job. Start being honest about your needs even if you get a little grief for it at first. Once people get used to your new boundaries, you'll be surprised how quickly things change in your world.

BUT WHAT DO I SAY? WHEN I NEED TO SAY NO.

Everyone has a friend who can't be trusted to keep dinner plans or a colleague who perpetually runs into the weekly meeting late and breathless. If that person is you or if you would rather tie yourself in knots than say "no," it's time for a life adjustment. Go back to your personal manifesto and remember what kind of person you want to be. If it's a girl who fulfills her commitments and honors her word, then learning to say no is a crucial skill. Be confident; your time is a valuable commodity and yours to share as you see fit. Here are some examples of what you can say to politely decline an invitation. I love having these in my back pocket so I don't get caught off guard by an invite and just panic and say "yes." There's something about being put on the spot that makes my head go blank, but memorizing a few "thanks but no thanks" one-liners makes me super prepared and helps me not overextend myself.

Her: I'm having a party tonight at my apartment. I know it's last minute, but everyone will be there. You have to come!

You: I'd love to come to your party, but my plate is very full right now and I'm taking a much needed "me" night to do absolutely nothing, but thanks so much for the invite.

Him: Hey, it was great meeting you. Let's do it again sometime, just the two of us. What about dinner and a movie on Saturday?

You: I'm super flattered you're asking me out, but I want to be honest. I'm not interested in going out with you romantically. It probably sucks to hear that and it's totally awkward for me to say, but I really respect you and want to be honest and not lead you on.

Her: You're still coming to the event tonight, aren't you?

You: I'm embarrassed to admit this but just want to be honest, I double-booked my schedule and I won't be able to show up tonight. I thought I'd have enough time to go to both events and just can't pull it off. I'm really sorry about that.

And lastly, here's one of my favorites—short and sweet.

Him: We would love to have you there to say a few words at our presentation next week. Can you make it?

You: Thanks so much for thinking of me, but I'm going to have to miss this one.

Period, end of story, and you don't need to say another word to politely decline anything. Too often we feel like people deserve an explanation when they don't—not if we don't want to share any additional information. A simple thank you, but no thank you is all we ever need to say. Let that be your mantra the next time you get tongue-tied trying not to hurt someone's feelings. Honesty can be hard, but it makes life *so, so, so* much easier.

STEP FOUR: REDEFINING PERFECTION

I find it fascinating that one of the key points raised about my definition of *perfection* was that, well, I didn't have one. One of the notes I was given by my editor whose job it is to ensure that this book makes sense was that I reference this idea of "perfection" throughout the book, but there is zero consistency. I said things like, "You're perfect as is," that "You're perfectly flawed," and that "Perfection doesn't exist." I mentioned perfection with regard to society's narrow definition and moments later celebrated just how perfectly we were created. If ever there were a confused and contradicting definition of *perfection*, it was mine.

The reason I'm even sharing this "behind the scenes," minor editing detail was because it was a red flag that not even I have a real grasp on what *perfection* means, and yet I feel its grip on my neck from the moment I wake up until I lay my head down at night. My idea of perfection has always played such a huge role in my life and worse, it has been running around my mind, concealing itself with so many different masks, that I haven't taken the appropriate time to call it out and face it straight on. More work had to be done on my end to think this through completely ... the following is what I came up with.

Perfection is defined as "The condition, state, or quality of being free or as free as possible from all flaws or defects." If speaking in literal terms, the idea that someone or something is inherently flawless is futile, therefore perfection is in itself in a living breathing entity impossible and unachievable. Perfection, therefore, is not real. However, our society, through its crafty, technological advances in airbrushing, has created a "perfect-driven" expectation. Everywhere we look, we see images of beautiful girls whose flaws have been deleted, erased, and enhanced into an unnatural and impossible standard. What does that leave us with? The chronic, "I'm not enough" syndrome. You know the one; the voice inside our head that picks out every flaw the moment our eyes lock on our reflection in a mirror. If it's not our big hips, it's our hairy toes, our thick thighs, our imperfect complexion, our tiny calves, our noodle-y arms, our flat or out-of-control hair, our imperfect nipples, our muffin top, big chin, crooked teeth, or our uneven ears. We judge ourselves by unrealistic, unattainable, impossible expectations and wonder why our self-esteem gets assaulted with the three thousand images we see every single day reminding us that we will never measure up.

So knowing that society has a distorted and unfortunate view of "perfection," one that completely annihilates our confidence, I have taken a rather brash and audacious step to redefine *perfection* altogether. Rather than reference it as an end goal, I'm going to turn it into an adjective to describe our "flaws," which I just so happen to think are the most beautiful things about us. I mean what the hell, right? If I'm going to redefine *perfection*, I might as well redefine *flaws* as well. Because I believe that our flaws are, well ... flaw-less. So yes, I will use the blasphemous word *perfection* to describe our awesome uniqueness because I think we are all perfectly and wonderfully flawed. Bam!

I have big, flat feet, my Texas hair is huge, my hips wider than most, and my impatience a challenge for both my loved ones and myself. My inability to sit still for long can frustrate, my insatiable hunger to change the world sometimes puts the people I love the most on a second priority tier, I'm not the best driver, and laundry and I don't always get along. I have a list of my insecurities, my fears, my doubts, my weaknesses, and my epic fails; but I also believe that rather than pretend they don't exist, to overcompensate for them or hide them altogether, I make a choice to accept them. Why? Because I am wonderfully and perfectly flawed.

Perfect? I am not. Trying to live up to society's bizarre and unnatural definition of beauty? Nope. I refuse to accept that. Do I think that we are perfectly made by God or whatever divine gnome made you and me? Absolutely. Do I believe that we are perfectly flawed, and those tiny chinks in our armor are what make us the most beauty-full? Abso-f-ing-lutely.

You see, I don't know who you are reading this right now, but I know what it's like to spend an entire lifetime trying to pretend that I'm okay, that I'm "fine." I know what it's like to carry the weight of the world on my shoulders, convincing people that I have it all together. I know how exhausting it is and how many nights I cried alone in my bed, too tired to carry the burden anymore. What I do know is the freedom when I decided that I wasn't going to pretend anymore. I remember the first time I spoke up for myself, that I had the courage to ask the guy I had a crush on, "What do you want with me? Because I know what I want (for the first time ever), and I'm willing to walk away if we don't want the same thing because I am worth it." I remember his jaw hitting the table and, yes, walking away. I remember setting boundaries, standing up for myself, saying, "This is who I am and I'm okay with it," and really meaning it.

I remember trading the cardboard version of me in for the real thing and learning to accept my "perfect" flaws as much as the things I was most proud of because, at the end of the day, they were all me; the wondrous, complicated, divine, and magnificent me. I remember the moment, the second I let go of the "pretty, perfect" game and I traded it in for the "real, candid, vulnerable, courageous" game. I remember the moment I redefined *perfect* for myself and it no longer had anything to do with airbrushing, makeup, or mistake-less life decisions, it was quite the opposite in fact. My redefinition embraced that of nature, that of our creator, and celebrates uniqueness; our freckles, our ADD, our spelling dyslexia, our shyness, our scars (both those visible and the ones our heart bears silently), our fair skin, our thick accents, our failures, our chicken legs, our stuttering, our birthmarks, our tiny boobs, our gapped teeth, our unpronounceable last name, our curlicue hair, or anything else we've been taught in the past to stamp as *imperfect* or *undesirable*. You damn well believe it's imperfect, it's awesome.

I understand that I'm battling a forty billion dollar beauty industry in this conversation, but that's what I signed up for in my life and every time I want to try and "fix" something on myself, highlight a flaw in the mirror or wish my body parts different, I think of you and it's all the accountability I need. We're in this together and we're building an army of girls strong enough to withstand the pressures of society telling us we need to be fixed in the first place and TRUST ME, I need the reminder as much as you do! So when I'm feeling weak, you can remind me of my divinity that transcends my physical attributes and when you're weak I'll remind you. Deal?

My goal is to sear into your heart and mind that all those things you think are *wrong* with you are wonderful. You, my dear (take a deep breath before you read this and really breathe it in), are PER-FECTLY FLAWED. No, you're not perfect, nor would you want to be, it's boring. You are unique and one of a kind. Some call those flaws, I call them uuu-mazing. Could you even imagine a world where we all embraced ourselves fully and we made the decision to feel enough, to feel confident, chronically beauty-full? We would have the freedom to focus on so many more important things, create the solutions to so many problems, and remind girls around the world that we are in this together.

EMILY GREENER (Cofounder, I AM THAT GIRL): Expectations. They almost exclusively come from what the world says matters. The expectations put on us by the world become the expectations we put on ourselves. We're frantic to be anything and everything other than simply who we are, where we are, right now. The constant internal (and verbal) "should" perpetuates the endless not enough-ness that lives inside our heads and hearts. When we're going fast, we "should" slow down, and when we are slow, we "should" be more productive. We "should" be in a relationship, be single, get better grades, do more, weigh less, fight harder, live longer, be stronger, smarter, more popular. I don't know about you but I'm exhausted.

What we aren't realizing is the fact that we are alive and breathing intrinsically ensures our worth. It's a fact. We just are. There is nothing we have to go do or consume to be worthy. Instead we have to strip ourselves of the "shoulds" so we can discover that everything we desire already exists within us.

It's been twenty-eight years and I'm just now truly aware of the critical voice inside my head. She makes me feel bad for being vulnerable, or for not being more successful. When my body needs rest, she calls me lazy. And when I prioritize myself over others, she calls me a bad friend. She tells me in order to have value and keep friends, I better use my gift to lift people up. If I'm not feeling particularly positive or high energy, I should just pretend or stay home all together. The word *should* immediately implies that it's not enough simply just being. Listening to her, it's easy to be constantly disappointed in myself.

Does anyone else feel me on this?

Well I'm here to tell you (and myself) that I'm fed up and eliminating the word *should* from my vocabulary. I'm done living by the expectations of what the world says I'm supposed to be. I'm going to practice loving myself daily exactly as I am and where I am.

Can you imagine if we took the *should*s out and just called it like we see it? Say, "I'm being lazy and eating food that doesn't give my body what it needs," instead of, "I shouldn't be eating this." Or, "I'd really love to meditate today because I know how good it makes me feel," instead of, "I should meditate (because it will make me a better person and if I don't I'm a failure at life)." How about some self-compassion? "I'm sorry, self, that you don't feel optimistic right now and whatever you're going through is causing you pain. I know we will get through this." *What?!* Acceptance for what is?! Revolutionary.

We are all beautiful works in progress. The more I learn about myself, the more I realize there's so much more to learn. And as I shed expectations, my journey of falling madly in love with *me* comes easier.

It's imperative to stop *should*ing all over ourselves. Join me?

You, beautiful soul, are 100 percent exactly as you're meant to be. Your endless worth is intrinsic to your very existence and to be able to look in the mirror and truly see yourself, and love what you see (or at least accept her) will be your saving grace from this big bad world. At our "best" and at our "worst" we are the only ones who have the power to love ourselves the way we truly deserve, fiercely and abundantly.

We have to be accepting of mistakes, ours and everyone else's too. It's the Golden Rule of mistake making; you have to forgive others' shortcomings if you expect them to forgive yours. As

Emily said, what we think are our imperfections are what make us unique, human, and remind us we aren't cardboard cutouts of ourselves. If the motives were right but somehow integrity was a bit slow behind it, well that's part of being human. I try to give people the benefit of the doubt and assume that those around me wouldn't intentionally hurt my feelings. So if they do, I let them know and trust they'll do their best to not do it again. The same goes for me. If I catch myself doing something ugly, messing up, or making a lame excuse, I give myself the benefit of the doubt. I ask myself what's really going on? Come clean with myself first and then with anyone I've let down. Then all I can ask of myself is to try and do better next time. That's it! No guilt, no shame, just walk on.

INTEGRITY: THE BEST INVESTMENT YOU'LL EVER MAKE

When we make excuses for not living up to our word, one of the most important things we put at risk is our integrity. Integrity is precious, terribly easy to lose, challenging to maintain, and extremely difficult to regain once it's lost. Why is it so important to be hard-core and what's the price of a flimsy sense of integrity? Integrity is the measuring stick to your reliability, your loyalty, and people's ability to believe in you and champion you. And when you lose it, you also lose their faith in you.

Integrity is hard to maintain because shortcuts are enticing and at the end of the day you are the only one who knows every decision you make. Integrity requires a strong personal accountability, and motivation can be fleeting. We've all been there, when we say how much we want to get to the gym regularly, eat better, or prioritize better and then suddenly that temptation pops in, that damn excuse gets used, and we forget our original goal. Integrity is tough.

It's keeping your word, being on time, and calling people back. Integrity is telling the truth when it's hard and when it's going to hurt feelings, and it's looking deep into your own motives and making them transparent to others. Integrity is admitting when you messed up instead of trying to cover it up, it's not cheating, and not taking advantage of a person when it would be so easy to. Integrity is doing the right thing. It's not succumbing to temptation, it's maintaining your standards when you're all by yourself and doing what's right (not just what's convenient) even when no one is looking.

It's true, consistency is hard in a world where we are going 100 miles a minute, overstressed, overscheduled, and overworked. Yet we are the most effective, best version of ourselves when we build up enough integrity that people just assume we will do what we say. People want to be around that kind of person because they can back up what they preach and there's a fundamental, unconscious trust that's created. The trick is to decide who you are going to be in spite of those around you and the choices they make. I'll be the first to admit that life is easier if you cut corners, there's no doubt about it. Many people just hope they won't get caught, and sadly the majority of them don't. But it shouldn't be about whether you get caught, it should be about the peace of mind in knowing you never will. Losing your integrity is a slippery slope. Watching your friends justify their behavior and tolerating it makes it a matter of time until you're doing something that you would have never condoned months or years before.

My dad told me once, "The true character of a person is not seen in their everyday routine or even in their greatest accolades; the true test of a person's character is witnessing the immediate steps after one of their greatest mistakes." Because we all make mistakes, it's not about how big they are or how messy they get, but who cleans them up the best.

I was working at Fox Sports (FSN) in downtown LA to help pay for graduate school. I slaved away during the day, attended school at night, and tried my hardest to get homework done on the weekends. I had no life. I barely slept and it was only a matter of time until I made my first major professional faux pas. I was in charge of booking all the travel for the directors, producers, and hosts. Because we send these teams of people all over the United States to cover every major sport, I was booking up to twenty hotels, rental cars, and flights daily. There were so many people going everywhere all the time, and once I overlooked the month entirely and booked one of our hosts for the wrong flight.

It was a simple oversight. I booked the flight for the same time, same day, just a month later. All of a sudden I received a phone call from him as he's waiting in the airport trying to get on a flight, arguing with the lady behind the counter who insisted he wasn't on the flight he was trying to board. Immediately I looked online and realized my very expensive mistake. Not only did I lose credit for the original ticket, but I had to purchase the last seat on the plane for three times the amount. I was horrified. Not only was he irate, but when everything was said and done I had cost our company over a grand.

I sat there in tears not knowing how I'd be punished and wondering if maybe I didn't say anything, no one would find out. Technically I book thousands of dollars worth of travel expenses daily so it would probably run under the radar, but I'd be chancing it if he decided to tell anyone. I finally got the courage to go to the head of Fox and just confess that it was an honest mistake. I felt horrible, irresponsible, and stupid to say the least. I knocked on the head honcho's door, who was known for being super intimidating. He immediately barked at me to come in. I blurted out my mistake before he even had a chance to ask me why I was interrupting his day.

"I don't know what else to say, I made a big mistake and I just wanted to make sure you hear it from me and not someone else. I mis-booked one of our hosts and it cost the company about a thousand dollars. Need be, you can take it out of my paycheck. I'm really sorry. It was negligent and I promise to pay better attention in the future. All I can say is I'll do my very best to make sure it doesn't happen again."

He sat there for fifteen of the longest seconds I can remember before snapping at me, "It's okay, Jones, thanks for letting me know and just don't do it again." That was it. He quickly shooed me out of his office and it was over. No dreading "the call" or wondering when or if he was going to find out or fire me for that matter. No terrifying lecture or public reprimand. I went back to work, stayed true to my promise, and never again made the same mistake.

The craziest part is that on my last day, not only did he attend my going-away party, but raised a toast to me, the lowly travel coordinator. He said, "I'll never forget the day Alexis walked into my office to tell me she had made an expensive mistake. It was that day that I knew I could trust her, that our company was lucky for having a woman like her on board, and the day her character blew me away." Are you kidding me? I wasn't sure he even knew my name, much less that he respected me that much. He made a point to tell me that if I never needed a job in the future, to not hesitate to call him.

You see, it wasn't my accolades or shining moments that he remembered, the revolutionizing organizational system I implemented, or all the times I had done things right. It was the way I cleaned up my mess when I screwed up that had earned his respect.

I learned that I'm not afraid to mess up anymore; I'm not afraid to take big risks and potentially fail and fall on my face. That's because I know that when I mess up or get the answer wrong, that I'm going to be the first person to admit it, learn my lesson, and move on. That's all we could ever ask of anyone; that's all we could ever ask of ourselves.

At twenty-one, I decided to start a nonprofit and, despite being young and not having much experience, I was shocked at how many people were willing to help me out, hand over their most important contacts, and offer life-altering advice. One of my mentors, a huge Hollywood executive, said, "Alexis, I'd selfishly go to bat for you because honestly, you make me look good. I have no problem calling in favors for you, so don't hesitate to ask me for anything."

I realized that when we have truly built a reputation on making good decisions, of unbridled self-discipline, unwavering work ethic with a strong moral compass, that in spite of circumstance and temptation, people are willing to invest in us. My career and my organization are thriving because people believed in my vision, and had the faith that my team and I could bring the idea to fruition.

My mom used to always say, "Pretty is a dime a dozen. You have integrity and people will line up to know you and work with you because your reputation will precede you anywhere you go, and it will get you farther than just being a dreamer or another pretty face." That could not be truer. People seek out our organization because they trust us, they know that we are professional, timely, respectful, honest, and we're known for working hard.

Integrity is the most powerful vehicle to success, to becoming a magnet to opportunity, and finding people willing to take a leap

CHAPTER 3: BE HARD-CORE

of faith to support you. You attract what you are. Stop making excuses, raise the standards for yourself, and watch the caliber of people you begin to attract rise right along with you.

Integrity is the most important accessory you'll ever have, it will never go out of fashion, get old, or fade. It's the greatest investment you'll ever make, and a noble fight you'll spend your lifetime pursuing.

BE HARD-CORE, SUPERSIZE YOUR DREAMS, AND LIVE WITHOUT REGRET

While excuses are a common way that we (attempt to) please others or avoid telling the truth, we use them most often to play it safe. Making excuses is the number one way we avoid doing something that we really want to do. They may start as pebbles in your path, but before you know it, they turn into massive, immovable boulders blocking you from your goals. If you want to pursue your passion, to change lives, and inspire those around you, you can't afford to make excuses.

> **TAMARA FERNANDEZ** (Actress/Writer): I'm still figuring out this thing called life. I grew up being a middle child and naturally assimilated into being a people pleaser. Weirdly enough, the main reason I find excuses for not doing the things I know I should, or for not pursuing the things I want most, is simply fear. I find that I can procrastinate with the best of them, without even being aware that the things I want the most, actually scare me the most. The fear that they may never happen is paralyzing. For the longest time I wanted to pursue acting but was too afraid to really tell anyone (silly, I know), because if no one knew then no one could truly know if I ever failed.

I feared being judged or not supported, and most of all, not being good enough.

Years later, after college, I finally came face to face with everything that I wanted living in a place where it was within my grasp, yet still chose the backseat in a film production company. I ended up having a conversation with a brilliant friend, and somehow he got me to admit this. It was scary to be honest and to expose my authentic truth about what I was most passionate about, but also weirdly empowering. After that he challenged me to follow through, to prioritize all my actions on things I needed and wanted to be truly happy, and not what I thought my parents, boyfriend, or friends expected of me. He said talking about it and thinking about it add up to nothing, and actually doing it and jumping in the water would be the only way to swim and see the ripples of its effects. I realized that I resist being vulnerable, and I naturally avoid getting hurt, but without taking the chance there would never be room to feel any ounce of the goodness or freedom of living truly honestly. I finally understood what the risk was about.

It became incredibly clear that I had two choices: I could do it—really do it—and jump in, fail, succeed, or maybe a little of both; or I could do nothing, and wait for it to happen, which really seemed dumb now that I had already waited this long and no one was walking around discovering me as some beacon of hidden talent. I realized that the easiest answer is rarely the answer for anything and the choice that scared me the most was the right one.

This translated through every medium of my life. To always choose the challenging path and to fight hard for what I want, whether it be my dreams, or more importantly my relationships. I realized that I had to be the same person about all my intentions—and some days it's easier being honest then others. It demands certain vulnerability to let people and dreams in, and risk letting them hurt you to possibly gain letting them shape you into the person you could have never imagined being.

My dream aside, so much of what I love and who I love makes me who I am. And pursuing people and paths that make me happy are what life is about ... the good kind of selfish. Surround yourself with what and who makes your heart truly happy. To get motivated, challenge yourself, scare yourself, and try to learn as much as possible about the people and the things you love because they will always continue to change and surprise you. Mostly love yourself, all of yourself. People accept the love and the dreams they think they deserve. Dream big, love big, and sincerely chase after what you want. Only once you get it, keep chasing and hold on for the ride.

Here's the truth: Most people are afraid to dream big so they live their lives with small dreams, with great self-imposed limitations, and with countless excuses to justify it. Living small and dreaming small is easy because you will never run out of excuses for why you don't want to do something bigger. Excuses keep you safe, comfortable, certain, and create an illusion of control. But they are the fastest way to burst your dream's bubble and knock down your hope-filled sand castle.

It's a powerful commitment to avoid making excuses and let the roadblocks of your life guide you to a different route to your dreams. Unfortunately that's where most people stop and turn around. My challenge to you is to stop letting yourself off the hook. You are the one who has to live with what you do with your life. There is nothing sadder to me than a girl who regrets not having the courage to even throw her hat in the ring. It's never, ever too late to go for it. I don't care if you're twelve years old or ninety-eight. This message is for all of us! It's never too late to take a leap of faith and hop on the bus headed in the direction of "Dreamville."

Of course there are no guarantees that you'll succeed. In fact, I can almost guarantee that you *will* have your heart broken, get knocked down, and be turned away at the door as many times as you'll succeed. But I can assure you that no matter the outcome, you will feel far more satisfied with your life if you give yourself the chance to try. You don't ever want to look back and wish that you woulda or coulda lived life with more guts or taken more risks. You want to look back and know you left it all on the field, you threw yourself into everything so fully that sometimes you got burned and that you learned from those losses just as you learned from the wins (most likely, even more).

So, be hard-core. Every time you want or have the opportunity to do something new or scary, encourage yourself to think of no less than three reasons why you *can* and will do it for the very reasons you fear that you can't. Welcome life's challenges and embrace the version of yourself that you'll meet when you make it to the other side—stronger, bolder, and a step closer to fulfilling your dreams or accomplishing your goals. Excuses don't allow you to grow, learn, or evolve—all they do is keep you stagnant and justify why you aren't where you want to be.

Here's the deal, you can't afford to play small. You have so many gifts to offer this world and you owe it to yourself (and to all of us) to be remarkable today.

CHAPTER 4

BE UNPOPULAR

"Forget conventionalism; forget what the world will say, whether you are in your place or out of your place; think your best thoughts, speak your best words, do your best works, looking only to your OWN conscience for approval."

—e.e. cummings

So you're officially passion hungry, you're learning to nourish yourself first, and kicking the bad habits and excuse making that prevent you from growing. But now that you've laid the groundwork for your internal growth, it's time to take a tough look outside and take stock of how the people around you are helping or hurting your progress. Are they the wind beneath your wings or your ball and chain? And no matter who you're surrounding yourself with in life, do you have the strength and the skills to dance to your own badass tune when the status quo just isn't cutting it?

Whether we succumb to its pressures or not, popularity is something that we are all aware of at some point in our lives. Whether it was middle school, high school, college, or the pecking order among your coworkers, the "cool kids" have always existed, as have the wannabes. Everyone wants to be liked; that's human nature. And there's nothing wrong with wanting to fit in and to have those around you admire and respect you. But all too often popularity trumps authenticity and we allow our "people pleasing" to come at the expense of our personal goals and values. Whether it's to your friends, family, or colleagues, when you start looking outside yourself to make decisions, you've lost a sense of who you really are and what you stand for.

Unfortunately, there's a culture out there right now that supports breaking each other down, that accepts backstabbing, gossiping, and bullying as the norm. There's a hierarchy plaguing our school system in which the "cool girls" aren't using their power to encourage and set a strong example, but to destroy and humiliate. After high school the popularity hierarchy doesn't vanish, it just gets more sophisticated. Instead of hallway chatter, it's gossipy emails at work and after-hours drinks discussing the latest he said, she said. The good news is that we aren't born catty and mean, we are conditioned to be that way. We are taught to be threatened by one another's success as opposed to being supportive and encouraging. Luckily because it is learned behavior, we can unlearn it and reprogram ourselves.

Recently, a girlfriend of mine was accidently copied on an email between two girl coworkers that were taking trash about her, "I can't believe she got a raise! She's such a kiss ass to the boss. It's so annoying. Maybe one of these days she'll realize that when we say we're 'busy' for lunch, the reality is we just don't want her to join ;) ha ha." Well, my friend is a class act and kept her composure even though she was deeply hurt. She hit "Reply All" and wrote, "I had no idea how annoying you thought I was, and it would have been a lot less painful if you were just honest with me about not wanting me to join you for lunch. I have to admit, this is one of the most hurtful things I've ever experienced, and sadly, I thought this kind of behavior stopped after seventh grade but it seems we don't outgrown being mean to each other, it just gets more sophisticated through email." When my friend got into her car after work she called me, humiliated and sobbing. At twenty-four-years old, this sting felt as powerful as it would have a decade earlier. When her cowardly colleagues realized what they had done, both girls were (obviously) mortified and apologized. We all know they would never have had the courage to say any of that to her face and now they were having to own it. But the wound inflicted by their reckless words left a huge heart scar and took serious time to heal. Not to mention, my friend was completely uninspired in her work environment and eventually changed jobs to not be around such catty, mean girls.

Likely, you've been on both sides of that story, and you know just how much meanness really does affect people. But even though gossiping with your girlfriends seems to bring you together, it actually tears us apart as a community of girls. The instant gratification that comes from getting a positive response to what you're saying feels good, like it's building camaraderie. But you know exactly what happens when your sharp words get back to the person you're criticizing. It's hurtful to them and makes you look like a jerk (a euphemism for what I really want to say). Gossip is a cheap way of getting attention, and there's no excuse for any of us to do it or allow it around us. Don't settle for a fractured, weak community of insecure and mean girls. I know it's a difficult temptation, but I also know that we're all better than that.

The way we relate to other people—to other girls especially—is hurting us. We have lost focus of who we are and what we stand for. We have bought into the ideas that we can't trust each other and that there's only one definition of beauty. Instead of relating to, sharing with, and supporting each other as community builders, we are knocking each other down. We need a shoulder to cry on when we are sad, encouragement when we are down, accountability when we stray, strength when we are weak, a calming voice when we are angry, and grounding when we're too proud. Community is intrinsic to girls and yet "mean girls" have replaced sisters, and catty glances have replaced supportive smiles. We've reached a breaking point, and our future as women rides on our ability to stop allowing ourselves to be spoon-fed a belief system that hurts us.

Have the courage to be unpopular. Be the one to have the guts to disagree and the confidence to stand up against the mob of yes-girls and say "no." I don't buy it that girls are mean and backstabbing. Sure these girls exist, but once you begin to speak your mind and follow your heart, you'll find that most people prefer honesty to deceit, integrity to spinelessness, blazing a new path to following the herd. This might not happen immediately, but even if you have to sit alone at lunch for a little while, in the long term it will feel immeasurably better to know you haven't compromised your values for something as insubstantial and hollow as popularity.

Start now and start with your circle of friends. Do you support each other? Do you have a habit of cutting other women down? Are you hanging onto a toxic friendship that brings you more drama and pain than it does happiness? Begin bringing into your life a group of like-minded women who support you and your dreams no matter how different they are. I was lucky enough to start out with a friend just like that, and she made all the difference for me.

MAKING THE TOUGH DECISIONS

I can't say I didn't have a great high school experience, because I really did. I played sports, I did well academically, I had great friends, I got along with all my teachers and didn't get into too much trouble. It also didn't hurt that my older brother was one of the most popular senior guys in school when I was a freshman. But looking back, like any fourteen-year-old freshman girl, my confidence rode on the approval of others.

Growing up on the "other side of the tracks" in a wealthy school district, I wanted to blend in with the opulence that surrounded me. But starting with the hideous, jaundice-colored Malibu my mom drove to drop me off at school, I did not always succeed in flying under the radar. Unlike the rest of Pleasantville where everyone's mom stayed at home and their dad made more than enough to support them, my parents

> "The woman who follows the crowd will usually go no further than the crowd. The woman who walks alone is likely to find herself in a place no one has ever been."
>
> —ALBERT EINSTEIN

were divorced and my mom worked two jobs. I remember being so embarrassed of where I lived that I'd do whatever I could to be dropped off anywhere but at my house.

As for friends, I had a myriad, from the soccer and volleyball jocks to the smart kids in my honors classes, but I never really felt like I fit in. My dad says that you only need one person willing to witness your life, willing to stand up for you, to protect you, and breathe life into your dreams. Growing up, that person for me was Miss Frannie Scott. She was my best friend, the one willing to believe in me when even I wasn't so sure.

I didn't drink in high school, so when I went to parties I was always the girl without a red plastic cup in her hand. I was probably more aware of this than anyone else, but it made me feel self-conscious. It's not that I was some Moral Molly. I didn't drink because partying was a luxury I couldn't afford. You see, most of my friends' parents were wealthy enough to send their kids to any college they wanted. (In fact, some of them had a safety net the size of the Pacific Ocean under them.) For us Joneses it was a different story.

My parents are both huge proponents of education, but sending *five* kids to school was no cakewalk. At the time I was looking to go to college, I had two other siblings already attending universities as well. My parents were already strapped beyond measure, taking out loans and sometimes struggling to pay the bills. I witnessed the sacrifices that they made for me. I watched as my mom came home after a long day at the office to cook dinner, do laundry, make sure we did our homework, only to then get ready for her night job as a bartender that kept her up until the wee hours of the morning. I saw how stretched everyone was, and I knew how much college cost, especially when you have three kids paying out-of-state tuitions at the same time.

So for me the tough decision was staying true to my desire to go to a great school in California. All the times I wanted to skip school, stay out late, not study for the test, or be lazy and ignore my homework, I just couldn't. I had my mind set on attending an expensive, out-of-state university, and I knew I wasn't born financially wealthy so it rode on my shoulders whether or not I could get the grades to earn a scholarship. At a certain point in your life, you'll have to realize the sacrifices necessary to make your dreams come true, and you'll be at the crossroads of the same tough choices. Will you be dedicated to the path that gets you where you want to go, despite it being far more difficult, or will you sell out to an easy breezy path that takes you in the opposite direction of where you really want to go? We are faced with these kinds of choices every single day, and fortunately we get to decide which path we take.

BUT, WHAT DO I SAY? WHEN A FRIEND IS UNSUPPORTIVE.

As much as it can hurt to be left out of the "in" crowd or face up to a mean girl, it's even harder to know how to react when a close friend is unsupportive. First, try not to take their words personally and just stomp off with your feelings hurt. As calmly as possible, ask why they said that or ask them to tell you more about why they feel that way. There may be something else going on. But that doesn't mean that you should endure these outbursts regularly. Tell them how their words make you feel unsupported and ask them not to do it again. If they don't stop, then you know it's time to reevaluate your friendship.

Here's how you might handle a situation like this:

Friend: I think it's a bit ridiculous that you want to go to Harvard and spend your life as a doctor overseas. Harvard is one of the hardest schools in the country, and you've never so much as been outside of the city and now you want to move to a different state for college and practice medicine in a different country?!

You: Wow, that's a pretty strong reaction. Why do you feel that way?

Friend: It just seems a little unrealistic to me, and as your friend I don't want you to be disappointed if it doesn't work out. (Which by the way, what they are really saying is that it seems unrealistic to *them*, not you! The power of projection!)

You: While I understand you not wanting me to be disappointed, I'd be exponentially more disappointed if I never tried. I know Harvard is tough, but why not me? I've worked my ass off for three years and it's always been a dream of mine. Plus, maybe I haven't seen the world, but that too is a passion of mine so I'm going to make it happen no matter what.

Friend: I guess it just all seems super out there.

> **You:** Yeah, it does but that's how I want to live my life, to go big or go home. And you not wanting me to be "disappointed" feels a whole lot like you just not being supportive. I know you love me and more than anything you're just going to miss me and the reality is it's super scary and I'll miss you too. But here's the deal, I have huge dreams and I have to chase them down and rather than prevent me from getting disappointed, I really just need a cheerleader in my corner. Can you be that for me?

At some point, for a number of reasons, I decided that I wanted to go to the University of Southern California, one of the most expensive private schools in the country. It was my dream school, and I proceeded to gush about it to my parents. In the middle of my sales pitch, my loving but realistic dad interrupted, and said, "Sweet girl, that sounds wonderful, but we just can't afford that. I'm sorry." And just like that my bubble didn't just pop, it exploded. I was heartbroken, devastated, and did what any disappointed kid would do. I threw a temper tantrum, spitting out phrases like, "Not fair" and "How come?"

Later that night, my mom had one of the greatest parenting moments of my life. She said, "Punkin [her term of endearment for me], I don't think you understand what your dad is trying to say. All he's saying is we can't make your dreams come true. He never said that *you* can't. If you want it bad enough, then find a way to come up with the money, earn a scholarship, work harder than everyone else. Because what I refuse to do is sit here and allow you to blame someone else for your dreams not coming true. You're going to let the first challenge you encounter stop you in your tracks? And for what, money? At least get creative with your excuses. If you really want it, then don't just find a way, make a way. Your dreams are in your hands, so start acting like it."

And in that moment, the challenge was set before me. If I really wanted it, then I had to earn it. So from that day forward school was so much more than just getting by and having fun. Like I said before, I made the tough decisions to not party because I simply couldn't afford to be distracted, unprepared for class, to forget about a test and not do well. I had to give it 100 percent all the time and have my grades reflect that. I poured myself into my studies, did every bit of extra credit, and sat with teachers during office hours. Of course there were many days I would have rather hung out with my friends and put school on the back burner. I just knew that for me everything was riding on whether I did well. I had no plan B, no safety net.

One Thursday night all my girlfriends were going to see one of our favorite bands play, but I had a huge test the next day. It seemed that my friends were always so carefree, so spontaneous, so wonderfully reckless, and I wanted to be that too. But at the same time I also realized that I had a bigger goal in mind and whether I liked it or not, I had a different road to take. So of course I stayed home that night, and it was one of so many times that I was truly envious that other people didn't have to care as much about their grades or work as hard as I did. And of course my friends

> "If I wasted my time trying to be like everyone else when I was 10 and 11, I wouldn't be me today. So if you are going to be the future rock stars, the future somebody, whatever you want to be, then you're wasting time trying to be someone else, because you'll never get around to being you."
>
> —PINK

gave me a hard time about being the "good girl." I would laugh it off, but there was always a part of me that felt insecure about it and wanted desperately to not stand out.

MISS FRANNIE SCOTT

Frannie was the only friend who never dogged me about my priorities, who didn't laugh at me for the ridiculous amount of studying I did, or criticize me for going home early to prepare for class the next day. She supported me when I needed it the most, helped me grow confident in my choices, and encouraged me to stay on my chosen path when the peer pressure mounted.

We may not have been the most popular girls in school, but after finding each other, neither of us cared about it all that much. I'd be lying if I said I suddenly didn't care at all what people thought about me, but Frannie helped me find me and be okay with myself. She gave me permission to just *be*, to define my unique voice and author my unique journey. The best part is that we were opposites in so many ways; her dream was to be a wife and mother (which she is now and is incredible at both!) and I wanted to run my own company and be the first female president. It didn't matter what we wanted to *do*, because we agreed about who we chose to *be*—accepting, supporting and encouraging one another's dreams, whatever they might be.

The situation I was in—not having my dreams fully financed—forced an issue into my life that I had to resolve then and there: how to take control of my own destiny. Though it was a frustrating lesson to learn, I feel lucky to have met this crossroads early because more than any other place, it is where I draw strength now. I proved to myself that I could set my sights on a lofty goal and achieve it.

I can still remember the day I received my acceptance letter to USC. With shaky hands, I opened it up and read the first line, "Alexis Jones, congratulations, you have been accepted to the University of Southern California and due to your excellent academic achievement, we would like to offer you a scholarship to attend." The beautiful thing was in that moment, I had never so confidently stood on my own two feet, knowing that I earned the right to my dream school. Nobody had done that for me, and to this day, it is one of the most rewarding moments of my life.

Of course it was a moment that I shared with Frannie—after all, I owed much of my success to her support. No one else knew just how hard I had worked or the hours of sleep I had lost. So after celebrating with my family, my first frantic call was to her. All she said was, "It was worth it, Jones. You deserve it." She made it seem like there was never any doubt I would achieve this goal (or any of my future goals), like she knew all along it was just a matter of time. Yes, I did the majority of the hard work, but it would not have been possible without my support system.

I hear a lot of people talking about their dreams, gushing about their latest goals and what they want in life. But rarely do I hear about the sacrifices that it takes to actually get where you want to go. I don't care if it's earning a scholarship to your dream school, getting the raise you want, completing the triathlon, or just deciding to eat well and get in better shape; every choice you make comes with consequences and sacrifices. And sometimes those sacrifices will make you stand out in a way that makes you uncomfortable and awkward, but they are always worth it.

What do you do when you're at a crossroads, deciding between the popular route and one less traveled? First, take a hard look at what you want and what you have to do to make it happen.

Be realistic with yourself. Are you still willing to sign up for it? I hope you are, because, like earning the right to attend USC, every time I set a tough goal for myself and achieve it, I feel invincible, invigorated, and ready to take on a newer, tougher challenge.

Second, hold on tightly to the friends and family who support you especially when you're younger and figuring out who you really want to be. People like Frannie help us make sense of the world, they talk us off the ledge when we want to write yet another text to the guy we have a crush on (who's totally not worth our time), they wipe our tears when the world is unfair, and they laugh with us over the silly stuff. Frannie and I get each other and we always will. We allow each other to mess up, forgive each other's mistakes, and hold one another accountable to who we want to be, not who we want to justify being. I don't know who your Frannie is, but you need one. We all do. We all need that person who tells you what you *don't* necessarily want to hear, who admits when you're being too dramatic, who's your biggest cheerleader, and who reminds you of the things that really matter.

WHO IS THE WIND IN YOUR SAILS?

Over the years, I have witnessed the power of living with a strong support system. While we may hope that we are tough or independent enough to make our own opportunities, the truth is, the help of a strong support system can mean the difference between success and failure.

I may not have had the luxury of wealth or a trust fund safety net. But that was *my* life challenge. Yours may look very different. Maybe you were born into privilege but never had a supportive family or friends. Maybe your challenge was dyslexia, a mental illness, a physical handicap, an unforeseen tragedy, experiencing some form of abuse, addiction, an eating disorder, or losing someone close to you. We are all gifted with some kind of adversity. I call it a gift because without a challenge there is nothing to overcome, and only in that space can we grow and see what we are really made of.

KATE FATTER (Trip Leader for Backroads): I can recall making a decision that made absolutely no sense to anyone around me. When I was twenty-seven, I decided that working and living in Austin, Texas, didn't quite satisfy my adventure spirit. I was surrounded with my wonderful family, fantastic friends, and endless entertainment. I had a good job and worked with amazing people. However, there was something missing. I still cannot put into words what I was missing, but I knew there was something I still wanted.

I applied for graduate school at the University of Boulder in Colorado while simultaneously applying for my absolute "dream job"—being a trip leader for an active travel company, Backroads. My GMAT scores were terrible and I was told that getting accepted to Backroads was about on par with getting accepted to Harvard. It wasn't looking good, but I thought I would apply anyway and see what happened. Six essays and four interviews later I had applied to both. I had devised all sorts of plans and contingency plans, but I never planned what I would do if I was actually accepted to both. And I was!

I had one week to decide between Backroads and grad school. And everyone around me had their own opinions. I listened to lots of opinions and found myself being swayed one way for a couple of days and then right back to the other side for a couple of days. I had the choice that "made the most sense" to my friends and family and the choice that my heart was in. After several stressful, "What am I doing with my life?"

---

moments, I decided to go with Backroads. It was a scary decision with more unknowns than I was comfortable with. But it made the most sense to me. Without saying so I knew everyone in my family was holding their breath until I realized I had made a mistake. Waiting for me to realize that this "dream" job was only short term and I would realize in a year that I needed to plant my feet firmly back on the ground and do the right thing.

So here I am. A year and a half later. Happy as I have ever been in my life. I have worked in Yellowstone, the Tetons, Vermont, the Canyons, Costa Rica, and soon Patagonia. I have met the most amazing people and have been able to travel to places I would have never seen had I chosen grad school. I am making a great living and learning more than I have ever learned in my life. I can honestly say that this job is the hardest job I have ever had, yet the most rewarding. I love my job!

My family now realizes that this was the best decision I could have ever made, even though it defied what they thought was the right choice. It was extremely hard for me to go against the grain and against what everyone I loved clearly wanted me to do, but it all worked out, as it always seems to.

Kate's family wasn't outwardly unsupportive, but she knew she was taking a leap that they didn't understand. So she took the risk to follow her heart, and in the process of living her dream she has met people who understand her goals and share them. While it's wonderful to have an unwavering support system, we're only human, and not everyone in your life is going to "get" all of your choices. The important thing is that they stand by you instead of trying to dissuade you from pursuing your passion. Just don't let even their unspoken doubts convince you to abandon what you really want. At the end of the day they just want you to be happy and so should you.

On the other hand, beware of the people in your life who voice their disapproval or seem to rain on every parade. Just like you are with your time and energy, you get to be selfish with who you surround yourself with because it is that crucial to your journey. The people in your inner circle influence you more than almost anything or anyone else, and so you must be conscious of whom you let in that precious space. You become what you tolerate, and most people in this world will respect you to the extent that you respect yourself and no more. It's your job to teach people how to treat you.

You may not even realize that a relationship has become toxic, which is why it's important to occasionally slow down and think about the people in your life. If you don't like the way you handled a challenge or feel confused or conflicted about some advice you received, that's your cue to pause for a minute and get back to your foundation. Focus on what you want, your long- and short-term goals, and your values. Then compare that to your advisors' values and the kind of support they're giving you. If there's a mismatch, there might be a problem. Sometimes we forget that we pick our friends, and that it's an honor, so start acting like it. Just like the president picks his cabinet of trusted advisors, surround yourself with people who edify, inspire, encourage, and challenge you.

TIME OUT! DO A FRIEND INVENTORY

Have you ever done an inventory of your friends? If not or if you haven't done it in a while, do one now. Write down the five people you spend the most time with and then start writing out the attributes you admire in them. When you really sit down and think about it, do you feel like these people inspire you, encourage you, challenge you, and respect you? Do they make you better and want to dream even bigger or fly even higher? Sometimes we're too nice when we should be a little more selective of the people we allow to influence us.

Also write down the things you want to improve in yourself, the places you need the most growth or guidance. Is there anyone out there who you think could mentor you or share their wisdom with you? Someone that could help bolster an insecurity or weakness? Maybe add them to your inner crew and schedule time to hang out with them. We are products of our surroundings so it's in your best interest to really think about the people you spend the most time with.

A friend of mine once told me about the "sphere" philosophy. The concept is that there are several circles in your life starting with you. So imagine drawing the first circle around yourself with chalk. The second is drawn around the first; it's a little bigger and it includes you and the people closest to you—your significant other maybe and your immediate family. The third tier surrounds that one and includes your best friends; the fourth tier includes your coworkers; the fifth, your acquaintances; and so on. Within these circles, you have the power to promote and demote people. Of course, the goal isn't to have a certain number of people in each tier, but to be clear with yourself about who gets to influence your world, whose opinions matter most, and whose you can live without. Of course, just because someone is in a fourth or fifth tier doesn't mean they don't serve an important function in your life. Your pals on your co-ed kickball team or fellow yogis keep you active and laughing, but you don't necessarily need to heed their career advice. There are friends you love to travel with, some you tell your most intimate secrets to, and others you work with. All of them serve a unique purpose in your life. Just know who gets intimate access to your heart and who to keep at arm's length.

Below is the list of what I value most in my closest friends:

1. Integrity—they have to be people of their word.

2. Loyalty—they have my back no matter what.

3. Honesty—when necessary, they can put me in my place and tell me not what I want to hear, but what I need to hear.

4. My biggest fan—they are interested in my goals, large and small, and cheer me on even when the odds are stacked against me.

5. Forgiveness—I have to trust that not if but when I mess up, they are willing to accept my mistakes and my apology.

6. Humility—they have to recognize we're all in this together and no one is more important than another and everyone deserves to be seen and heard.

7. Passion—they are searching for or have found something they love and lead a life filled with purpose, inspiring me to do the same.

8. Sense of humor—they don't take life so seriously, and find humor even in dark times.

9. Authentic confidence—they believe in themselves and have the courage to speak their truth, granting me permission to do the same.

10. Selflessness—they are willing to fight for things bigger than themselves.

Of course, if you create a list of things that really matter to you, you'd better make sure you embody them yourself. Creating a list of what you expect in others is a great way of tapping into what really matters to you and what kind of life *you* want to lead. Don't be harder on your loved ones than you are on yourself. Hold everyone in your inner circle to a high standard, starting with you.

To start thinking about what kind of attributes you need in those around you, imagine what you'd write if you were posting a job description to fill the position of "your friend." It may sound silly, but it's a useful exercise. What would you want or need from the person you would hire?

BUT, WHAT DO I SAY? WHEN MY FRIENDS START TALKING TRASH, AND I WANT OUT!

One of my favorite quotes is by Eleanor Roosevelt; she said, "Great minds discuss ideas. Average minds discuss events. Small minds discuss people." I've always taken it to heart so when my friends and I get together we try to talk about ideas, interesting new things we've learned, what's going on in the world, and often how we can make it better. That being said, there are times when all of us find ourselves in a conversation that turns petty and devolves into gossipy chatter about the people in our lives, especially their perceived shortcomings and imperfections.

I recently ran into some old friends from my hometown who invited me out for a drink. Within minutes they were talking trash about the same girls they had issues with in high school, recounting the same silly stories only with newfound enthusiasm. After twenty minutes of not saying a word and letting the toxic conversation turn to superficial, mean chatter, I smiled, stood up, and said, "I'm sorry girls. It's been great catching up. I just wanted to pit stop and say hi, but I actually gotta get going." As much as I wanted to say how bored I was and scream, "Get over it already!!" I politely hit the eject button and evacuated the situation. The moment I stepped away, I felt like I could breathe again.

Now I'm not going to pretend that I never say mean things behind people's backs, but I can say that I make a concerted effort not to. I do my best to surround myself with people in my life who, when I do start getting catty, lovingly remind me to knock it off. My mantra is you never know what he or she is going through, and if you're really that upset, then bring it up to them directly, not about them to someone else. If not, then stop talking about it. Surrounding yourself with loving, kind, and compassionate people provides a powerful accountability, and their positive influence will make a huge difference in your life.

My friend Josie struggled with "fitting in" her whole life. Instead of picking friends who supported the person she was, she sought the approval of the people who seemed to be special, thinking she would become special in the process. She didn't understand that she was enough, exactly as she was—until something profound happened that forced her to.

JOSIE LOREN (Actress and Activist): When I was in middle school, I desperately wanted to be a member of the "cool crowd." They wore adidas sneakers, Nautica jackets, and had their own table in the cafeteria. Not officially, but it was understood. Naturally, I begged my mother to buy me these items, but she made me wear the school uniform even though it wasn't mandatory. I could have died.

I couldn't wear the same clothes, but I could change other things. Unlike myself, none of them were enrolled in the school's academically "gifted" programs, so when the cutest boy in the clique started talking to me, my conversations turned from academics to video games, clothes, and movies. That's what he liked, right? Unfortunately, I was never accepted into this group. That hurt. But what I remember even more poignantly was the feeling that came when I abandoned myself.

It's sad to admit, but ever since I can remember, I have found myself chasing. I chase friendships, romance, careers. Now that I'm a little older and a tad bit wiser, I realize what I'm really chasing is status, confidence, and validation. It comes from a place of insecurity. I don't think I am enough, so I fill the void with what I believe will make me whole in the eyes of others. Each person or thing I chase holds something that I have convinced myself I lack and they possess. If only I can be this person's friend, my social life will twinkle with success and people will know I'm cool. If only this guy would date me, I'll know I'm attractive, smart, worthy. It's a debilitating way to think and live your life, and the consequences are steep.

When our self-worth resides in the eyes of others, we compromise who we are to accommodate their lifestyle. I was in a relationship for two years where I spent the majority of my time chasing his love and seal of approval. I changed every aspect of who I was to fit his model of the perfect woman. Everything from what I wore to what I ate and thought was tweaked to his liking. With every choice I made to accommodate him, I lost a little piece of me until I didn't recognize who I was anymore. My bad habits got the best of me and finally drove me to hit rock bottom.

When I thought things couldn't get worse, my father was diagnosed with stage 4 lung cancer the same day my grandmother, the heart of my family, suffered a massive stroke. Life knocked me down, and for the first time in my life, I couldn't pick myself back up. There was no fight left in me. I was numb, empty. But a funny thing happens when you find yourself face down on the ground. You stop trying and you start "being." Every layer of superficiality that I had carefully tailored was stripped away leaving me with the purest form of myself. I had no energy or desire to impress anyone or anything. The idea alone of chasing anything exhausted me. At the time I thought it was weakness, but I see now that it was truth. From that place of purest truth, I began to live my life for me and my loved ones instead of for others.

Life works in mysterious ways and in the face of tragedy, beauty began to bud all around me. I found that in making the choice to stop chasing, I weeded out the negative energy in my life. The people who didn't accept me for who I was disappeared, and for the first time in my life, I was grateful. It left me with pure goodness. Suddenly, I was surrounded with honest, genuine people, who loved me for everything I am—the good, the bad, and the really bad. Connecting on a real level with people became my daily goal and my life became rich with poignant, powerful moments that were bursting with love. I realized life is a gift. It's not a guarantee, and it's too short to fill it up with superficial, empty moments that look dull and depressing on your life's canvas. Make it beautiful. Make it bright. Make it count.

This year has brought trials and tribulations that I thought would never come my way. Life has been relentless. But if given the chance, I would not erase one tear, one scream, one hug, one fight, one moment. They have brought me to the place I find myself today—in a loving relationship with myself and the ones I hold dear to my heart. The only thing I ever want to chase is truth.

PROTECT YOUR REPUTATION

So we've established that going along with the status quo is an impulse to resist and that surrounding yourself with a stellar support system is crucial to blazing your own trail in this world. Got it? Good. But that doesn't mean that you should be careless about what others think of you. You only have your good name once, and once it's gone, it can be nearly impossible to get it back. Your reputation matters. You may not like that fact, but it's true.

Reputation matters because it's the very first impression people have before they ever get a chance to meet you, and it absolutely impacts the way they view you. You're starting out in a good light and most likely they assume you can be trusted. It's like being on the winning team; the mere fact that you win says something about every member, including you. Unfortunately, the flip side is also true. Being associated with less-than-trustworthy friends or a shady organization can put you at a disadvantage. When meeting new people you may first have to convince them that you can be trusted, that you're not like the others.

Having the reputation that you're the real deal makes you unimaginably influential because people believe in your abilities, they trust you to do what you say you're going to, and are willing to support you along the way. A good reputation is more important than where you went to school, who your daddy is, and more important than your resume bullet points. It's why you are hired above the other girl and why you're given the raise. No matter if the task is large or small, take pride in what you do and do every job like your life depends on it. That's because it does! We are judged (and judge others in return) constantly. So you have a choice whether your acquaintances, colleagues, and people you've never met swap stories about how terrific, loyal, and capable you are or say the exact opposite. You can either have an incredible PR team talking you up or a team of people showcasing a video montage of your lowlights.

Recently a young woman approached me who wanted to be involved in I AM THAT GIRL. The first few times I met her I thought she was lovely, sweet, and obviously passionate about working with girls. But a few weeks later I learned that her actions did not exactly match her ideology. She had posted pictures of herself on social media outlets in which she was wasted and half naked. And when I asked around about her, more than a few people dismissed her as being just a "drunk party girl." It seemed that no one took her seriously and they certainly didn't recommend her as a good candidate for I AM THAT GIRL.

The next time I met with her and she expressed how much she wanted to get involved in a leadership role at the organization, I was honest. I told her that I wasn't sure if she knew, but that she had a terrible reputation in the eyes of many people who knew her. She was horrified and said that while many of her friends partied hard and were in the drug scene, she wasn't like that, but people frequently assumed that she did too. I said that by the look of the pictures she was voluntarily posting for the world to see, I understood their assumptions. Though she may be smart, savvy, and confident, the online reputation she was creating was quite the opposite. I explained that I couldn't afford to involve her in our organization because, even if it wasn't true, she was giving the impression that her personal life conflicted drastically with our mission and our ideals. Not that we don't have fun at IATG and let our hair down, but we take our job as role models seriously and can't afford to have anyone who tweets pictures of themselves holding a tequila bottle, doing body shots with only bikini bottoms on. Authenticity is a cornerstone of our business, and one bad apple, one person who doesn't practice what they preach, could spoil *our* good name.

This wasn't easy news to deliver, and I know that it was difficult for her to hear. It was an eye-opening experience because she didn't realize just how badly her reputation had been damaged by her actions. She certainly didn't fathom the impact of social media, of creating a negative on-line reputation, and that it would keep her from a job she truly wanted and seemingly had a passion for. The interviewer at your dream job, a potential client, an admissions board, or a professor, no one, owes you the benefit of the doubt, and they may dismiss you without an explanation. It is your responsibility to safeguard your reputation because it is a powerful and fragile thing. Make your good name one of the attributes that helps you realize your dreams; don't let losing it be yet another hurdle.

REMI NICOLE (Singer, Songwriter, Actress): As a teenager, I was always very strong minded and confident and had a lot of good friends, but once I was in my twenties, my career as a musician started to take off and a whole new group of people were introduced into my life. For a while it was infectiously fun and I really did have a great time. However, along with those new people came a lot of issues that I had to deal with, ones I hadn't dealt with before. The main one was being around people with astronomical levels of insecurities. These people were the types many others look up to, and their outward bravado would explain why, but deep down they were riddled with insecurities that really affected their actions. They became bitter, jealous, unhealthily competitive, and generally unkind when their insecurities hit high levels. They made unwise choices that often made things worse. I found myself, through associating with them, entangled in webs of deceit, lies, drama blown out of proportion, and general disarray.

I started to feel uncomfortable, as their behavior brought out my own insecurities, and suddenly I started to question myself more than ever, which made me try to mould myself differently. As ridiculous as it sounds, there was even a part of me that enjoyed the darker moments. There seemed to be a romance in the melancholy. It seemed to be "cool" to be unhappy and as a musician I thought it helped. However, that was such an uncomfortable feeling that I knew it couldn't be right. It took me until all of this passed, much later into my twenties, to realize that being yourself is all you can do in life. There is no other option. Every other option makes you feel uncomfortable in your own skin, confused, and empty, and that is no way to live. I realized if I couldn't be myself around certain people, or if I felt the need to try and be someone different, or indulge in negativity to be "cool," these were not the people I needed to surround myself with. They were not bad people, mostly, but they were not good for me and I was fortunate enough to realize that in good time.

Sometimes you have to make those choices and cut out the things in your life that don't have a positive impact on you. I learned that when I was around people who were open, honest, and secure with themselves it really brought out the best in me and helped me to grow at lot more, secure in the knowledge that I was being myself at all times, which really was all I could be.

I have been lucky all my life with the friends I have acquired, the good and the bad as you can learn from everyone, but I strongly believe that to have good people around you and to keep them around you is one of the most important factors that will shape your life for the better.

Unfortunately, it can be easy to get sucked into a world or a group of friends that is not good for you. Sometimes, as with my prospective intern and Remi, you don't even realize how you've changed or the negative effects your friends are having on you. Be sure you're checking in with yourself regularly, listen and look for signs that something isn't working, and if you discover that you need to make a change in your life, don't be afraid to do it. You'll be glad you did.

A MORE SUPPORTIVE CULTURE
STARTS WITH YOU

I believe in a world where girls empower girls, a world in where we are each other's biggest supporters and our greatest cheerleader, a world where we are taught to celebrate one another's gifts, not to be threatened by them. I believe in a world in which girls use their energy to solve the world's problems and inspire others to do the same, where girls recognize their limitless potential and remind each other who they are and what they are meant to do in this world.

Do you believe a world like this can exist? It can if you begin to create it. Start where you are and build a world for yourself that is full of supportive people who share your dreams. I dare you to have the courage not to be popular, not to make striving to fit in your top priority. I dare you to choose weird over normal, to hip hop dance to the rhythm inside your soul, and, when necessary, fight for something that doesn't make sense to anyone but you.

We are all perfectly flawed human beings, works in progress. Grant each other permission to be who you are. Be gentle with yourself and with the people around you. Protect your reputation and refuse to compromise your values. Listen to the advice of your closest circle of advisors, but not if that takes you down a path your heart knows is the wrong one. And above all, trust yourself enough to follow your own lead and go where your heart wants to take you. You may not change the whole world right away, but I promise you'll make the community of *you* a much brighter place.

PART II

SOARING 101

The second part of this book is all about learning to soar as high as your heart wings dare. In part I we chatted a lot about the importance of getting quiet long enough to really listen, to think for yourself, to speak your truth, and to discover your unique purpose. We talked about cultivating an unwavering confidence and creating a personal constitution, your go-to when life's greatest storms hit and your little boat starts getting tossed around. But now that you have a solid foundation of who you are and what you stand for, here comes the best part.

Now you get to show off all the hard work you've done by jumping in head first and using it in real life. In chapter 5 I'll cover the biggest problem most of us struggle with, and one that so often prevents us from making our dreams a reality: fear. Obviously we all smash into it at one time or another, but if you're going to be the most awesome version of yourself, you're going to have to learn how to coexist with fear and let it fuel your fire. In chapter 6 you'll learn how to make peace with your past mistakes, not allow disappointment or rejection to trip you up, and quickly bounce back from your epic failures so your dreams and goals don't suffer. In chapter 7 we'll assemble your dream team of people who will fight alongside you, challenge you, inspire you, and guide you. We'll talk about how to maintain those great relationships, and soak up all that they have to share with you. Finally, we'll wrap up chapter 8 with me reiterating why it's super important to really know and love yourself unconditionally. I hope I'll convince you to get off that boring, perfection treadmill, and inspire you to start sharing your unique gifts and talents with the world.

In short, we're going to walk you through how to be the most badass version of you, also known as being THAT GIRL.

You down? Then flip the page already!

CHAPTER 5

BE BOLD

"Whatever you can do, or dream you can, begin it. Boldness has genius, power and magic in it."

—Johann Wolfgang von Goethe

So now that you've practiced nurturing yourself better, tapped into what you really want in life, and even stood up for yourself, made your own decisions, and fought for what you believe in once or twice, what happens next? Now, it's game time! This is when the rubber hits the road, when mama nudges you out of the nest because you're ready to fly. Scared yet? Great, that's the point, because magic lives where fear and excitement intersect.

Mark Twain said, "Life is short, break the rules, forgive quickly, kiss slowly, love truly, laugh uncontrollably, and never regret anything that made you smile. Twenty years from now you will be more disappointed by the things you didn't do than by the ones you did. So throw off the bowlines. Sail away from the safe harbor. Catch the trade winds in your sails. Explore. Dream. Discover." That has always been one of my favorite quotes because it so perfectly captures the abandon of living a fearless life. So follow Mr. Twain's advice and live the heck out of life. Savoring the good parts and taking risks despite the fear and doubt that naturally comes along with it is the most you can ask of yourself and just might be your greatest achievement.

JENNY SMART (Badass): Anxiety is something that I have struggled with for most of my life, but it wasn't until my junior year in college that it really started to affect my day-to-day activities. The day I returned to the University of New Hampshire for my second semester of junior year I had my first real panic attack. I had no idea what was happening. I felt very faint and short of breath and thought I was just having a dizzy spell. Over the next few weeks I kept having what I thought were asthma attacks. I just could not catch my breath. I had gone to the doctor and they couldn't find anything wrong, so I just figured my asthma had kicked in again and it was something I would have to deal with. It wasn't until I had to make a trip to the emergency room because I was having chest pains, and my face and lips were tingling and numb, that I found out I was having panic attacks. The doctor gave me a box of tissues because I was sobbing my eyes out—relieved I wasn't having an actual heart attack—and a prescription for Ativan. And with that, I was cured!

Just kidding. It is now four years later and I still suffer from debilitating and painful panic attacks and anxiety. Like most people, my anxiety goes hand in hand with depression. So depending on how healthy I am mentally, my anxiety is either almost nonexistent or out of control. At its worst, I'm having anxiety over my anxiety. Which is exactly as healthy and fun as it sounds. My anxiety paralyzes me with fear. It stops me from hanging out with my friends and family, from chasing my dreams, and doing anything that remotely puts me out there. Last December I lost my job, and all of my fears and anxiety about not being good enough came true. I was not capable of doing what I came out to LA to do, I failed, and I needed to go home.

I decided I would extend my trip home for the holidays, thinking that three weeks in the tiny town I grew up in would help me out. After about three days on my parents' couch with nothing to do but let my anxiety eat me alive, I realized it was probably the wrong decision. However, it did get me to the breaking point that led me to the best and funniest life-changing decision I've ever made. I was going to stop holding myself back, try *every* new thing that came my way, date *everyone*, and everything would change and life would be perfect. I called it the "Year of Yes." I immediately told everyone, because that's what you do when you come up with the best idea ever, and waited for the first insane, life-changing event to come my way. As it turns out, looking for crazy, life-changing events doesn't actually work, and to be honest the first few months of my Year of Yes were basically me doing a bunch of stupid, embarrassing things that did not help me at all.

Then something kind of amazing happened. One Sunday afternoon these three boys showed up at my house to go on a hike with my roommate and they asked me to join. After they tried to convince me for way too long, I finally agreed. Yes, I will go on this stupid hike with you. The hike ended up being insane, so hard, but so fun. It pushed me way out of my comfort zone, both mentally and physically, and I had to trust that these people I didn't even know had my back. By the end of it I was bruised, freezing, and starving, but also happier than I had been in what felt like forever. I had found a group of people who were smart, hilarious, and inspiring, and I couldn't wait to continue our friendship. This was what I had been waiting for. I didn't have to backpack through Europe (I want to!), jump out of an airplane (I don't want to!), or do any other crazy cliché thing to change my life. I just had to be open to going on a hike with new people, and through them I met the greatest group of humans who I have had the most incredible, and yes, life-changing experiences with.

Finding a wonderful support system where I have decided to live my life and follow my passion has been the best thing to come out of my Year of Yes. My anxiety will always be something I will have to live with, but with the support of my friends, I am slowly working past the fears that have been holding me back from experiencing life.

The people who have done, seen, and accomplished amazing things in this world have done them not because they lack fear, but in spite of it. The same goes for everyday life. Jenny wasn't trying to invoke world peace, she just wanted to get off the couch and do *something* without being paralyzed by her anxiety. And she found a way to do that, with a little help from some new friends who inspired and supported her. She decided to live boldly, which was clearly outside of her comfort zone, and she is. To live boldly is what separates those who are truly the authors of their own lives from those who allow their story to be dictated by others. To live boldly is to choose what you want out of life and then to stalk it, chase it, and not rest until you've captured it.

To be bold means that, like Jenny, you will soar so far outside the universe of your comfort zone that you will get laughed at, maybe stared at, and if you're lucky, I mean really lucky, people will call you crazy. I wear that label with pride—it just means I'm willing to do things that someone else is (or thinks they are) too scared to do. Unfortunately, living a bold life makes you an open target for gossip, envy, and jealousy. Being the captain of your ship is a power that most people dream of, but never have the guts to take, and that can make them resentful. Don't worry about these people. I lived so much of my life worrying about what other people thought of me, concerned with how I would be judged, or what "they" would say. I don't exactly know who "they" are anyway, but I know I spent too much time making sure they liked me and they approved. And I'm here to tell you it was all a waste and a diversion from the great things my life is trying to offer me.

I know this is a confrontational statement, but I believe it's true; you will never achieve your dream if you let other people dictate your choices and don't exercise the boldness that every single one of us possesses. While boldness doesn't guarantee your success, you will have a much stronger chance of your dreams not being overlooked. Sheryl Sandberg, COO of Facebook, gave an incredible TED talk in 2010 on the notion of girls needing to "sit at the table." She even wrote a book entitled *Lean In*, where she talked about her experiences in the corporate world. She found that most girls don't make their voices heard, negotiate their own salaries, or even believe in their own abilities as much as men do and because of it, women in the workplace are suffering. She thinks women need to have more guts, more "Listen to me, I have a great idea!" I agree with her and it's not just in the corporate world that girls are shrinking from their potential. I think that boldness is magical, and if used correctly, it will open doors, create opportunities, and manifest dreams.

> "You gain strength, courage and confidence by every experience in which you really stop to look fear in the face."
>
> —ELEANOR ROOSEVELT

So how badly do you want it? How badly do you want that dream job, the big promotion, a relationship with a family member you've not spoken to in years, the chance to travel to a foreign country, acceptance to your dream school, or the adventure you've been daydreaming about? You can't afford to keep this passion inside, your dream relegated to dancing only in the living room of your mind. Who knows what embarking on this journey will bring you—it might not even be the dream you think you have, but a different one waiting around the corner of your next adventure. You deserve this, and trust me even if you don't yet believe it yourself, you are worth it.

YOU HAVE TO DREAM IT BEFORE YOU CAN DO IT

Before you can take that bold leap into your future, of course, you'll need a big juicy dream to leap *for*. Dreaming, much like faith, is one of those things that requires you to believe in something you have yet to see and for many imagining a world different from your own can be virtually impossible. Yet it's a powerful and necessary skill to cultivate.

Many of my friends have taken serious leaps of faith. My dear friend Adam created Pencils of Promise after he realized his passion for creating educational opportunities for children across the world. Bobby, Laren, Jason, and Jed have inspired me with their organization Invisible Children, fighting to end the longest running war in Uganda. Two of my friends, Yael and Adam, both creatively fighting cancer through their organizations F Cancer and Movember. My fellow Texan, Blake Mycoskie, created TOMS (and Friends of TOMS) after a life-changing trip to Argentina where he saw children without shoes and wanted to do something about it. And so many others, Scott at Charity Water, Sean at Fallen Whistles, Ellen at 30 Project, Nyla at Mama Hope, Elizabeth Gore with Girl Up, Somaly at The Somaly Mam Foundation, Jamie at TWLOHA, Haley at Girl Talk, Laruen at FEED, Rachel at The SOLD Project, and Scott at the Children's Cambodian Fund, just to name a few. Check out their organizations by the way, because they are redefining what it means to be a rock star and making the world better at the same time. I have an endless list of phenomenal friends who have dedicated their lives to fighting for others, and who have courageously "found a way" to do it. But before any one of them took a single step, they knew what it was they were chasing, they knew their WHY, and they knew they would stop at nothing.

Too many times, I have come across girls who lack the ability to just close their eyes and imagine their lives better, envision their dream job, or visualize their ideal relationship. They live by what they see, what already exists, and in that space there is no room to be your own author. But the world desperately needs you to be awesome, to dictate life on your terms, not sitting down, waiting for someone else to give you direction or permission. One of my favorite quotes by artist and writer Flavia Weedn is, "Cut not the wings of your dreams, for they are the heartbeat and the freedom of your soul." I truly believe that when we stop dreaming, the essence of our souls *is* lost along with our unique contributions to the world.

> **MARJA HARMON** (Singer, Actress, Broadway Performer): Getting the courage to say, "Why not me?" can be easy. I've found that keeping that courage and confidence in a world and an industry that will try to shake it is the difficult part. As a child I never looked at a performer and thought, "I can't do that." My family and friends never said, "She can't do that." In fact, it was the opposite, when I voiced my dreams to my parents and peers, they encouraged and supported them. They became dedicated to helping me find opportunities through training and performing that would give me the tools and guidance I would need to enter this very intangible and subjective industry.
>
> Any disintegration of confidence and self-esteem I had along the way came from self-doubt that was aggravated by outside

influences such as the media, negative peers and colleagues, and my own insecurities. It came from placing a lot of focus on destructive opinions and destructive people, and not on the positive opinions of my loved ones and most importantly me. Through influence, young women learn not to love themselves, their bodies, their talents, their choices, and to think "I can't" or "I'm not good enough, smart enough, talented enough, pretty enough." We are born with this innate confidence and slowly the insecurity demons wiggle their way into our heads and this becomes the battle we face for the rest of our adulthood.

No one in my support circle was telling me I couldn't be on Broadway. The only person who could get in my way was me by letting those demons impact my confidence. I needed to prepare myself for that, for what happens when my self-esteem gets low? What happens when I have to face rejection after rejection at auditions? How do I keep going forward? And even though I've had some wonderful successes, and played dream roles, and been on Broadway, those are still things I struggle with.

This is a business where you give a lot of yourself and are constantly putting so much of yourself out there even before you have the job! You are at your most vulnerable when you are in the audition process trying to get the validation of having them pick *you* out of so many. I've not gotten roles because of my weight, skin color, height, etc., and it's impossible to not take those rejections personally. If auditioning and booking jobs was solely based on how you sang, acted, or danced then it would be easier to handle certain outcomes. Knowing that there is an aesthetic and subjective element can lead you to focus on everything else, except yourself, and I can guarantee that the key to being incredibly unhappy in this business and in life is to start comparing. Whether it's comparing yourself to another girl at an audition or comparing your career with another person's career, it will ultimately lead to unhappiness and self-doubt. Especially in an age of social media where we can have a front row seat to the highlight reel in everyone's life, this can lead to a lot of focusing and coveting of everyone else's accomplishments and not your own. I have no control over what another girl wears, sings, and looks like. Every thought I spend worrying about those things is taking energy away from me to be *my* best.

I realized that if my self-worth was based on whether or not I get this part, whether or not this casting director or critic likes me, or whether or not this person thinks I'm beautiful or talented, then my happiness will mirror the roller coaster ride that is this business, and I didn't want that. We are all unique, and each and every one of us has something different to bring to the table. Every day I remind myself I have something special to offer, in fact all of these women do. Every woman here is talented and has the resume to prove it, it's just who is right for this specific part, this specific opportunity among so many opportunities.

Over the years I've had to find the balance of understanding what I can control, accepting what I can't, and never forgetting that I'm unique and have something to offer to the stage and to the world, and to know the only person who can really take that away is me. Now of course, I have to remind myself of these things every day. The insecurity demons will wiggle their way in every now and then, especially in an industry such as this. My confidence comes from appreciating the moments I get a chance to live my dream, and hopeful for the new opportunities that will eventually come, and trusting the voices from those dearest in my life and not listening to those demons!

Whether or not, like Marja, your dreams were encouraged from an early age, we are all entitled to dreaming big dreams and going after them, and yet so often we face obstacles that prevent many of us from taking that leap of faith. Dreaming requires an ability to imagine a world that you can't yet see and revel in it as though it's already your reality. It doesn't matter where you are from, your class, ethnicity, educational status, gender, race, sexual preference, or age, dreaming is one of the most special gifts we are all born with, and we must protect and fight for it against naysayers and skeptics. It's the reason why the story of Peter Pan is so beloved—to remind those of us who have lost our way that a world of possibility and wonder lies just two stars to the left and straight on till morning.

CHOOSE YOUR OWN ADVENTURE

To this day, the most courageous thing I have ever done was when I decided to follow my heart, packed up all my belongings, and moved out of my apartment in LA (where I had been living for ten years). It was terrifying because I didn't know exactly what I was doing or where I was headed next. Naturally, I had several mature and logical reasons for doing this, but not a single one of them was good enough to actually do it. They never are. I made this decision, like all of the best ones in life, with my heart guiding the way. Logic is often overrated. It's only in the kitchen of your warm, beating heart where you cook up the best stuff.

I told a friend that I'd do anything to pack up and move to Europe for a few months, to go on an adventure, and for the first time in my life have no clue where exactly that adventure would take me. (Full disclosure: I recently fell in love with a man who lives in Spain. Not a bad incentive.) My friend's blunt response to my daydream was simple, "Then do it." Ugh, she used a dose of my own medicine on me, and it was humbling to realize just how much preaching I had been doing about chasing down a dream while my cozy, comfortable world had gotten a little too cozy and a little too comfortable.

Of course, soon after that conversation the logic police showed up. "I mean honestly, Lex, I was kidding," I reprimanded myself. "Obviously you can't just pack everything up to chase love on a European adventure. You're not a kid anymore and last time I checked, you don't live in Never Never Land." I decided there was no good reason I couldn't up and leave. I have a job I can technically do from anywhere. I'm young, not (yet) married, don't have children, not in serious debt, not suffering from a debilitating illness, or running from the police. Now is the time—before one or more of those conditions changes—to do something mildly crazy and ridiculously exciting. Plus, every bit of it scared me, which is the exact reason to do it. I wasn't going to let fear paralyze me like a spider caught in its web. Decision made.

Now, I'm not so Pollyanna that I can't see there are real life responsibilities and paying your bills is necessary. I just don't believe that "growing up" means giving up on life as an adventure. You should be seeking out fun, practicing spontaneity, and doing things that don't make a whole lot of sense. No matter where you are in life, whether you're a student discovering your passions, a new mom learning how to raise your first kid, a single young professional chasing your dream career, reinventing yourself in your sixties or somewhere in between—don't let anything or anyone hold you back from what you really want. If you're not happy then change something—do what you have to do to stay true to yourself. If you need an adventure, then create one.

You have this one, precious life and you alone dictate the colorful resplendence of your mural. You decide the spectacular spectrum of shades and brush strokes you'll use to illustrate your story. And while I can't fathom what life has in store for any of us, I do know that life is not too short, but rather, far too long for you to waste another day not seeking out every adventure calling your name.

There are a lot of unspoken rules in life—society's invisible stipulations for "normalcy" and the unspoken pressures to fit in. I say, to hell with that. No person made history or caught the tail of happiness fitting in, staying quiet, and flying under the radar. We are all on the adventure of our life, with no idea where we are going exactly, what we are doing, or any other details to the story. I'll keep you posted on where the wind blows me, but in the meantime, start charting out your own expedition and keep me posted where *you* end up. Who knows, maybe our paths will cross on our journey back to our very own Never Never Land.

TIME OUT! CULTIVATE YOUR INNER ADVENTURER

Okay, so not everyone is like me. I'm a big picture girl for sure, and sometimes I can't stop dreaming up new ideas and adventures long enough to pick one to execute. But maybe you're more detail oriented or have the kind of mind that is naturally geared toward executing what's in front of you. That's great! Just as I need people like you in my life to help me focus on and run with my ideas, you're going to need people who help you think up new dreams and adventures.

But that doesn't mean that you can't also cultivate a dreamer spirit yourself. It may just take a little practice. Just as you do with exercise or tackling long-term projects, create a habit of checking in with your dreams on the regular.

Make a list of your favorite things—the things you love to do, the things you are drawn to, lose yourself in, or stay up late thinking about. Next, pick one and spend an hour thinking about and researching all the ways that you could become actively involved in that field.

I keep a list entitled "Burner." It's all the crazy ideas I think up when I have a few minutes to myself. I write down things that interest me or that I want to learn more about. Like I said, I'm a big adventure dreamer, but dreams aren't about the size, they are about the uniqueness and the creativity that only you can imagine.

A good tip for dreaming is to start thinking outside the box. As a warm up, I'll just start imagining something that is completely and ridiculously outrageous. For instance, I'll imagine that I'm going to start a business where I train miniature elephants (that don't technically exist) who also happen to talk (not possible) and fly (also not possible) as pets for mermaids (interesting) who just so happen to fancy them. Then I'll spend ten minutes mentally creating a commercial for these adorable creatures. Do I end up cracking myself up most of the time? Obviously. But, it gets my brain juiced up to think outside the box and that's the warehouse of awesome. Think about the most impossible things you can, even if it makes you laugh out loud because it's so absurd, and then, when you say something like, "I want to ignite the twenty-first century women's movement," (my goal in this lifetime) it will sound surprisingly reasonable.

Dreaming is a gift you give yourself and the *one* place you should be able to create and imagine anything with no judgment. The main reason we don't dream is because we shut down the possibility before we even get the idea into our brains. Let go and dream. Big, if not downright huge.

GO FOR IT

So if you haven't sailed off on your big adventure just yet, I get it. It's normal to feel hesitant about taking a step into the unknown especially if you can't anticipate what's around the corner, but that's not a good enough reason to sit on the sidelines. Who knows, going after your dream just might bring you something even more wonderful than you originally thought. Don't limit yourself to what you can imagine—the world has so much more to offer.

PENNY ABEYWARDENA (Head of Girls and Women Program and Associate Director of Commitments at the Clinton Global Initiative): At the start of my career I asked myself, "Do I do what I'm good at or do I do what I'm passionate about?" The answers to these questions don't have to be mutually exclusive. That said, early in one's career it can often become (and more often is) apparent that the skills you want to cultivate don't neatly dovetail with the type of work you admire.

It was just after college, while working concurrently for a boutique investment firm and a well-known human rights organization, that my crisis of conscious hit. Obviously. Many say I was asking for it: Who can work in finance during the day and steep themselves in human rights advocacy at night and *not* face a moral dilemma? Given these circumstances, my crisis was rather status quo, but the pressure of it took me by surprise. I loved both jobs but for very different reasons. My finance job challenged me to build skills I knew I needed such as a burgeoning talent for sales. Selling people on ideas has been a powerful tool, core to my success. The nonprofit job, on the other hand, developed my awareness and passion for issues related to girls and women and a deep admiration for the human rights researchers around me. I spent a lot of time dreaming of being an activist on the ground, uncovering and addressing human rights abuses around the world. The reality, however, was that this line of work didn't take advantage of what I was good at.

I found the answer to my dilemma through fund-raising for nonprofits. It was a challenge to leave my previous positions and step into this critical, albeit not overly celebrated, role within the nonprofit sector. Fund-raisers need to fully understand the content and possess excellent communication skills in order to translate and pitch their work to donors. However, it was a surprisingly hard shift in ambition to go from wanting to work in a program to a job in development. I found myself constantly second-guessing my decision to leave finance and enter this underappreciated, sometimes mocked fund-raising role. However, as the years passed and my skills sharpened, the fact slowly dawned on me that this might have been the smartest thing I could be doing. Without quite realizing it, I had acquired significant program expertise while having sharpened my "commercial" sensibilities. Ten years later I find myself in a job that perfectly capitalizes on both.

The journey to understanding your professional self inevitably takes you to the question: Why do you do what you do? It is easy to ignore and difficult to tackle, but take it on. The benefits of understanding the role of passion as well as your skills and talents in your decision making will be indispensable as you take on your career. A long-term goal may require early sacrifices, and the best way to capitalize on that sacrifice is by understanding why you do what you do.

Even though not being able to predict her future career made her nervous, Penny listened to her gut and then stepped out into the unknown. Without focusing on what she really wanted to do and accomplish in her career, Penny would have had a much more difficult time making the bold step into the world of nonprofit fund-raising. Even though she faced ridicule over her choice and sometimes doubted her path, she was able to cling to the knowledge that she was putting her talents to good use in a career that she felt passionately about.

Whether it's planning your next career move, choosing a college major, taking off on an adventure, or making any new, slightly scary commitment, if you have the passion, then have the guts to throw your hat in the ring. Swallow your pride and ignore the naysayers (you included!). Nothing great or exciting that you want to do in your life is ever going to be handed to you on a silver platter. You might have to fight for it whether it's you against your inner skeptic or you against the world.

"You miss a hundred percent of the shots you never take."

—WAYNE GRETZKY

Keep in mind that getting what you want is not necessarily the goal here, and that's because the outcome of your actions is not always in your control. The real victory is in knowing that you are the kind of person who takes a shot every time, regardless of whether you're guaranteed a basket. Recently, a girl came up to me after one of my talks and said, "Alexis, I know you keep preaching this idea of 'just going for it,' but I've been doing that and time and time again, it doesn't work out. So what's the point of putting myself out there if things never work out the way they are supposed to? Don't you think at some point it's okay to accept that it's just not meant to be?"

I completely understand where she was coming from. If you've tried every single door, looked at the same situation from every angle, and still you aren't making any progress, then sure, maybe it's not meant to be. Or, I should say, maybe it's not meant to be exactly as you had imagined it. Like Penny, sit down and think about what you really want in the broadest way possible. If you can't become a doctor, think about what you thought you'd love about a medical career and find a new way of getting that. Don't just walk away from your dream without exploring the other ways you can achieve it.

This girl wanted to go to art school and had applied time and time again. She had met with successful artists to get their advice, called the deans of the art school, emailed her portfolio, and cold-called people looking for a way in. Yet time and time again, she was getting doors closed and professionals advising her to maybe try something else. I asked if she had tried everything, and I mean everything? Her response was an exasperated, "Yes," to which I responded, then try something different. Sometimes we're not listening when God, the universe, or whatever you believe in is trying to tell us something, and beating a dead horse does us no good.

A month later, she shot me an email saying that she had taken my advice and tried something different. She knew she was passionate about art and wanted desperately to learn more about it and work in that field. But this time, instead of banging her head against the art school door yet again, she applied to work at a very prestigious museum. They were impressed with both her theoretical knowledge of art as well as her experience as an artist herself, and thought she had the potential to be a phenomenal curator. Here was a chance to put her many skills to good use that only came along when she opened her field of vision to accepting more than she initially imagined. She was suddenly living a brand new dream. So worry less about the exact outcome and more about staying in the game. Your boldness will be rewarded somehow, even if it's not how you had imagined.

MAKE SURE YOU CAN BACK IT UP

While I'm a huge advocate for being bold and breaking the rules when you need to, you better be able to back it up when tested. There is nothing more frustrating than doing all the work to chase down an opportunity and then when the opportunity presents itself not being ready or prepared to properly execute it. I don't believe in luck. I believe that luck is what happens when hard work and preparation slam into a fantastic opportunity. I also believe we are the ones in charge of creating that awesome opportunity.

Now if you know anything about me, you know that I grew up in Texas with four older brothers and that I'm borderline obsessed with college football. Don't judge me. When you are raised with wolves, you can't be surprised if you behave like one. In addition to four big brothers and an incredible daddy, I was also spoiled by having one of the best high school football teams in the state, only to then graduate and attend a school with one of the best college football programs in the country. Needless to say, college football was in my blood.

I was in grad school at the University of Southern California, my alma mater, the year blogging hit the online scene. The beauty of blogging was that it provided a platform for the everyday Joes or Janes to make their voices heard in a public setting and leveled the playing field with professional media outlets. Our quarterback, Matt Leinart, was and still is one of my dear friends; our head coach was the dad of my sorority sister; and our quarterback coach, Yogi Roth, was my best friend in grad school. Given that I had full access to our team, coaches, and practices. I figured why not start a blog about USC football that gave inside access to a team everyone wanted to know more about? We were the number one ranked team in the nation at the time going for a history-making Three-Pete (named for our head coach Pete Carroll) by potentially winning three national titles in a row, something that had never been done. The entire nation was watching and wondering whether we were going to make history or fail wonderfully trying.

In weeks, we had hundreds of thousands of people reading our posts. My cofounder Nathan and I were contacted by the *New York Times*, the *LA Times*, *Sports Illustrated*, ESPN, and Fox Sports wondering who we were and why and how the hell we had inside access to the best college sports team in the country. For the non-sports watchers, ESPN is the Oprah

> **"The question isn't who's going to let me; it's who is going to stop me."**
>
> **—AYN RAND**

of sports television, and it was one of my little girl dreams to be a sideline reporter. I knew my favorite ESPN TV show *College Game Day* was coming to my campus so I got ready. I wasn't sure how I was going to do it, but I knew that if I got the chance to meet anyone on their production team, I wanted to be prepared. I spent weeks memorizing every USC football statistic for the past ten years. I made hundreds of flashcards, studying stats, reading the book *Football for Dummies,* and racking my dad's sports almanac brain. Even though I didn't, I prepared as if I had an interview lined up for my dream job.

Then it happened. One of the producers from the show got my number from the sports office. Opportunity presented! They were trying to recruit as many students for the live broadcast and had heard I was the girl on campus who could get the word out. It helped that I had told everyone in the office that I was dying to meet someone, anyone from the show (you have to enroll people in your dreams because if it's not on their radar, how can they help?). The producers thanked me in advance and said in return for my help, they'd gladly get me tickets to the game (which I already had). However, before they hung up, I asked (just out of curiosity, wink-wink) where they were filming the show. Without thinking the producer gave me the location and laughed saying, "We're working on East Coast feed, so we have to be there at 3:30 a.m., gonna be an early morning. Anyhow, thanks again for rallying the troops."

My mission was set. I knew more USC football facts and had just presented myself with an opportunity to meet the producers, the hosts, and the entire crew for my ESPN dream job. I went to bed extra early and was dressed and ready for work at 3:00 a.m. I waltzed right into where they said they would be, beating everyone by half an hour. Only the makeup artist, some of the lighting guys, and two assistants were there. I saw a huge breakfast spread, so I sat down at the main table awaiting my future boss. Eventually, the three hosts and two producers along with other staff members came walking in sleepy-eyed with uncombed hair. With every arrival, I was given a double take, followed by a confused expression, but not one of them said *anything* to me. They sat down, joining this strange girl at their breakfast table, and then asked me politely to pass the milk for their cereal.

It took twenty more minutes of sitting there until one of them finally asked, "Sorry, but who are you?" All the guys started laughing (proving it was on all their minds). My simple and confident response, "I'm Alexis Jones, I work for you." Naturally they were really confused, not knowing how to respond. "You're Lee, right?" I asked as I looked at the producer I'd chatted with the day before and whose voice I had recognized. He nodded. I said, "I'm smart, I'm hard working, and I know *this* football team better than any of you. I think it's in your best interest to have me work with you. Especially if they go to the championship this year, you're going to need an expert on USC. Also, worst case scenario, you say no and I go home and go back to bed … but I'm really hoping that's not the case." I didn't even bat an eye because I knew every bit of it was true. He paused for several seconds, almost like he was waiting for me to back down, but I didn't because I was more than ready for this opportunity. I'd earned that confidence through endless hours of studying, over weeks of tireless preparation.

He looked around him to the other guys sitting at the table, in hopes of some kind of help. They just started laughing and smiling. "Why not?" one of them said, "I mean, she's here, isn't she." The others agreed, "I mean it takes guts to just show up and, like she said, worst case, today is her first and last day." He smiled, shook his head, and said, "Wow. Okay. Yeah, sure, we'll see what you got." In the end I was a huge asset to them over the next several months, and I was given the opportunity to work with them and stand on the field for the biggest college football game in the history of the game, the 2005 Rose Bowl. Over the next several weeks, I was tested time and time again. But as I had promised, I had insider access to the team and I knew stats better than anyone. I earned the right to work with them, I just needed to create the chance to let them know.

Now, I would never have had the audacity to show up that early morning and stare down a producer had I not been able to back it up. It would have been professional suicide and I would have been laughed out of the room if I was that arrogant, gotten the opportunity, but hadn't done the homework. So you better know what you're getting yourself into and if someone is going to stick their neck out for you, gamble on you, give a "no name" a big chance, you better be prepared and not let them down.

It's easy to talk the talk, but delivering on it is what separates the good from the great. You have to earn it, you have to do the dirty work, put in the long hours, humbly pay your dues, and when you get the chance to shine, shine so brightly people can't take their eyes off you. Authentic boldness is knowing that you can back it up. Otherwise, you're just another entitled princess who thinks you deserve something you haven't begun to earn. Arrogance will get you nowhere in life and only builds a reputation that will repel opportunity like the plague.

Also, you never start at the top nor would you want to because it wouldn't be meaningful if you did. When I realized I wanted to be a motivational speaker I didn't start by giving talks to thousands of people. My first talk was to six girls and then thirty and more and more from there. Only after countless hours of preparation and hundreds of unpaid talks can I now confidently share my life experiences with thousands of people and get paid to do it! I have worked on my personal life and read a myriad of books on relevant topics, I compassionately engage with people on a daily basis to better understand the human experience, I do deep internal self-inquiry, and I'm up to date on important and relevant statistics. When I finally stand up on stage, boldly giving my advice to a group of people, challenging, inspiring, and encouraging them, I do it all without the fear of being a fraud. And that is such a powerful and influential place to stand, knowing you are exactly where you should be.

Boldness requires you to be the real deal. It requires that you are what you preach. The product of being authentically confident is that you *get* to be bold. LeBron James gets to shoot the three-pointer with two seconds left in the game because of the countless shots he had taken in practice. He earned the right to shoot the game-winning basket. So it's not just about how badly do you want it, but more importantly, are you willing to do the work? Are you willing to work harder than anyone else out there? Are you willing to be the first one there and the last one to leave at the end of a very long day? That is the fuel to boldness. Remind yourself that when you're bold, you are the captain of your ship and you can point your boat in any direction you please.

KNOW WHEN TO LET GO

There is a certain amount of blind faith required in being bold. There is only so much you can do personally to "make something happen." I'm willing to do 90 percent of the work, but this is where my faith kicks in, that last 10 percent. I believe we can only get ourselves so far with preparation, and then there is that last leap of faith required to make up the rest.

Confession: I love the Indiana Jones trilogy. There's this awesome scene at the end of *Indiana Jones and the Last Crusade* where Harrison Ford, playing Indiana Jones,

> "Faith is taking the first step even when you don't see the whole staircase."
>
> —MARTIN LUTHER KING JR.

has miraculously passed through this lethal maze and the final challenge between him and his treasure (the holy grail) is traversing a huge chasm. Because he doesn't "see" a bridge he's left with only one option—to close his eyes and take a leap of faith onto an invisible bridge. His hope (and what his life depends on) is that a bridge will appear that will prevent him from falling hundreds of feet to his death below. Luckily (and sorry to spoil the ending), as he clenches his heart, closes his eyes, and takes one terrifying step, a bridge magically appears under his foot and his faith is rewarded with safe passage.

I sometimes think about that scene when I'm facing something in life. I work so hard and the most difficult part for me is, after I've done all I can, to throw my hands up and trust that it's either meant to be or not. I tend to be a type A, "can do anything" control freak, so giving up that last 10 percent is more painful than all the legwork I've done for the previous 90. But that's where my personal faith kicks in and I couldn't write this book without including my secret advantage, the ace up my sleeve. My faith plays a major role in my life. Regardless of what religion you ascribe to, whether you believe in God, Allah, Jesus, Mother Nature, or purple polka dotted unicorns, I encourage you to snoop around that area of your life and to feed your faith and spirituality the best way you know how.

JACLYN BELL (A Mere Human Being): The eternal optimist. I have been called this. I have called myself this. I have worn that badge of honor around on my Girl Scout sash in this life not only to courageously pursue all of my endeavors, fears, and dreams but to refute the jaded realism that seems to be taking this world by storm. However, there came a time recently where I was forced to humbly realize that a perpetual attitude of butterflies and babies was not courageous at all. In fact, it was cowardly. I mean, how can an eternal optimist grieve, be sad, or feel depressed? Well, they can't. And that's not okay because we are merely human beings. God and I wrestle a lot about that actually. Me being a mere human, that is. And He always has to put me in a full nelson and pin my face to the mat in order for me to actually accept the fact that I need Him and others in order to get through this crazy life. In fact, I would say I spent all of last year with my face on the mat.

You see, last year I lost my Papa. Except he wasn't the cute grandpa that I only saw at family Christmases filled with generic conversation and bad jokes. He was my advisor, my confidante, my hero, and my father. He raised my siblings and me when our parents chose to renegotiate their contract on parenthood. At the ages of six, eight, and twelve our birth dad walked out on us for a life of looking at the bottom of a bottle and my mom went with him. And so the three of us were taken in and taught everything we know by the most loving, faithful, Godly man we've ever encountered.

With his death came the conditioning of my menial human heart and mind. I can assure you, nothing prepares you for when you lose your favorite person on this earth. Every ounce of strength and faith inside you leaves you desperately searching for answers that sometimes just aren't there. Searching for something, anything, to dull the ache of that person's absence. For months I begged for the faith and courage just to endure. But there's no irony in the fact that you find holiness in, well, the holes. In dark places that are empty and desperate and lost. You see, faith isn't believing in something really, really hard. Hebrews 11:1 tells us that "Faith is being sure of what we hope for and certain of what we do not see." And so with a lot of faith, a lot of acceptance, and a lot of love from my beautiful friends I feel blessed to have made it to the other side. Don't get me wrong, I've got some pretty gnarly scars and Band-Aids everywhere, but I'm still here. I believe that there is meaning amid mess and pain, that more will be revealed, and that truth and beauty will somehow prevail. It must be that pesky eternal optimist in me.

There will be times in your life when you need to beg for immeasurable faith and courage just to endure this world. You will lose something or worse, someone. You will be scared. You will be beat. You will fail. You will lose your badge of honor and trade it in for a badge of humility. And that is okay. You are merely a human being. I encourage you to embrace the hurt.

Cry a whole bunch about it. Learn from it. Cry a whole bunch more. Take from it just as it has taken from you. And then peel your face off the mat and move forward.

Through losing her Papa, Jaclyn learned that not only could anything happen in this life, but she could endure it and move on. That kind of confidence only comes, unfortunately, from surviving something very difficult. But you can practice letting go of the control (you think) you have over your life and how it will unfold. That's where faith comes in.

My faith allows me to be bolder than I could ever be with all the preparation and memorization in the world. I believe that if something is meant to be, it will. That means I *get* to be courageous because I know that when things don't work out as planned, I'm still precisely on the path I'm supposed to be on. Even though I don't always understand it at the time, I trust things will unfold perfectly and not even I can mess up what I'm meant to do in this world. Maybe it's naïve or childish to believe in a world where there's an unconditionally loving God that has my best interests at heart (and I'm not asking you to agree with me), but I'll admit this—that crazy, awesome belief absolutely works for me. It makes my life brighter, my purpose stronger, and my courage bigger.

However, on the flip side of that coin, people sometimes use religion and faith as an excuse to be passive. I don't believe that while you sit at home, God magically hand delivers everything you've prayed for while you're on your butt watching TV. While I do think the God of my understanding *is* capable of anything, I don't believe that if you stay cooped up in your room praying, your dream husband will appear on your doorstep, your future boss will magically find your phone number and offer you your dream job, or that God will melt away those extra pounds. I believe you have to do the legwork, you have to chase down whatever you want trusting that the desire has been placed on your heart for a reason; you have to fight for your passion, your dreams, and chase down everything you can to make them your reality. Then you patiently wait for God and the universe to show up for the last 10 percent, trusting that whether or not that last 10 percent looks like you thought it would, it works out exactly as it should. It's a delicate and humble dance with the Divine, and something that I work on daily.

In fact, I remember when I decided I was going to be on *Survivor*, I made an obscene amount of phone calls to people I thought could help me, asked my best friend to help me make an audition tape, meticulously filled out an application (rereading it to make sure there were no errors), attached the perfect picture that encompassed my personality, drove to the production company, had the courage to actually get out of the car, and eventually snuck in and got the chance to talk to the producers in order to (hopefully) convince them to cast me. I just remember thinking regardless of whether I get cast or not, I can walk away from this dream knowing I did everything in my power to make it happen. But then after my 90 percent was up, I also had to let go and trust that it was either in the cards or not, but either way, I knew there was nothing more I could have done.

Yet, let's be honest, letting go and being detached from a certain outcome, especially when we really want something to happen, is difficult. "Getting over it" is so much easier said than done—what are we supposed to do, just stop caring? Well, kind of, yeah. We can really only control and care about our own actions. We can't control what people think or say or how they choose to feel or act. We can't control what happens the moment we walk out the front door or whether our loved ones live long or short lives. Surrendering to this reality is a powerful exercise, and is as rewarding and as difficult as "living in the moment." Sure, ideally, we would all learn to breathe deeper and appreciate exactly what we are experiencing in the moment. And yes, ideally, we would detach ourselves from the reactions of others, from our own expectations and hopeful thinking, but often we allow that thing or that person to get right under our skin and irritate us to death.

TIME OUT! THE POWER OF SILENCE

I believe in the power of silence, stillness, meditation, prayer, and just being. It's the most important thing I do. Sure I've worked very hard over the years, but my life is too rich, has worked out too serendipitously, for me to take all the credit. There's also a luxury in believing that there's someone else or something else who has a hand in how my life turns out. Like I said before, I believe that I, Alexis Jones, cannot mess up my life's master plan. So in every choice I make, in every star I shoot for, I give it my best and then close my eyes and trust that it all goes exactly as it should, regardless of the outcome. I envision that the right people come into my life at the right time with the right keys to the right doors. Then I let go and patiently wait for more to be revealed.

How do I get still, just be, pray, meditate, or get silent? There are so many ways, but my favorite way of doing all of them simultaneously is finding a quiet place where I'll be uninterrupted, sitting comfortably on the ground (what I prefer but completely up to you), maybe sitting on a pillow with the wall behind me, close behind me in case I get lazy and start slouching. I close my eyes, I put my hands on my knees, and I just start to breathe.

Then I start to focus on taking long breaths in and out, consciously trying to relax my muscles and let my shoulders fall. Then I try to just observe my thoughts. The first few minutes tend to be an internal dialogue (a.k.a. a fight) about all the other things I *should* be doing to be more productive than "simply sitting and doing nothing." I mentally write to-do lists and panic about things I've forgotten and am just now remembering. It takes about three solid minutes before this barrage of thoughts (seemingly uncontrollable) stops pouring in.

If I can make it through those first three minutes without breaking my session to jot something down, to make that quick phone call or whatever else I've decided is more important than my morning ritual, my mind starts to finally calm down.

I love visualization so I always imagine a door appearing right there before me, my hand gripping a beautiful old handle, and opening up into another world, as if I walked through the wardrobe just like in *The Lion, the Witch and the Wardrobe*. I imagine a tiny cottage, my relatives and friends who have passed away always greet me, and I sit on the couch of my tiny little house with my creator (who shows up in different forms depending on how creative I feel that day) and we just chat. We chat about life, love, heartbreaks, my recent victories, my fears, and my current dilemmas. Whatever comes to mind, I silently share and then I await a wisdom that transcends my understanding, an indescribable compassion and grace that helps guide my thoughts and my actions into a more loving direction. I swear when I open my eyes things are physically brighter and I feel more secure, more grounded, more confident, and more me. My veins pump faster and my heart beats stronger. I appreciate myself, my loved ones, and all that I have more and focus on what I'm lacking less. In that space I'm able to connect with the best parts of me, to really see me in all her infinite brilliance.

This all may sound silly to you but somehow that little couch, in that little cottage, sharing my life and just sitting quietly, makes me a better human. Regardless of whether this works for you, I found something that works for me; which inspires compassion as opposed to impatience, love as opposed to fear, and creativity as opposed to rigidity. I don't know how you best connect with yourself. For some people it's attending a traditional church, synagogue, or mosque; for others their "religion" is running, it clears their minds. Some people go on a long stroll in the park, read an inspiring book, have coffee with a dear friend, do yoga, watch sermons online, volunteer at the local homeless shelter, or any other way that puts them in touch with themselves and allows them to exercise love. All that matters is that you're silent long enough to hear your own thoughts.

I believe that our divine creator exists in the hearts of every single one of us, so I do my best to be quiet and still long enough to hear that voice speaking from within, and more often than not I get pointed in the right direction. Prayer doesn't have to be fancy, meditation doesn't have to be complicated, and getting quiet can be as simple as that, just stopping what you're doing and listening to your own breath. But either way, I encourage you to create a daily practice of being still. I'm working on twenty minutes a day, in the morning before I jump into my busy schedule, and while there are days when it's the last thing I want to do, by the time I'm done, I realize it's my favorite part of the day.

We are never in control. Even in the moments when we feel we are the most. All you can do is work hard, throw yourself into the deep end, believe the impossible is possible, and then close your little peepers and take a leap of faith. Like Indiana Jones, I've found that that bridge shows up sturdy under my feet every time, even when it takes me to a destination I wasn't anticipating.

LIVE YOUR LIFE (IT ISN'T ANY GREENER SOMEWHERE ELSE)

The flip side to dreaming big and chasing your goals at all costs is that you can get caught up in the fast pace and excitement of searching for a new adventure and forget to appreciate the one you're already on. Dreaming is essential to manifesting your future, but it's all too easy to sink into the trap that life is always greener somewhere else. Part of dreaming is being content where you are at in this precise moment, choosing happiness now instead of your happy being contingent on "when all your dreams come true."

While you can create any opportunity you want, it's also true that you should, as they say, "be careful of what you wish for, because you just might get it." Often the reality of your dream is different than what you expected. For instance, my dream was to be a motivational speaker, to travel all over the world, and to write books. Well, that is exactly what my life is now and while it has incredible perks, I also live out of a suitcase. I now have the work life I dreamed of—lots of travel, different every day, no boss, no office—and while it certainly has some beautiful benefits, there are also some serious challenges to not having a "normal" life. It was only once I had the life I'd been hoping for that I began to discover the beauty in simplicity and routine—and all the things I once swore off began whispering sweet nothings to me. I had to accept that I chose this life of uncertainty; I sought this lifestyle, and patiently awaited its arrival. So how could I have the audacity to question it now? Then I had an epiphany.

It is not about my job, whether it's still satisfying or burning me out. It's not about the pros and cons I can write down and mull over, and it has nothing to do with grass of any kind or their varying shades of green. It's not the amount of traveling I'm doing, the growing pressure of settling down and starting a family, or any other outside factor I could point at. It's about making a choice to enjoy the life I'm living right now with all of its inevitable positives and negatives. And that requires digging deep into your soul on a daily basis and making the choice to be joyful, not because you have the perfect job, found the love of your life, or won the lottery, but just because you chose to be that way.

It's so easy to "live in the moment," in theory. But doing it is so much harder. We have to give up on comparing our lives to what we think we could be doing or who we could be with. Trust that you are capable of making good decisions for yourself. Then when the going gets tough or you begin to doubt yourself remember that you made the best decision with the information you had at the time. When we live in a "grass is always greener" mentality, nothing is ever good enough. It's an insatiable hunger for the next big thing or the next big adventure. Our challenge as twenty-first-century girls living in a world of endless choice and instant gratification is learning to value and cherish the bird we have in our hands, not the two fluttering up in the sky. Learning to be grateful for the here and now is a daily practice that we could all use more of.

The same goes for our expectations of other people, particularly our significant others. When we cling to our childhood fantasies of "happily ever after," not only are we putting unrealistic pressure on the other person but setting ourselves up for disappointment. For instance, I have a girlfriend who is forever meeting and then being let down by her Prince Charming. As soon as the guy fails to meet just one of her unspoken expectations, she immediately crosses him off her "potential" list. The ironic thing is that on several occasions, I thought there were some great guys who she overlooked or didn't give a proper chance because they didn't fit her (unrealistic and impossible) standards.

Part of the challenge of dreaming is also not losing sight of what's sitting right in front of you when you've constructed an entire idea of someone or something in your mind. When we decide that our dream guy, dream job, dream anything comes in a very specific package, we tend to be disappointed when we don't see what we were looking for. It's a terribly limiting habit because by doing this we can rule out some fantastic packages just because they don't have the right kind of bow on top. Be open-minded to the opportunities that come, allow life to surprise you, and accept that maybe what you think you want isn't the very best thing for *you*.

As singer, songwriter Maia Sharp sings, "You were my whole flat world, until the day I discovered it was round. You were my favorite movie, until they started making them with sound." Be willing to see past the scope of your life experience and trust that what lies out beyond the horizon is better than anything you can currently fathom. A dream that you begin will only reach its full potential when you let it free to progress in its own way.

Life's timing is strangely perfect and not necessarily synced with our rather impatient, internal clocks. If you can forget everything you've heard about the way it's "supposed" to be, and trust that it will be exactly as it should be, you will be able to live a more satisfying life.

STOP WAITING

The world will try to convince you to play it safe, not dare too much or dream too big, to color within the lines. Don't listen to it. There is nothing more life threatening than resignation because the moment you settle for complacency and compromise who you are, you've lost the best part of life and squandered the potential that lies within you. Don't believe it's okay to show up every day at a job that you don't love or one you do just for the money. Discard others' expectations; hold tight to your own. The beauty of life is that it is your own, so dare to live it.

Choose what you will and will not settle for, not only from others but more importantly from yourself. Become what you believe. Prioritize life by what genuinely makes your heart smile. Love fearlessly. Abandon hesitation. Do everything. Imagine. Create. Surprise yourself. An uncommon life is for those who are willing to take leaps of faith, chance fate, and bask in the uncomfortable. It is worth it. Life is magical, intoxicatingly surprising with unforeseen twists and turns on a Technicolor roller coaster. Prepare yourself for the road less traveled, for an uncommon life. Accept your fate, but also know your life is what you choose to do with it. Take a deep breath. It begins when you say!

> **INGRID VANDERVELDT** (Dell Entrepreneur in Residence and Creator of the Dell Innovators Credit Fund): If I had the opportunity to sit down with my twenty-one-year-old self, I would tell her that everything is perfect. I would also tell her that there is a divine order to everything, and that the saying you always hear about, "Things happen exactly as they are supposed to," is in fact true.

That being said, had I known that concept then, I would have accepted the total awesomeness that is *me* (and you for that matter), and I would have kicked butt even more. Or would I?

When I was twenty-one, I pushed myself to be accomplished. I had (or was in the process of earning) a master's degree in Architecture and had run and won the office of National Director of the American Institute of Architecture Students. I was also elected National Student Director of the America Institute of Architects. That said, even with the external accomplishments, I would find myself questioning my capabilities at times, and would feel down when people told me no. Instead of seeing the no as part of the process to get to a yes, I would find myself at times questioning if I was good enough.

Instead, had I accepted my "awesomeness" (wink), I would have finished school, hopped in my car, driven to Los Angeles, and worked my way into television even earlier. That said, had I done that, I would have missed out on business school and the opportunity to learn that not only could I create environments and opportunity from nothing (architecture), but that I could balance a checkbook and learn how to create wealth through business, while earning that TV show along the way!

Had I accepted my "awesomeness" when I was twenty-one, I could have been Jenny McCarthy (or so I wanted to believe). Had I become Jenny 2.0, I might not have ever broken the party girl perception and gone on to be trusted by investors, customers, and employees who enjoyed that I was fun and yet serious enough to make sure we would build something great together.

Had I trusted my "awesomeness," I could have married someone totally rich and famous and would have missed out on meeting the most amazing, confident, strong, and highly generous man who is my husband. His confidence grounds our family and provides the backbone of our family, which allows me to go out into the world and impact billions.

Had I trusted my "awesomeness," I could have blown my millions of dollars on cars, houses, and trips (I did some of that) and missed out on the chance to learn that, instead, I can actually make a difference in someone's life by using the money I have to inspire and create opportunities for others.

Had I trusted my "awesomeness," I might have missed out on the opportunity to learn that completely "failing" in some ventures and opportunities has made me who I am. I wouldn't have learned that it isn't the money and fame that gives us the platform to impact the lives of others but rather being in service that can change the world.

So if I was talking to my twenty-one-year-old self, I think I would tell her: "Accept your awesomeness and allow that confidence to enable big things to unfold. Balance that understanding with the deep 'knowing' that there is a divine order in everything. The fastest way to realize the fullest life you are meant to live is to take your hands off the wheel while still remaining in the driver's seat, listen a lot, and go forth confidently."

I would tell her to stop spending more than she makes (paying off credit and interest often is more important than the great sale I just "couldn't miss out" on).

I would tell her to always look within and operate from gratitude.

And I would tell her to stop wearing the Laura Ashley one-piece jumpers.

Boldness is the vehicle to get you from point A to point B, from your current reality to the place where your dreams come true. No one is going to do the work for you, and who you choose to be is more powerful than any resume. So when you want something, you have to be vocal about it. If you want something, no one knows until you say it, and the more people who know, the better the chances of them helping you make it happen.

Humility is a beautiful thing, but if you aren't willing to be bold, you will often be overlooked. There's a fine line between seeking attention and actually being able to back it up, but there's not a stronger combination than knowing what you're made of, being the best candidate for the job, and confidently letting your future boss know it as well.

On a recent cross-country flight I sat next to a woman half a century older than me. Her name was Joyce, her hair was a brilliant white, and her hands were spotted, wrinkled, and soft. Within minutes of takeoff I knew I was in for a treat, and over the next several hours Joyce shared her beautiful wisdom with me, the lessons she had learned along the way, insight that only comes with experience, and advice that only a woman of her age can bestow. I'll never forget the emphasis she put on what she called "really living." She said if there was one thing I took away from our talk, she hoped it would be the importance of dancing full out with no regard to who is watching, unconcerned with impressing or outshining. Dance brilliantly, dance loudly, and dance as if your life depended on you pouring your entire heart out on the dance floor. Looking back on her life, she said the only things she ever regretted were the things she shied away from, the opportunities she was too scared to take, and the adventures she passed up. She said, "So dance with all your might and make up for all the dances this little old lady sat out."

This life is too short for you to waste it wondering, "What if?" Joyce taught me that. So be bold. We all have it in us, even you, my dear, whether you know it or not. It just takes deciding to punch your pride in the face, to forget about what "they" think, and to go for it. It means making the choice that you are willing to put in tireless hours of work and that you are unwilling to quit, unwilling to back down, unwilling to be distracted or deterred. Boldness is a choice we are all presented with, a state of mind, a way of being. If you don't try, you won't succeed. If you don't shoot, you'll never score. If you don't leap, you'll never know what you are made of, and you'll wake up at the end of a very long life and wish you had danced more.

Be bold and I promise, together, we have the potential to move mountains.

CHAPTER 6

BE RESILIENT

"You may encounter many defeats, but you must not be defeated. In fact, it may be necessary to encounter the defeats, so you can know who you are, what you can rise from, and how you can still come out of it. "

—Maya Angelou

Often it feels like simply finding your passion or making the decision to act is the biggest hurdle to achieving your dreams. But once you begin chasing after your dream, you might be surprised that doors don't suddenly open up to you. It's possible your work has only just begun. That was the case with Shaun Robinson when she began her fledgling career in journalism.

SHAUN ROBINSON (Emmy Award-winning Journalist and Author, *Exactly as I Am*): Young women who are aspiring reporters often ask me what it takes to be successful in the world of journalism. My answer is always very simple: perseverance. I remember when I was first starting my career in my home state of Michigan. I was working in a very small market, reporting and anchoring. It was one of my first jobs where I was living on my own—away from the comforts of my parents' home, struggling to make ends meet. Even though I didn't have much money, I was very excited about this new chapter in my life.

I was bringing new story ideas to the morning meetings, learning how to edit, perfecting my writing skills, making important contacts in the community—everything I needed to do to become a good reporter. Despite my best efforts, the news director was always critical of my work. Even though I was really trying to be a standout journalist, he found fault after fault. This was so discouraging to me because I felt reporting was my calling—I knew it was something I wanted to do since I was a young girl.

One day, after a very long week and only two months after I was hired, the news director told me he was letting me go. He was going to give me two weeks and that was it. He added that he didn't think I had what it took to make it as a reporter. Talk about a crushing blow. I remember, in that moment, I felt like the world was ending. Here I was getting what I thought was a chance of a lifetime, and instead being told by the person who hired me that I wasn't even cut out for the job! I remember going back to my apartment and just crying my eyes out. I was too embarrassed to even tell my parents.

But I did not have a pity party for long. I said, "Okay, I don't like this situation, but I know what is in my heart and I know that I won't let anyone stop me from realizing my dreams." So, the very next day, I started poring over all the broadcasting trade magazines that listed jobs for reporters. I made a list of all the ones that sounded like they would be a good fit, and I mailed resume tapes to them (which I had learned how to edit myself!). Within ten days, I got an offer at another station, in a much larger market! I remember going to my news director—before my two weeks were up—and telling him that I got this other fabulous reporting job in a bigger city. His jaw fell to the floor. But I didn't gloat. I just thanked him for the opportunity and finished my assignment for that day. It was an amazing feeling.

Perseverance will take you a long, long way. It will make a great difference in your life—the difference between achieving your goals and just sitting back wishing things would change.

Perseverance means not taking no for an answer. It means just because one person doesn't believe in your dreams, you aren't any less enthusiastic. There is a saying that I have on a small Post-it Note on my wall that goes: "Always remember that you are braver than you believe, stronger than you seem, and smarter than you think." You must believe in yourself when no one else will. I find this is especially true for women. Oftentimes, we may not fit into the "boys' club" or may have to work twice as hard just to be thought of as half as good as our male counterparts. Never let this discourage you. Don't guarantee your failure by quitting.

If you haven't experienced something like this yet in your life, I have some bad news. You will. We all get the wind knocked out of us from time to time, get disappointed, betrayed, lied to, heartbroken, manipulated, or let down. Failure and rejection are part of living a full life (if you don't take any chances you may be spared, but I doubt it). That's why it's crucial to develop a strong sense of resilience, a confidence in knowing you can and will get back up no matter the circumstances.

It is precisely when everything as we know it is turned upside down that we have the opportunity to transform, evolve, and grow. This life is not about avoiding obstacles, it's not about sidestepping pain or avoiding hurt or disappointment. Life is about moving through those obstacles with grace. And sometimes that grace involves clenched fists, a tear-streaked face, and some four-letter words, but it's about choosing to keep going even when it gets hard.

Life is going to hand you some brutal circumstances that you have absolutely no control over, but what you choose to do with those circumstances makes you who you are. We are not entitled to this life, we're not all guaranteed a healthy, happy ninety-some-thing years. The only things we have control over are the choices we make and the attitude we carry with us. Be strong, persevere, and you'll reap the rewards of knowing that you are a participant in life, not a victim.

BOUND AND REBOUND

Resilience is that ability to get back up when you've been knocked down. Sometimes it's a monstrous, life-altering punch like losing a loved one, but no matter how big or how small the blow, you have to cultivate a confidence that each time you fall, you will rise again.

My experience on *Survivor* was my greatest life lesson on re-silience. Maybe it was the thirteen days of not eating a real meal, breaking my finger on day one, hacking my foot with a machete on day seventeen, or blowing out my knee on day thirty-one. It could have been the six days of torrential rain, the days without drinking water, or the scorpion-infested jungles that left me stung on three separate occasions. Whatever it was, something about that majestic country, Micronesia, and that challenging game changed me forever.

On *Survivor*, it felt like Mother Nature was out to prove just how much stronger she was than little old me. Trust me, she was. If I woke up with less than sixty-five new mosquito bites, it was a good night (unlike the one night when a curious rat got stuck in my hair). At one point, sick from bad fish, we resorted to trying a boiled bat. Needless to say, I had every reason in the world to be a brat, we all did. We were a bunch of soaking wet, starving city slickers sleeping on the cold wet ground for weeks. But focusing on what I didn't have, or what I wished I had, did nothing for me out there.

I'll never forget the storm that began on night seven—it was the worst any of us had ever seen. Waves of ice-cold rain crashed on us one after another, and we sat helpless under our pathetic attempt at shelter. Rain began funneling through the holes in our patchwork roof, and before we knew it, water was pouring into our shelter like a dam had broken.

To make things worse, I hadn't slept in days and began hallucinating that I could hear my dad's voice, probably my mind's attempt to cope with the situation at hand. Every time I closed my eyes, I heard him say, "Sweet girl, come on, let's get you out of here," and saw his hands reaching down for me. Only I'd open my eyes and he wasn't there. After several hours, I was out of tears. I was terrified, it was dark, and I was shivering uncontrollably and willing to do almost anything to make the suffering stop. The storm went on for 9 more hours before it let up. And every minute of those 9 hours (a painful 540 of them), I had to find a reason to not go completely insane.

I remember waking up the next day, stiff from sleeping on top of Mikey B—one of my closest friends out there—to keep me off the ground, crawled out of our embarrassing excuse of a shelter, and saw the sun. A smile burst onto my face, quickly accompanied by streams of grateful tears. I had literally weathered the worst storm of my life and against all odds I had survived. For the first time in my life, daddy's little girl had no daddy coming to save her. I found what I was made of out there, I discovered that I'm tougher than I thought I was, I'm stronger than I thought I was, and, whether it was true or not, I had beaten

Mother Nature (or I could at least go nine rounds with her and live to tell the tale).

During *Survivor* I spent thirty-three days battling constant mental, physical, spiritual, and emotional challenges. Every day I had to get up bumped, bruised, cold, demoralized, hungry, thirsty, and tired and find a reason to keep going. Of course, I could have quit. There were days when it looked like quitting was the only sane choice I could make. But every day I chose to be strong. I learned that resilience is not pretending you're not upset, hurt, or disappointed; it is finding the courage to choose a positive attitude in spite of whatever storm you're experiencing, it's deciding if you're going to focus on the pain and the hurt or cling to your faith that at some point, the sun will come out again. True resilience is when the worst storm of your life rears its ugly head and rather than lay there defeated, you hunker down, dig your heels as deep as they can go, suck it up, and withstand wave after wave until you see the rainbow.

> **"Believe in yourself and all that you are. Know that there is something inside you that is greater than any obstacle."**
>
> **—CHRISTIAN D. LARSON**

Whether it's a recent break-up, not getting that cushy job, your inability to meet someone special, getting in an especially epic fight with a loved one, relapsing into an unhealthy habit, or any other of life's complicated and messy moments we are all sure to encounter, resist the urge to strap on your Wonder Woman cape and pretend to be okay. You're not fooling anyone and it won't get you very far. Instead, admit that you're having a tough time—at the very least to yourself—and take this precious opportunity to be honest. Please don't invalidate yourself or your circumstances to soften the blow. Breathe in the pain, have the courage to feel every bit of it, to cry as long as you need, to curl up in bed and pull the covers over your head until you're ready to face the world again. Then when you've given yourself a chance to feel it all, even if it's only with two percent of you, get up and move forward.

I have no doubt you'll feel scared, wobbly, and unsure, but even that is a good place to start. The only real chance of failure here is if you don't have faith in yourself that you're stronger than you think you are, and, despite how much it hurts right now, every day that passes will be a fraction less painful.

A friend once told me that pain is our friend. Trust me, I know how ridiculous that sounds. But the more I thought about it, the more what she was saying made sense. When we feel physical pain, it's our body trying to communicate that something is wrong and that pain prevents us from seriously harming ourselves. The same is true when we feel emotional pain; it's a signal that we need to change something in our life. We don't have to like pain, but can appreciate that it's a great way to get our attention and communicate to us that change is necessary. Now when I experience some kind of pain, I pay attention to it and see where and how I can immediately change something in my life. I may not enjoy it, but I am grateful for it. So rather than avoiding disappointment and the instability it causes in your life, stop what you're doing and listen to what your pain has to tell you. If you don't, you're missing a terrific opportunity to make a choice or a change that can mean all the difference to your future.

THE THREE STEPS TO BEING RESILIENT

Over the years, and through many failures and heartbreaks, I've learned that there are three basic components to becoming stronger and more resilient. Without these strategies, it's possible to get there, but the ride to resilience is certainly smoother when

I practice having a positive attitude, finding the silver lining in every tough situation, and forgiving others and myself for making mistakes or causing pain.

STEP 1: HAVE A POSITIVE ATTITUDE

The saying "Attitude is everything" is cliché for a reason. It's true. Having a great attitude is the first step to becoming resilient because of the sheer power of your mind. By doing nothing more than thinking positively you can shed light onto a dark situation. Of course the opposite is also true—negativity is like trying to walk wearing lead shoes. And a negative attitude can both prevent you from moving past a tough experience and even turn a potentially positive situation into a dead end street. By choosing to use the power of your mind for good instead of evil, you will be well on your way to becoming a woman who rebounds from adversity with even more depth and experience than you had before. If you believe that each negative experience has a lesson to offer or a tool you can add to your bag of tricks, you'll find a way to make it so.

From the time we're little girls we're fed this terrible "Happily Ever After" story that promises that, at some specific point in the future, we'll have it all and when we do, we'll be happy. When we finally have the "perfect" body, dream job, hot significant other, swanky apartment, *then* we'll be happy. Always waiting for that one thing we're missing means that we have an excuse to be discontented bystanders to our own lives, looking out for that fantasy on the horizon and missing all of the potential opportunities that sail by every day. Sadly, I have heard many girls justify their whining because they don't have this or don't have that. The reality is that 95 percent of the time you won't have *every* thing you want, and as long as you're putting your contentment in exterior things you will never attain it.

ANONYMOUS GIRL: My close-knit family has always been my rock and stronghold. Any time I'm having a less than perfect day, I call my mother or father and talk to them for ten or fifteen minutes. Even if it's nothing about my day. My father always has a way of putting everything in perspective for me. If tomorrow I woke up and the world was ending, would I still care about the huge spelling error that I made in an extremely important email to one of my company's Fortune 500 clients that in turn made me look like the most incompetent employee in the company? Not nearly as much as I would care about the well-being of my loved ones. Jobs come and go, we make mistakes so we have the ability to make wiser decisions, and we are put in awful positions so that we have the chance to rise.

There is one experience in particular that has shaped me and made me much stronger and wiser than I ever gave my-self credit for. When I was a sophomore in high school, I dated a senior. I was desperate to be cool and liked, and with that desperation came poor decisions. I started having sex with him at fifteen. He left to go to college and we continued to date. At one point I traveled to visit him in college, and while I was there, I allowed him to take pictures of me because he said he needed something while we were apart. I agreed to this and a year later when we broke up in the fall, and he was bitter, he showed these pictures to his friends, and his friends gave them to their friends, and so on. These photos spread like wildfire throughout my whole high school. Even graduates from years ahead had seen the pictures.

It wasn't until the spring when I found out my entire high school, and then some, had seen semi-nude photos of me. The

---

worst part was when I realized all of my friends (all but one best friend who made me aware) knew/had seen these pictures circling the school, and no one said anything to me about it even though they knew I was completely unaware. I felt completely humiliated and dehumanized. Guys would walk behind me down the hallway and I could hear them chuckling and making fun of me. Girls looked at me like I was trash on the street. I knew that the word got out even to the teachers because they treated me like I was some troubled teenager. In reality I was one of the very few high school students who never drank, never snuck out at night, never did drugs, never hooked up with multiple guys, and never yelled at my parents or disrespected teachers or authority. Yet I made this one (terrible) mistake, and I felt like I was being burned on a stake.

I took a few things away from this. I knew who my true friends were. It might have been a little uncomfortable for her to bring this up to me, but my one friend knew that this was greater than her momentary discomfort. To this day, we are the best of friends. I know I can count on her any time of day and the same goes for her. It also made me realize that people will always use other people's mistakes to feel better about their own. People will ridicule and gossip to transfer the judgmental light. I remembered my dad always told me not to point out the splinter in someone else's eye when we are blinded by the stick in ours. That has always stuck with me.

Instead of becoming bitter or lashing out at the "friends" who let her down, she decided to take this opportunity to improve herself. She bonded with a loyal friend and learned a valuable lesson about how to treat others. Like this girl, positivity is a choice you must make at the start of every day. It can come in the form of happiness, appreciation, tolerance, kindness, or humility, but it's not always an easy choice to make. Like integrity, it requires digging deep into your soul and making the choice to be joyful, not only on the days when you land the perfect job, find the love of your life, or win the lottery, but also when you're at rock bottom. When you screwed up and everyone's talking about it, find something positive to cling to. Who's supporting you? What are you learning? What will you never do again or always do in the future?

It's so easy to look outside yourself for the answers, for someone to hand you a free ride to happily ever after, but contentment in your life and yourself isn't given, it's earned. You must work for it every single day. So stop asking yourself whether your job makes you happy, or your body, or your relationship. You are the only one who can make you happy. The grass is only greener when you let it be.

> **"Life isn't about waiting for the storm to pass. It's about learning to dance in the rain."**
> **—VIVIAN GREENE**

Decide right now that in spite of your endless to-do list, your broken heart, your work drama, the ten or thirty pounds you need to lose, the terrible economy, and all the other excuses you make for not being happy with yourself and life, that for the next three minutes you're going to get obnoxiously happy. Set a timer if you need to. I don't care if you do it as a joke. Your thoughts become your reality, and you just so happen to be sitting in the commander seat, so change the setting to "Happy" and watch what happens.

Then when you get good at being positive for a few minutes at random, try to do it through a boring class, a difficult meeting, or a dinner with your least favorite client or family member. Resist the urge to roll your eyes and judge. Then say to yourself, "Thank you [annoying person, frustrating situation, etc.]

for helping be become a more patient, loving version of me." Even if you don't believe it in the moment and your anger wins out, you'll be more conscious of your strength. Next try it for a whole day. Decide that no matter what happens today, you won't allow it to crack your attitude, or upset your mood. Bear in mind that I'm not asking you to slap on a fake smile and pretend that everything is fine. Absolutely not! I'm challenging you to appreciate the good along with the bad, knowing that you are being made stronger. I'm asking you to have that difficult conversation and then allow the negativity or hurt to fall away. I'm suggesting that you go to that dreaded dinner and then, instead of reveling in all the stupid things she said and why she really is your least favorite person, either say nothing negative or challenge yourself to find at least as many positives as you did negatives. Pretty soon you'll be in the practice of rebounding more quickly and more efficiently from challenging situations. You'll find that your mind starts picking out the positives before you even ask it to.

We can't control the outside world, what cards we're dealt, the way people act, or any circumstances for that matter; the *only* thing we can control is who we choose to be in spite of them. Here's where you get to work on your personal resume, develop your patience, compassion, acceptance, forgiveness, resilience, understanding, and unconditional love. It's weight training for the intangible characteristics that make us good humans. So be grateful for the chance to grow into a better version of you (or throw a fit and scream into your pillow for two minutes, then be grateful).

You and you alone get to choose what glasses you view the world with. They will color every circumstance so choose a pair that is going to make your world rosy. Being an optimist is not the same as being naïve or ignorant, in fact, it takes far more discipline to extend tolerance over judgment, faith over fear, and love over hate. Choosing to be kind in the midst of an often-dark world and among inconsiderate people is the real challenge here. Be a source of light—that is the real test of living well.

STEP 2: BE WILLING TO FAIL

Someone once told me that true success is nothing more than having the willingness to mess up time and time again, until you finally have the patience to make it happen. Resilience is just that, having the courage to get back up and trusting that it's a matter of time until you get your big break. This is why being willing to fail is step two in becoming strong and resilient. Being positive in your mind and then turning that mental strength into action is a knockout combination.

There have been so many times in my life when I thought, "If only this would work out, then I would be happy." Of course, more often than not, it didn't. So I have become an expert at picking up the pieces and moving on in spite of the setback. When I was a senior in college, I auditioned for a new reality TV show that had just come out. After four callbacks, the executive producer called to "unofficially" congratulate me because I was "99.9 percent sure to be cast in the show." (Hint: Watch out for that .01 percent. It can bite you in the butt.) Of course, I immediately called my family and closest friends to tell them the great news. And I was thrilled—I had just landed my first job out of college without breaking a sweat. That is, until the producer called a few days later to say how sorry she was. It seems there was a last-minute cast change, and I had been the only one who they replaced. I was devastated. I was embarrassed and disappointed. Much worse and more humiliating than anything else, I had to tell all my friends and family that it didn't work out.

This was one of the first times I had really been disappointed about missing a big opportunity. It was also my first chance to see how I was going to react in the face of being let down by the big bad world beyond home and school. Naturally, I was disappointed, but I remember waking up the next morning with a slightly more positive feeling. I thought to myself, "Well it didn't work out, but that's okay, there's something out there even better for me."

I didn't let that disappointment, nor the thousands that have happened since, define me. I certainly didn't let it create a fear that prevented me from trying again. This ability to quickly forget and move on is sometimes called a "quarterback's memory." They say that the best quarterbacks forget about the interceptions and stay focused on throwing that game-winning touchdown. If you're focused on your mistakes, the fear of messing up again will lead to exactly that. I've also heard that the best athletes are the ones with the shortest memories because like a quarterback, when a goalkeeper misses a save, or a softball player strikes out, your team can't afford for you to sulk about the mistake. They need to know your head is in the game and to trust that you're not going to be distracted and do it again. My dad used to tell me after I made a mistake and missed a goal in soccer that to throw a fit and pout was giving in to my ego and spoke more of my pride than my humility to get back in the game and give it my all. He said that real athletes shrug it off and are working twice as hard when the next ball comes. There is a true grace and confidence in being able to make a mistake and quickly move past it. It's part of being human, and the most successful people are those who let their mistakes roll off their back like water off a duck's feathers.

TIME OUT! THINK LIKE A QUARTERBACK

Just like when a quarterback throws a terrible pass that's intercepted by the other team, when you make a huge mistake (especially one that everyone in the entire stadium, room, your life witnesses), you can't afford to lose your cool and focus on your mistake. Instead, practice thinking like a quarterback to get back on your feet and back in the game. Here's how:

1. Practice telling yourself something encouraging—make it your mistake mantra. Mine is, "You got this, girl." Make it simple and easy. Say it as many times as you need to prevent the judgmental, guilt-ridden funk that often follows your biggest blunders.

2. Figure out the lesson you can take from it. This may not happen right away, but take the time to seek out the silver lining. No matter what you think, one always exists.

3. Create a game plan in case you're faced with this challenge again and plan your new strategy in the midst of it.

4. Take some deep breaths and release the mistake. Imagine that with every breath in you are breathing in love and compassion, and with every breath out, you're releasing harsh critique and resentment. Breathe as long as you need to get it all out of your system.

5. Make a definitive decision (this is a choice after all) to *move on* and let it go. When your mind goes there to remind you what an idiot you are, say your mantra again, "You got this, girl," and breathe in more love and compassion.

6. Get back out there and kick ass.

You may be tempted to play it safe so you can avoid failing, looking bad, or making a mistake. Some may argue that never putting yourself out there at least affords you a safe and comfortable life. I disagree. You may not regret it today, but someday you will come to realize all the opportunities you missed. Along with avoiding big blunders, you'll also miss out on great successes and at least a few adventures.

I was sitting in an LA restaurant recently when I overheard the guy at the table next to us making fun of our waitress for being "just another actress in LA." When the waitress came over I asked where she was from and what she was pursuing. Sure enough, she was a struggling actress, but her backstory was riveting. She was a small town girl from Ohio who against everything her parents believed in, decided she wanted to act. With no help from her family, she packed up everything she owned and without knowing a soul in LA, having a place to stay or a job, she drove across the country to pursue her passion. She was willing to dream big and potentially fail miserably, but my goodness was she courageous.

Then I turned to the guys behind me to dig a little deeper. I had a hunch that these guys who were so judgmental of the waitress were pretty insecure about their own lives. And sure enough I found out that the guy making fun of the waitress had lived in LA his entire life, had never been out of the country, grew up very wealthy, and currently didn't have a job, but was living off his parents' money and comfortable as a clam. I said, "Don't you think it's ironic that you're willing to make fun of our waitress when it seems as though you have never dared to do anything half as brave as her?" His silence said it all.

You see it's easy to point and laugh at people who have failed, especially in massive, public blunders, but wouldn't you rather be the person daring to go for it than the one on the sidelines commenting on other people's lives instead of living your own? There will always be judges and critics who like to offer their commentary on your life, but don't allow what they will or won't say about you to prevent you from taking a risk or living the life you dream.

In order to go where you want to in this life, in order to reap the massive rewards that you've dreamed of your entire life, it's going to take irrevocable mistakes that may haunt you for weeks or months or years. Those battle scars are also signs that you've played the game and you're headed in the right direction. There is not a successful person out there who will tell you their journey was flawless. Quite the opposite, the most successful people I know have horror stories of making huge, earth-shattering mistakes. They have heart-wrenching stories of humiliating bloopers that would make nine out of ten people never try again, but that's where their secret lies. They swallow their pride, brush off the embarrassment, get their head back in the game, and keep shooting. They know that one of these days they are going to score, and it's the faith in believing what they haven't seen that carries them.

Success is in the hands of those willing to fail time and time again. It is something you earn. When a new crop of interns comes to work for I AM THAT GIRL, one of the first things I tell them is, "All I expect is for you to fail." Of course they look at me totally confused, and I explain, "If you aren't failing on a regular basis, then you're not trying hard enough, you're not taking enough risks, and you're not growing." I would rather have people who fail because they were going for something out of their reach than someone who hangs out safely in the baby pool all day never failing, but never creating or discovering anything great.

When you're facing a challenge, visualize the stronger version of yourself who is waiting on the other side. Whether you win or lose, you'll have experienced something new or difficult or scary, and that will *at the very least* help you grow. Making a practice of thinking this way will help inspire you to be grateful after and even in the midst of a challenge. You'll be focusing on the benefits you're receiving instead of dwelling on the negatives, and, next time, you'll feel less scared to fail and more excited to learn something new even if that means failing your way to something better. Remember that feeling disappointed is part of the process of realizing your dreams. Don't worry about the unknown or fear what the future will bring—don't over think it! The only thing you need to know is that you're not going to give up no matter what. After that, bring on the challenge and trust that the girl on the other side of it is stronger, braver, and maybe even a little wiser.

STEP 3: FORGIVE YOURSELF

Step three in becoming stronger and more resilient is to forgive yourself. As you did when laying the foundation for your integrity, resilience can only come when you are willing to leave your failures and mistakes in the past and don't allow them to stop you from becoming the person you want to be.

Forgiveness is the ultimate ingredient in resilience; it takes astounding courage, an unprecedented amount of love, and rare humility, but it also heals our wounds more than any other method. Remember that when you forgive someone for hurting or letting you down you are not only helping them, you are also giving yourself the gift of freedom—freedom from resentment, the discomfort, and the weight that holding a grudge brings. Often dwelling on your mistakes or the mistakes of others holds you back from moving through a tough situation.

LAUREN ELFORD (Austin Chapter President, I AM THAT GIRL): "Sit still, shut the $%# up, and don't move." I was fourteen years old, high on cocaine, and tied up in a garage. My mouth was duct taped and as I turned my head, I saw them taping my best friend's mouth. "If you tell anyone about this house, we will kill you." After scaring us enough to where they believed we wouldn't say a word, we were released, and my friend said, "Come on, let's go smoke this," and walked away from another near-death experience, nonchalantly.

I lived a step away from death for about six years. I tested every limit. I was reckless. I had no sense of authority. If someone can tie you up and threaten your life and you are only worried about the next hit you're taking, something ain't right, honey.

I remember the day my dad told me how he and my mom had a serious conversation about if I would die before I turned eighteen. Something triggered inside of me that made me feel I was meant to live. I was meant to survive that night in the garage, poisoning myself with drugs and alcohol, and I was meant to *become* a woman. My transition into the woman I am now (graduating from a university, working full-time, drug free, etc.) wasn't overnight, and there was no moment I can look back on and say, "Wow, I had it all figured out and that's where I changed." Just because I made an extravagant transformation in myself and began dictating my life on *my* own terms doesn't mean I don't get tempted or stray from the path. I am surrounded by sin, and I haven't forgotten how good it feels. This time around if it won't better me, I walk away. When things in my life weren't adding up, I had to start subtracting. This meant friends, boyfriends, jobs, and even the city I was living in. I had to do *me*. And the reward was a life of freedom.

The most rewarding part of this journey is to look back at my past and say, "I conquered you." I put every bit of my time, energy, and life into getting high, creating lies, passing drug tests, etc., and now I'm putting that same amount of time, energy, and life into becoming the me I'm meant to be, a woman people are proud of. I was that girl that went to rehab twice, sold drugs, and was called "a slut," and now I choose to be THAT GIRL who has class and confidence, who is dreaming and doubting, making mistakes and succeeding, but can accept my pitfalls and look at my scars to remind me where I came from. If I can make it, perfectly and wonderfully flawed, so can you!

I believe that the most important days in your life are the day you were born and the day you find out why. As I walked away from my first meeting as I AM THAT GIRL Austin president, I had my why. I used to question why I lived what I lived and what good came from it, and decided that if someone can look at my troubles and have them speak to them in a way that they let me take the fall for it, my job here is done.

I think back to that house quite often, and the crazy thing is no matter how high those people are today, they won't ever feel the kind of high I feel from turning away from that life, and turning into the woman I am becoming.

Simply getting through your blunders and embarrassing moments builds your resilience. Being willing to embrace your flaws as much as you do your triumphs makes you unstoppable. They both make you who you are and, after all, everyone has both darkness and light in their past. Isn't it always more interesting to hear about a famous or successful person's faults and missteps? Knowing they have overcome tough challenges just like the ones you face is even more inspiring than thinking they've skipped through life without a single blunder. So why would it be any different when it comes to you? Who are you hiding your mistakes from anyway? Don't deceive yourself that the people around you can't see the truth or don't know what's happened. Take a deep breath and reveal those chinks in your armor, your latent character flaws, your mismatched socks. You'll be one step closer to forgiving yourself and moving on to the bigger and better moments that await you.

Sometimes we hit a grand slam and other times we're destined to strike out. But never, never can we hang up our jerseys and walk away from the game. Too many people sit in the stands of their own lives, watching the action below but not having the courage to be on the field where everyone in the stadium can see their mistakes on display. Don't let that be you. Most of us have made some big mistakes, maybe ones we're ashamed to even whisper because they seem so horrific. Here's a little secret: so has everyone else, especially the seemingly "perfect" people. They are called skeletons in a *closet* for a reason—we'd much rather keep them locked up where no one will ever find out about them. But really, we're not hiding the skeletons from the people in our lives as much as we're hiding them from ourselves. We'll frame our accolades, our achievements, and our shining moments, and then shove our mistakes, disappointments, and most terrifying blunders in the closet.

Rather than pretend they never happened or forget them altogether, accept your skeletons, or at least let them out of that deep dark closet to air out now and again. Instead of letting them become big scary monsters that you try to hide from the world, relive them as many times as necessary in order to get comfortable with them and find their silver lining, that life lesson that leaves you better. In losing thousands of dollars in a poor business decision, I learned the importance of unwavering attention to detail. In not winning *Survivor* I learned the significance of integrity. In nearly losing her life to drug addiction, Lauren (one of my personal heroes) learned the importance of rededicating every day to health and growth, and even greater, she found the humility and courage to share her story with others in hopes that they don't have to go down the same road.

Louisa May Alcott once said, "I am not afraid of the storm for I am learning to sail my ship." Aren't we all? No age, maturity, wisdom, or intelligence will prevent you from making mistakes. We make them from the time we are born until our last breath, but those who live life best are the ones who choose what they will take from each moment and how they will use it as strength in the future. So stop pretending you haven't made mistakes, pull your skeletons out, and choose to take pride in all aspects of your life. We're not custom cars built with everything exactly to our liking. We are mismatched, stained, ripped, scratched, and (at times) totally broken down. But with every bit of wear and tear our character is built richer, more beautiful, and more unique.

IT TAKES REAL GUTS

When you've been disappointed or beaten down so many times, it takes real guts to get back in the ring. It's easy to shrink away from challenges, to hide in the face of difficultly and tiptoe past adversity. But that's not you. It's not our nature and it certainly can't be our habit if we want to achieve all that we are meant to in this lifetime. Your ego will tell you it's okay to quit, that not trying is better than losing. But if you give in to this little voice in your head, you'll disappear into the sea of mediocrity and worse, regret.

You need to make all the mistakes you have to in order to grow and become the best version of you. You need to get back up each time and not lose faith or focus. Whatever it is you want in life, you're only going to get it (or hold on to it) if you're willing to fight. My mom told me once when I was in the depths of a hard time, "This too will pass." The truth is, it will. It did. And getting through it and learning something from it will prepare you for the next hard time.

So take the time you need, sit in the bottom of that barrel, sulk, scream, punch a pillow, cry until there is not an ounce of tears left in your eyes. But then when the anger is out and the resentment purged, move on. Not next month or next year; do it now. You are the only one with the ability to pick yourself up by the bootstraps and keep moving. So get to it.

If it's a broken heart, nurse it but then put your cards back on the table. If it's losing a friend, let your heart mend but then be willing to trust again. If it's a mistake that costs you your job, learn the lesson and move on. If it's a sick loved one, revel in the fragility of life and the importance of love. The people who live life the best are the ones who get back up, not the ones who avoid the obstacles, but the fearless ones seeking out the ultimate challenge that comes in the form of humility, forgiveness, acceptance, and resilience. This life is not for the faint of heart. Resilience takes bravery. So take a deep breath and decide that you are going to be the kind of person who gets back up. No. Matter. What.

CHAPTER 7

BE A SPONGE

"And, when you want something, all the universe conspires in helping you to achieve it."

—Paulo Coelho, *The Alchemist*

Humility is a beautiful thing. Reverence for those who have come before us is essential for understanding where we have come from and where we are heading. Why spend your time reinventing the wheel when there are so many incredible people out there who have already done it? It would be a travesty not to tap into what took them a lifetime to learn. Whether you know exactly where you're headed and have a million questions or need a little help finding your passion, surround yourself with as many mentors as possible. The reality is that the greatest map we have to our life's awesome quest is actually imprinted inside the walls of our heart, and the constellation of stars guiding us along our journey are the phenomenal people we are surrounded by. They are keys to getting things done quicker, more efficiently, and with fewer battle scars.

YVONNE RANDOLPH (Lifestyle Designer): Now, it may be because I am the firstborn, or because my parents always seemed to have it pretty much together, or perhaps because I grew up in a very religious home. Wherever my need to be perfect came from, I can tell you, it's hard work! It's not easy knowing everything. The pressure is tremendous. I remember knowing. Everything. When I was twenty-one.

I was certain about most things. I had to be. If I didn't *know*, how could I be considered smart or interesting or valuable? There was little room for the beauty of learning. I felt that somehow I was just supposed to have all the answers, have it all figured out by osmosis. I felt as if there was a dark ocean that threatened to sweep me away and being perfect was my life preserver. I believed that if I did not offer an opinion then I was irrelevant, and the fear of rejection kept me anchored firmly to my views. A pretty lonely way to live. It often didn't matter where I got my information as long as I felt that I could contribute and have a voice (however misinformed or uninformed). How could they not see it my way, the true way? It was a burden not initially born of arrogance, but of fear. I desperately wanted to be admired and liked. Epic fail.

Now, I know very little about very little. My body of knowledge just scratches the surface of subjects that at one time I felt I had figured out. In fact, the more I am exposed to, the more I realize how immense, how deep, and how wide every subject is. My lack of knowledge is hard won! My imperfections have taken work. It has been a journey filled with the difficult lessons of failure, rejection, and humility. I'm still working on it. But if I could go back and offer any wisdom, it would be to let go. To start at the beginning. To know nothing and then learn. Step by step. Slowly and with the grace and the self-compassion to accept your mistakes, missteps, and detours. I would offer the glorious gift of knowing this one thing: You are right where you are supposed to be right now, and it will change. Spread wide to possibility your arms and your heart and your mind. Look at every side, every angle. Let others guide you. Listen and absorb the beauty of life through the eyes of the other. Another culture, another religion, another lifestyle. Be generous with your acceptance and withhold your opinion. Let life unfold with hands that are open.

So in this new skin that I live in, this place of becoming, I find my strength not in knowing, but in learning. My identity is more found in who I love than in who I feel I need to be. I can smoothly answer, "I don't know," and find power in my acceptance of the grandness and enormity of this beautiful life and my beautiful, learning mind.

Would I have taken my advice when I was starting out? Would I have listened and thought, "Wow, life could be so much more than I ever imagined!" Probably not. Remember, I already knew everything.

Don't be afraid to learn, no matter where you are in your journey. You'll be surprised how far the simple acts of listening to others and asking questions can take you. Even if you *think* you know a lot or have read a lot about a certain topic, always be seeking and gathering more information, particularly from people who have actually done it. There is something drastically different between theoretical knowledge and experiential knowledge. It's the difference between reading about a far-off country and visiting it. Being there to soak up the sights, smells, tastes, and the feeling of a place firsthand changes you in ways that no book ever will. In class and through reading, you can prepare yourself only so much for what lies ahead of you. Experiencing life is how you learn the practical lessons, where you make the mistakes, and where you're challenged to grow.

I certainly believe in reading as many books and articles as possible (*Half the Sky* by Nicholas Kristof and Sheryl WuDunn is my newest life-changing pick). But in the beginning of any new venture, no matter how well read you are, you will be inevitably short on experience. That's where mentors come in. You'll learn from their experiences as you begin to have your own, and you'll gain a new perspective that only comes from someone who has been there.

Throughout my life I've called on the advice of trusted mentors—from my mom to my favorite professors at USC (thank you, Christopher Smith)—but it wasn't until I decided to launch a business that I learned just how valuable mentors really are. I had just completed my undergraduate degree when I began to put my dream of starting my own empowerment nonprofit for girls into action. I was determined to ignite a revolution, and I didn't have the faintest clue where to begin. I had a degree in international relations and zero business savvy. I had been pretty good in math growing up, but knew nothing of how to write a business plan, how to raise money, how to do accounting, or how to create an effective organizational chart.

But rather than drown under what I didn't know, which was a lot, I decided to call the people who did. In fact, I cold called twenty female executives in the entertainment industry. I explained to their assistants that I was a recent college graduate looking to interview their bosses for ten to fifteen minutes on how to effectively run a company. The twenty women I approached were experts across the board, from finances, to production, to PR; all were at the top of the food chain so they had obviously done a few things right on the way up. I figured if even three of the women granted me interviews I'd be lucky to pick their brains.

To my surprise, not just one or two, all the women called me back and in a single week I had twenty scheduled interviews with the most powerful and influential women in Hollywood. I was shocked they were willing to make time for me, but also knew the ball was now in my court to capitalize on this opportunity, ask the right questions, and take full advantage of the chance to meet and learn from these women.

I meticulously read their bios, learned about their backgrounds, their companies, and anything else I could find. I walked into each of those meetings knowing what I hoped to gain from each of them. I told them my goal and asked what advice they had. I inquired about their life's journey and what challenges they had run across, what major mistakes they had made along the way, and to what they attributed their success. I asked who their mentors were and about their dreams, motivation, and battle scars. I was a sponge soaking up their years of knowledge, advice, warnings, and suggestions. It was one of the most mind-blowing experiences of my life.

> "Hug and kiss whoever helped get you—financially, mentally, morally, emotionally—to this day. Parents, mentors, friends, teachers. If you're too uptight to do that, at least do the old handshake thing, but I recommend a hug and a kiss. Don't let the sun go down without saying thank you to someone, and without admitting to yourself that absolutely no one gets this far alone."
>
> —STEPHEN KING

Though each meeting was scheduled for fifteen minutes, not a single woman met with me for less than an hour. They were as eager to share what they'd learned as I was to listen. From the VP of Walt Disney to a head finance woman at Fox Sports, they shared with me the good, the bad, and the ugly of what it had taken for them to be where they are today. They described the choices they had made, the sacrifices they had made, and their life's greatest blunders. I watched women laugh and cry as they nostalgically recounted their complicated, messy, wonderful, and surprising journeys.

I still draw on their advice. "Don't ever comprise what you believe in, *ever!*" said one of the women. "Don't do what I have done. I sold out and yes I have a fantastic job that pays me far more than any human should make, but I don't love what I do and that is something I have to live with every day." Another woman said, "Looks only get you a foot in the door (if that), so build a reputation based on your work ethic because that only gets better over time." My favorite bit of advice was, "Play more! I wish I hadn't taken life so seriously, that I would have flirted more on the weekends, worked less during the week, went out more with my friends, spent fewer nights in the office, and made the relationships in my life more of a priority."

As I shared with each of these women my vision for I AM THAT GIRL, my borderline insane dreams of starting a nonprofit, publishing my first book, being a professional storyteller and a motivational speaker, the single most common bit of advice they gave me was, "Go back to school and get the tools you need to make it happen. The last thing you want to be is another dreamer with a great idea but without the tools to properly execute your goals."

I figured these women knew what they were talking about so the following week I applied to graduate school at the University of Southern California (where I had just earned my undergraduate degree). I didn't have the money, I wasn't sure I'd even be accepted to the number one communication school in the nation, but what the hell, you only live once.

These women guided me in the right direction and illuminated the exact path that got me where I needed to go. I was accepted to the grad program a month later, applied for loans, and found a woman (the mother of a friend) willing to let me live in her garage (converted into an apartment) while I worked to gain my wildly expensive education. Thanks to the twenty women who contributed their time, invested their energy, and encouraged me, I was on to the first step of manifesting I AM THAT GIRL.

What I learned from those magnificent women was, don't underestimate the number of people out there willing to invest in you, willing to take the time to share their wisdom, their advice, and their guidance with you. When I walked into each of the women's offices, I remember saying how humbled I was that they were willing to meet with me, especially knowing how busy they were. The surprising response from most of them was, "You know, most people just don't ask. I'd be happy to work with more girls, but it seems like people just assume I'm too busy when (in all honesty) I'd love to share my story with more girls." I love sharing this insight because I remain in shock at the amount of people who were and are willing to selflessly make time for me, all because I was/am just willing to ask.

Life is a crazy adventure with snares and traps behind every corner. It's like being alone in the jungle at night trying to make your way through uncharted territory. Mentors are the lanterns that light the path, guide you in the right direction, and point out some of the obstacles before you trip over them. Having already traversed similar ground, mentors know many of the shortcuts and hidden treasures along the way. That's not to say that you can't figure out how to get through it yourself, no mentor can prevent you from occasionally getting lost, confused, backtracking, and starting over again and again. There are certain life lessons that no one can teach you except yourself, but mentors can ease those epic fails and make the journey more enjoyable.

Find people who have already done what you're trying to do and use them to speed up the process. Why make all your own mistakes when you can learn from theirs?

WHAT MAKES A GOOD MENTOR?

A good mentor is someone who has done what you want to do and been where you hope to be. I have mentors for all different areas of my life: business mentors who have been successful and are willing to share their trade secrets with me and accountability partners for my faith that encourage me to stay focused on the bigger picture and, when things get hard, remind me why I am doing what I'm doing. I have mentors for my personal life too, the friends, wives, and mothers who I aspire to be like one day. Some of my mentors have known me all my life and others are new friends, but all of them continue to encourage me and challenge me along this crazy adventure.

Regardless of what area of life you're focusing on, find people who will be personally invested in you and who are willing to take the time. There are plenty of "busy" people out there, but you want to find the ones who make time for you. Think carefully about and be clear with the people you ask to be your mentor. I make sure they know why I have chosen them and what it is about them that is so inspiring to me and what I think I have to learn from them. This will also help them tailor their advice, at least at first, to what part of their journey you are most interested in.

Mentors come in all shapes and sizes and it's not always necessary for them to be older than you. The majority of mine are, but if you are changing careers or getting into something new, chances are there will be younger people who have lots of experiences to share. Depending on who they are, I discuss the amount of time I would like them to spend with me. For some it's a weekly phone call, for others it's a monthly coffee. How frequently you get together depends on your schedules and what you're hoping to learn from them. If you'd like your mentor to help you make progress in a particular area, your meetings may be linked to the milestones you set. But no matter how frequently or sporadically you meet, you want someone who's not going to sugarcoat their life experience or omit their failures. You need your mentor to be candid with you, to be willing to tell you what you don't want to hear, and to let you know when you are far off track.

One of my favorite professors, Warren Bennis, once told me that if necessary, you should "stalk your mentors." Now he didn't mean that literally, but once you find someone you want to learn from, it's up to you to seek them out. After all, there is no downside to asking. Some people really may not have the time, but it's usually not personal if you get turned down. You'd be surprised how many people will say yes, and the right ones for you may be honored. I am shameless when it comes to finding a new mentor and am not afraid to contact someone several times if I don't hear back from them. If they are super busy, you can often fall between the cracks, but it's not an indication that when you do finally get a hold of them, they are more than happy to play that role in your life.

For instance, a girl who heard one of my recent talks on I AM THAT GIRL asked if she could pick my brain about a new organization she wanted to start. Immediately I thought, "Sure, of course, I need to write her back," but then I moved on to something else and forgot altogether. She emailed me again, and again her email got buried under the hundred plus messages I get a day. She emailed me again and again and again until I finally set aside the time and made her a priority. In all honesty, part of me just wanted the girl to stop inundating my inbox, but it proved to me how determined she was to talk with me, and how do you say no to someone who is that relentless? You don't. The irony was I ended up thanking *her* for "staying after me" because I just needed the constant reminder.

Sure it took a month, but I finally scheduled a "twenty-minute" talk with her. And just like my meetings with my first mentors, I was on the phone with her over an hour and a half. Why? Because she was asking all the right questions. It doesn't end at being persistent. Once you get that first interview with your potential mentor, *do not* take their valuable time for granted. She was more than prepared and had obviously done her homework. She knew my entire life story it seemed, from my early modeling days, to the red carpet gig, what I did in grad school, my stint on *Survivor*, and founding and running I AM THAT GIRL. She obviously valued my time and my insight, and I was happy to chat about the things I had learned along the way.

In fact, I was so flattered that she had taken such an interest in me and was so passionate about using me as a resource that I found myself wanting to help her anyway I could. You could tell she was a girl on a mission and that is inspiring for anyone to witness. I not only ended up sharing all the lessons I had learned along my journey, but offered to help promote her on our website, to offer other influential people from my personal Rolodex who I thought could also help her. She was patient with my busy schedule and certainly persistent, and I have no problem helping people along their path who are serious about where they are going, especially because of all the help I was given along my own journey.

At the end of an interview when I thanked my mentor for taking the time to meet, they often said how grateful they were to *me* for calling on their help, saying that it made them feel good to know they were giving back. I thought they were just being polite until I became a mentor to others. Nothing feels better than contributing to someone else's life. I can certainly remember all the people who played massive roles in my life, and so having the chance to be that for someone else is ridiculously rewarding.

Allow yourself to accept the selflessness of others and their desire to mentor you—you're worth it, my dear. And for where you are headed and what you need to do in your life, you can't afford to walk in the dark. Look up different women and men in the areas of your life that you need the most guidance. Then start your search. Find someone who's doing exactly what you want to be doing and find out everything about them, search high and low until you build a powerful network of people who simply won't allow you to fail.

TIME OUT! BADASS MENTOR REQUEST CHEAT SHEET

Making a list of people you would love to learn from and then contacting them is easier than you may think. Between the phenomenon of social media and everyone's personal information just a Google click away, there's no excuse not to find a way to connect with whomever it is you admire.

That's step one. Here's a checklist of the other things you'll need to do to start and maintain a relationship with your mentor:

- Identify five individuals (known or unknown to you).

- If you don't know them, then Google them, find a contact number, and schedule a time in your schedule when you are going to cold call them. If you don't, you'll make excuses not to and never get around to it.

- Then say something like this, "Hi _____, it's _____. I'm calling today because I have put together a list of mentors and you were at the top of the list. Due to all the incredible work you've done from (list the things they have done that inspire you) to (add more here), I'd love to pick your brain and hear a little about your life story. I also know how busy you are and I value your time, so I was just hoping that you'd have twenty or thirty minutes sometime this week or next that I could pop by and chat with you. I'd also be happy to pick up some coffees or treats if you let me know your favorite kind. It would really mean a lot to me. Do you think that would be a possibility for you to share your experience with me?"

Remember, if you get the person's assistant, you can use that same script in the third person. Just let the assistant know why you're calling and what inspires you about their boss. Remember that they are the gatekeeper so you want to make sure you leave a good impression on them as well, thank them for their time, and let them know how much you appreciate them passing on your request.

- When you are talking to your mentor, start by thanking them for their time, then dive right into your questions and be mindful of time so that you end exactly when you said you would. If they are in the middle of speaking, you can say, "I don't mean to interrupt you, but I want to let you know that our twenty minutes is up. Obviously, I'd love to continue listening to you, but I wanted to respect your schedule if you need to go." Usually the conversation continues, but you at least let them know that you are mindful of their time and it's incredibly respectful.

- My grandmother taught me this one—always, always, always follow up with a handwritten thank-you card. People remember few things (especially today with the convenience of email) as well as a handwritten thank-you card. You can follow up saying that you'd love to continue these talks if they have time in the future (offer them another date) and if not, you wanted to thank them for taking the time in the first place. I go out of my way to mention something specific that they said, that really stuck with me.

- Last, just like life, some people will dance in and out throughout your journey, some will only cross your path once, and some will choose to spend a lifetime with you; the same goes for mentors. Organically you will know if they are meant to be in your life for a short period or for a longer period. But setting up regular meetings and establishing a long-term relationship should be discussed after you've developed a strong connection. Like any relationship, it takes two to tango, so don't assume they are in for the long haul if you haven't talked about it.

FAMILY AND FRIEND MENTORS: TOO CLOSE FOR COMFORT?

Whenever I have a major life decision to make and I go to my mentor council for their perspectives and advice, I tend to make a far better decision than if I had approached it alone. Without fail they point out things I would never have thought to consider, offer their expertise on those issues, and ask all the right questions that help me clarify the situation and understand what's right for me.

My council of mentors doesn't stop at professionals, however; it's also full of friends and family. Of course it might be hard for you to hear the truth or take constructive criticism from your inner circle, but it's worth it to listen and be open to others' perspectives.

SUSIE CASTILLO (Television Host, Author, and Former Miss USA): Feeling supported by those we love and respect is nourishing to our souls. I was raised by a single mother who couldn't have been more supportive of my goals throughout my life; even when, at seven years old, I told her that when I grew up I wanted to be a garbage truck driver. I remember she was cooking in the kitchen when I ran in to tell her my dirty future job plans, and she said, "You can be anything you want to be when you grow up!" I remember those simple words giving me an incredible amount of confidence. From that moment on, I truly believed that I could accomplish whatever my heart desired. My mom said so and so it was!

But as important as it is to be surrounded by people who support you wholeheartedly, I believe it's *much* more important to have the utmost belief in yourself and what you want to accomplish in life. If you don't believe, there's not a thing anyone else can say or do to help you or support you. On the flip side, when naysayers come your way, but you totally believe in your abilities and your dreams, nothing they can say will leave you with self-doubt.

I write this because I have lived it.

My career dream had always been to work in the entertainment industry, but at age twenty-two I was still looking for the right opportunity. And after graduating from Endicott College in Beverly, Massachusetts, I saw that opportunity—one that could help me get from point A to point B: the Miss USA Pageant. I researched all things "Miss USA," I worked hard to

---

prepare, and that fall I competed in the Miss MA USA Pageant, the preliminary pageant to Miss USA. I studied pageant footage (no, I'm not kidding!), exercised hard, ate right, believed in myself … and won! Suffice it to say, I was thrilled that my dream was becoming a reality, one step at a time.

But at one point in the months after the Miss MA USA Pageant, as I was preparing to represent my home state in the 2003 Miss USA Pageant, I got into a heated conversation with my boyfriend of four years. Why? Because he said to me, "Why are you doing this pageant? You're not going to win." Now, it was never my dream to be a "pageant girl," but this was a huge opportunity. Winning the Miss USA Pageant would be a great stepping stone that could get me where I ultimately wanted to go in my career. The exposure would help me tremendously in reaching my lifelong goals, and he knew that, so I was shocked at his words.

Of course my feelings were hurt. I immediately thought, "How dare you say that. This means so much to me!" But the really cool thing is that because I was brought up to unwaveringly believe in myself, I mostly thought my boyfriend was totally wrong. That said, I knew he loved me as much as I loved him, so I wanted to get to the bottom of why he said something so unsupportive and hurtful. When I told him how his comment made me feel, he very quickly apologized and admitted that the words came from his own fears. He saw how driven I was and actually had a strong feeling that I *would* win the pageant! He said what he said out of fear that once I became Miss USA, I might break up with him for a celebrity. Becoming Miss USA meant that I would move to New York City and have a year of extensive travel, speaking engagements, red carpet events, and rubbing elbows with celebs, and I can see how that could scare a guy. Turns out his fear of losing me drove him to say what he said in a moment of weakness.

After talking about it, we both learned something very valuable that day. We learned that when people say they don't believe in you, it's actually quite possible that they really do believe in you, but are afraid of what your success might mean for them. In fact, it has nothing to do with you and everything to do with *their* fears and self-doubt. Remember that those in your life, supportive or not, are there to teach you invaluable lessons. Look deep within yourself and ask, "What am I supposed to learn from this?" I believe there's a lesson in every situation, good or bad.

By the way, the boyfriend in my story is now my husband, and we've been together for eleven years. We talk about everything and are honest about our feelings at all times, which brings about incredible strength and support for one another.

No matter which mentor you're talking to—someone from your work or home life—it's best to remember that their opinions are only there to guide you. Your mentors are people too and their advice is often based on their personal experiences. That's what you want! But for that same reason, keep your own values and goals in mind. Especially when you are talking to close family or friends, you may find that your mentor's advice is mixed with their love and concern for you. As in Susie's case, there may be moments when opinions may even be muddled by jealousy, fear, or anxiety. So be compassionate with your mentors, keep your wits about you, and check back in with yourself before heeding anyone else's advice. It's your journey, after all, and you're the one who has to answer for your decisions.

As for me, my mom is one of the greatest mentors in my life because there's not a woman who knows me better and her immeasurable life experience always holds a lesson for me in times of need. I'll never forget the first time I got my heart broken. I was sixteen years old, and I thought it was the end of the world. I was crying hysterically in my room when my mom came walking in and with a sweet smile, said, "Honey, this too will pass. I know it doesn't feel like it now, but trust me." She proceeded to rub my back and tell me about her first heartbreak and how she never thought she'd meet another guy who she'd loved as much as him. She then shared how mistaken she was and reminisced about the "loves of her life" (yes, plural). Despite what my sixteen-year-old self thought, she was right and I did fall in love again. And yes, when I got my heart broken again, she was there to help me pick up the pieces and remind me that this was still not the end of my love train and every new relationship would bring a new and exciting adventure as well as an important lesson.

My mom's advice is priceless not because she's some prophet, psychic, or genius, but because she's been through it. There were times in her life when she felt hopeless, confused, lonely, or overwhelmed but she managed to navigate the scary waters and has insight for me in the moments I find myself in the same dark waters. Her advice isn't always my perfect solution, but it always lends a new perspective.

That's what mentors are, a pair of fresh eyes through which you can view the world. And no matter if it's coming from your mom or the top executive in your field (or preferably both!), the more options and perspectives you have the better choices you can make.

MY MENTOR ROSTER

My mom is my go-to mentor on anything and everything going on in my life. She is always my first phone call and my most trusted voice. Along with my family she is in good company with many others who make up my phenomenal mentor council. Check out how I balance the roster with both male and female mentors from every part of my life and who have a variety of personal and professional experiences. This is a good example of the kind of scope you should build into your mentor roster. I've included some details about them below so you can see what people in your life can fill these kinds of roles for you and what characteristics to look for. Obviously I have many more mentors and so will you throughout your life, so make a list first of the roles and positions you want to fill and then start hiring the right people!

DADDY JONES (MORAL COMPASS)

My dad is the go-to person when I know I need to be told something I probably don't really want to hear. He's my moral compass, my reality check, and the person who makes sure I'm not getting "too big for my britches." You know those moments when you know you're doing something you probably shouldn't, or you're about to do something that you know isn't right? That's when I go to him because he doesn't allow me to make justifications for what I want to do, as opposed to what I know is right. My dad is the mentor that keeps me "shootin' people straight," as he would say.

BUT, WHAT DO I SAY? WHEN I'M SITTING DOWN WITH MY MENTOR.

It's easy to feel tongue-tied when you're sitting in front of your mentor for the first time. Here are some examples of questions you might use:

Who were your personal heroes growing up? Now?

What is your favorite childhood dream?

Who in your life has the most influence on you?

How did you choose your mentors? How did you ask them? How often do you meet with them?

What are you most proud of in your life?

What was the biggest mistake you've made both personally and professionally? What did you learn from it?

What's your biggest strength? Where do you struggle?

What did you wake up stressed about this morning? How do you handle stress, pressure, and high expectations?

What does your daily routine look like?

I'm (your age) years old. If you could sit yourself down at my age, what advice would you give him/her knowing what you know now?

What inspires and motivates you personally and professionally? What shuts you down?

What do you want to be remembered for?

Do you have a personal motto? Where did you learn it?

What goals are you currently striving for? Do you have a plan on how to achieve them?

How do you balance work and home life? (Ask this especially if you're talking to a badass professional woman who has children.)

ILLY (CHIEF INTEGRITY OFFICER)

Illy is one of my best friends and one of my greatest life mentors. He keeps me on the path for what I'm meant to do in this lifetime and won't let me stray even for a second. When I doubt myself and worry about whether I'll accomplish my goals, his steadfast encouragement reminds me, "Of course you will." He makes sure I don't give up, sell out, or settle, period. He's forever holding me accountable and rarely tells me what I want to hear. He's methodical and filled with integrity, grit, determination, wild creativity, and unconditional love.

SETH (REAL MAN AMBASSADOR)

I have learned so much from his advice and ability to prioritize, manage, and creatively explore options I didn't know existed both professionally and personally. He's a marvel of a man, a polished professional powerhouse (who also happens to have fabulous fashion sense). He fights for women, supports, loves and encourages them. He and Eva's (his wife) decisions to adopt two precious children is also a reminder that compassion is a verb and not an adjective. I admire him professionally almost as much as I admire him personally, and that is saying so much.

EMMY (SOUL SISTER)

She's my best friend and my cofounder at I AM THAT GIRL. Emily is my soul sister and much like Frannie (my bestie I grew up with) she helps me make sense of the world. The good thing is, unlike most friends, she's willing to stand her ground and tell me what she really thinks and feels, which like many of my mentors is not always what I want to hear. We're yin and yang, opposites in a lot of areas, and often our strengths make up for one another's weaknesses. She often believes in me and gives me courage to do things I might never have tried without her. In fact, I often say, "She is the method to my madness," and without her I AM THAT GIRL would never be where it is today.

"HE" (FELLOW SUPERHERO)

I call Dave "He" and he calls me "She" because we both loved He-Man and She-Ra growing up and always said we were brother and sister superheroes. Dave is the guy *everyone* needs in their corner, because he has one of the best work ethics that I know and reminds me that nobody is going to do it better than me. He is also one of my biggest faith accountability partners. He and his wife re-inspired my faith when I had drifted away, living and working in the craziness of LA. He always reminds me of the bigger picture, to exercise my faith, grace, compassion, humility, and kindness above anything else. He reminds me to always give people the benefit of the doubt and, even in LA with shark-infested waters, to do what's right, not what's easy or convenient.

ARA (THAT GIRL POSTER GIRL)

She is the cool big sister I always dreamed of when I was given four older brothers growing up. Ara is the woman I strive to be in so many ways, and she has taught me a lot about work ethic, about actions speaking louder than words, about the fashion world (since she might be the trendiest girl I know), and about professional prowess balanced with femininity and grace. She taught me about really "showing up" in life for the people you love and expecting them to do the same. My admiration for Ara is unimaginable and one day, whether she knows it or not, we will work together on some company/ project and it will be epic.

HANCE (DREAM BUILDER, FIRE STOKER)

Hance is a fellow passionista, a *huge* dreamer who finds time in his schedule to have six-hour coffees with me if need be. We're the guy/girl version of each other and few people have ever understood me the way he does. He's my endless inspiration, challenging me with the question, "Why not you, Jones?" So often we assume that our greatest confidants come in the same sex, but often they are found in just really great people, boys or girls. Hance is one of those, who helps give structure to my dreams and grounds my stargazing eyes in order to actually make my goals happen. He brings the heat as much as I do and reminds me it's okay to be me, exactly as is. There's just an unspoken agreement that we've danced in past life times together and we're sure to dance in them again in the future.

Those are but a couple of the many mentors that rock my all-star roster. Everyone is different, providing a wild array of experience, expertise, and influence on my life, but every one of them is vitally important to the overall person I am and will turn out to be. Few things are as important as developing your dream team of people, who literally do not *allow* you to fail.

BE A WISDOM SPONGE

Seeking out and learning from mentors is a key step in realizing your dreams. Get into the habit of asking for the help and advice of people you trust. If you have any illusion that you should know more than you do or feel shy or hesitant to sound ignorant in front of more experienced people, it will be especially important that you create a practice of consulting other people. I asked a very smart woman, Professor Adler-Baeder, what she wished she had learned from a mentor when she was starting out, and this is what she told me.

FRANCESCA ADLER-BAEDER, PHD (Professor of Human Development and Family Studies at Auburn University and Director of the Center for Children, Youth, and Families): What do I wish someone had told me in my twenties? Pace yourself. No one ever mentioned that. To the contrary—the message for young women of promise is to go at life full force. Seize all the opportunities, work really hard, develop and use the gifts you've been given, and leverage them to make a difference in the world in a big way. To whom much is given, much is expected, right? I am part of the first generation to receive this "encouragement" at many levels—societally, within my community, from family and friends, and internally. Once we moved away from the prescribed daily activities focused most exclusively on home and hearth that our mothers had implemented, we opened a world of possible contributions through our work—both in-home and beyond—and most of us sought to cram a resume as full as we could possibly imagine.

It is my only lament about our liberation as women. So well-intended, but the result is that we quickly normalize a daily schedule of fluid boundaries between work and personal life that if we look closely reveals we're essentially working all the time. There's a (secret) pride felt in the length of our resume and the amount of tasks on our daily to-do list. We find ourselves in conversations with others acknowledging the insane number of hours we're working, our regular operation on very little sleep, and our terrible eating habits, not as a lament or a call for help, but as a sort of bragging point that seems to impress others.

I can feel my stress levels rising just thinking about the passionate, focused, hard-charging young woman that I was for two decades, and I have such compassion for her. I think of you and the kind of young woman you must be to be reading this book. I can feel your energy and passion and drive to make a difference—and I want to take you by the shoulders, give you a long hug, and say slow down. Sleep, exercise, eat well, lounge with friends and family and loved ones, and read and watch inspiring, thoughtful stories as part of your daily routine—not just for special occasions. It is part of your work here too. If not, the chance of you hitting an emotional and physical brick wall around your mid-forties to fifties is huge. I speak from experience. Receiving a diagnosis of breast cancer floods you with a million different thoughts and emotions. I have determined through my own research that predicting cancer development or any other serious physical condition is a complex, multifactor puzzle; there is no linear causality and no singular cause. But I do know that several pieces of that puzzle are in my control—namely, lifestyle choices that would better serve to keep my cortisol levels predominantly at a low level and my immune system strong.

As I pursued a myriad of accomplishments I would always say, and mean it genuinely, that I wasn't stressed (in the psychological sense). I loved my work—I was just busy. The problem is the body experiences "busy" as stressed. My daily schedule now looks much different than it did five years ago, and I am not alone. So many of my female colleagues have "woken up" to this important and simple truth. Work less. It will be enough. Because chances are you will have a longer, more consistently inspired life within which to manifest your vision for your life's contributions. You will prune the *shoulds* from your schedule and plans, and focus on *want tos*. You will become more mindful of the many ways, large and small, that you can impact others—and that small can be powerful. I believe that a measured, paced life-span approach will ultimately serve you and our world best.

Ask the turtle if she feels like a winner.

There are people like Francesca out there doing what you want to do who have many thoughts about their own life choices and who would be more than willing to share them with you. Find these people, figure out what they did, study every aspect of their lives, and if they have the time, beg them to be your mentor. Don't reinvent the wheel, don't stumble around in the dark crashing into obstacle after obstacle. If you want something bad enough, make it happen.

It's not cheating to learn from others' mistakes, it's called beating the system. Trust me, you'll make plenty of your own mistakes in this lifetime. If you can avoid a few here and there it's only going to get you where you want to go faster and with fewer bumps and bruises.

In the meantime, people want to help you. It feels good to give back, so you're really giving them an opportunity as much as you're asking for one. Their life experience is precious to you; it's like the secret shortcut manual for your favorite video game that teaches you in minutes all the tricks it takes other people months to learn. It gives you a leg up and better equips you for the incredible life adventure awaiting you. Your secret weapon is the repertoire of mentors you collect, the dream team you construct. They're your biggest fans, your support system, your guiding lights, guardian angels, inspiration, encouragement, accountability, and some will be your lifelong cheerleaders.

So put together an unstoppable force of people who will shower you with wisdom, share their life lessons, and push you in the direction you're already headed. We all need a crew of the best, brightest, and most talented people in our corner. Take the time to pause and intentionally and thoughtfully curate your mentor list. Like a new president taking office, you must assemble a cabinet you can trust to guide you and counsel you in their specific area of expertise.

Find them, learn from them, and soak up every bit of wisdom they share with you. I certainly don't want to speak for them, but I can only imagine that anyone you would ask would be honored to one day call themselves your mentor.

CHAPTER 8

BE OF SERVICE

"We're not on our journey to save the world but to save ourselves. But in doing that you save the world. The influence of a vital person vitalizes."

—Joseph Campbell

To be "that girl" means being the best version of you, perfectly and wonderfully flawed. Too often we look outside ourselves and think "that girl" has it all, but we don't realize that what we admire in her already exists in us if we were just willing to recognize and exercise it. I've been asked in multiple interviews what my definition of beauty is, and I can sum it up in two words: authentic confidence. There is nothing in this world that is more beauty-full than a human being who knows her worth and is comfortable in her own skin. Authentic confidence is when you know who you are and what you stand for. You're unshakable, a force to be reckoned with, and no one can take that away from you.

Plenty of women paint on a façade of perfection and pretend to have it all figured out while in truth they face the same doubt and uncertainty as the rest of us. I know there have been times when I tried hard to live up to the unrealistic, unattainable guidelines for that image of perfection and that no one knew the real me—even I didn't know her. I was so busy being everything to everyone else that I never got around to just being me. The truly beautiful shine so brightly that it's hard to keep your eyes off them, and it has absolutely nothing to do with what they look like. Their eyes conceal nothing, their confidence seeps out of their pores, their beauty radiates from their smile, and their charisma rolls off the waves of their laughter. We all know people like that, who embody such a bold, powerful presence that you can't help but be magnetized to them.

To be "that girl" means that you're allowed to make mistakes, change your mind, start anew, and reinvent yourself. "That girl" is in all of us. It is the pearl that we sometimes forget or misplace, but never lose. Most of us have to go looking for her, dust her off, and shine her up a bit, but she's always and forever the most beautiful part of us. She is timeless, not affected by gravity, wrinkles, or gray hair.

To be "that girl" just means you're going to give life your best shot, that you're not going to make excuses or justifications, that you're going to go for it, whatever that means for you. It also means you're going to be an example of true beauty in the world and encourage the same for all the other women in your life. Being "that girl" means you are a constant work in progress—you're willing to be vulnerable, flawed, and compassionate and are someone who stumbles and falls but isn't afraid to admit her shortcomings in the midst of her magnificence.

YAEL COHEN (Founder, F Cancer): When my mom got diagnosed, I was shattered. I will never forget the small room we sat in, with my mom's scans plastered on the wall, where we heard for the first time that she had cancer. In that moment I broke.

I quickly pieced myself back together because there was work to be done, and I had to save my mom's life. Or so I thought. Which now seems utterly ridiculous, but at the time it was an honest reaction to a situation I just didn't know how to handle.

For weeks I was a headless chicken making arrangements for the upcoming surgery. But at night, when no one was around to distract me and there were no more arrangements to be made for the day, that's when I fell apart. I didn't feel like I could really open up to any friends about what I was going through, so I never cried in front of friends or family. That is not to say I didn't cry. I cried a lot—alone. The one person I share everything with is my big brother Ryan, and this was no exception. Poor him. At the time, Ryan lived in London and there was an 8-hour time difference. I would call him at all hours, crying hysterically. Sometimes there were no words, just sobs. Ryan was the only person who ever heard me cry throughout the cancer. I think the only reason I was able to hold it together was because I could fall apart late at night and Ryan would piece me back together over the phone. Thank you, big brother.

I tell everyone that it is natural to experience fear, sorrow, anger, and grief—among other emotions— typically considered "negative" in today's culture when you are going through something this traumatic. It's essential to our mental health to be allowed to scream, cry, and shout, "This sucks!" Because it *does* suck; that's the reality. I was unable to follow my own advice though, and I didn't want to cry or show my deep sadness because I thought I had to be strong for my mom. I thought, "Who am I to cry? I have to be her rock." I was wrong. I needed to cry and maybe my mom needed to see me cry.

One of the most important things I've learned over the crazy journey that has been the last four years is to be honest—with yourself—and ask for the help you need. It is so easy to convince ourselves that we're okay, that we're fine with something that isn't good enough, or that we can handle it alone. Whether it's how much you're struggling with a situation, a friend who isn't a real friend, a man who doesn't deserve you, or a situation that makes you uneasy, we have to first be honest with ourselves before we can be honest with anyone else.

I had trouble admitting how much I was hurting when my mom got sick. I thought that, because I wasn't the patient, I didn't get to feel that way—I had to be strong. Learning to be vulnerable was really the strongest thing I could do. It helped me not only heal, but to build a movement that has helped hundreds of thousands of people on some of the worst days of their lives.

As I've said time and again throughout the book, your journey to your most beauty-full self starts by listening and understanding what it is *you* want for your life, whether it's for next week, next month, or next year. And remember to call on your team of supporters—even if it is a team of one—to help you sort out your thoughts and feelings. Listen to their stories, consider their advice, and regardless if it's not right for you, it will give you more clues about what is. People have a way of guiding us in the most unexpected ways and when wisdom is called upon, it always shows up. It may not be what you were hoping for, or arrive in the way in which you thought she would, but she'll find her way to you. She will tell your heart exactly what it needs to know and guide your feet in the right direction if you let her.

My mom has always been the first person I go to when I'm feeling off track or less than sparkly. Maybe because her compassion, resilience, self-authored constitution, and childlike enthusiasm for life inspire me daily. Or maybe it's because, in spite of her life's circumstances—not coming from wealth, experiencing abuse, getting married and pregnant at sixteen, raising five children as a single mom and defying all odds—she's a warrior in civilian clothes and someone I will forever look up to. Either way, I can't discuss "that girl" and not mention the woman who inspired it all. The irony, of course, is that when I asked her to write something for this book, she gaffed and said, "I can't imagine I have anything important to share." I beg to differ, Mom. I want to share some of her wisdom that has helped me so much over the years. Here are my mom's precious and wise thoughts about what is most important in life.

CLAUDIA MANN (My Mom, My Hero): I was married and pregnant when I was sixteen. My husband went off to college across the country while I lived with my parents, finished two years of high school in one, and had our child. I then followed him to school and worked, kept up the household, and cared for our child while he attended college. Four years later we were divorced; he had four years of college under his belt and I still had my secretarial job, making barely enough to pay for day care, an apartment, food, and my car. I got my college degree at forty-three years of age.

I learned a lot in those first four years. First and foremost, don't get married or pregnant while you are still a child yourself. Grow up, finish school, and should you be married in college, even if it takes a little longer to finish, make sure you both leave with your degree.

Always be honest with yourself and others. Earning back trust is much harder than maintaining that trust with truth.

Always be on time. Everyone's time is as valuable as yours. When an opportunity arises for an advancement, or job

---

recommendation, people remember that you were the one always on time and that you were dependable. Your name will go to the top of the list.

Learn when to say no and mean it. Be true to yourself. My father once said if you ask advice from five different people you will get five different responses. Figure out what you want yourself. You cannot please everyone and will be lucky if you can please yourself most of the time. Trust yourself.

Look people in the eye when you talk with them and listen to them. Listen carefully. A good listener is much more valuable than a good talker. Be a good friend and you will find that in turn you have good friends. I have found that my true friend is that one I can call when my car is broken down in Tennessee and the only question he asks is where I am, and gets on the road and heads in my direction all the way from Texas.

Remember that you are human. You will make mistakes. Do not let them define you.

Our journey through this life is like a river. It is a constant flow, sometimes going faster, sometimes slower, and sometimes getting stuck in the eddies going round and round. You have to view life in its whole. You cannot pick out a single mistake, or accomplishment, and say, "That is what/who I am."

Don't waste time on regrets. They are backward looking and based on situations you cannot change. Learn from your experiences and move on.

Take time for your family and friends. Work hard and be the best at whatever it is that you do. If you work at a hamburger stand, make the best hamburger in the world and when you hand it to that customer, make them feel as if you waited all day just for them to come by.

> Love, love, love. Love yourself, love your family and friends, love life and the many blessings it bestows upon you. Be thankful each and every day. Be kind and forgiving. Let things go. Holding on tightly to things doesn't open the opportunity to what may come your way in the future.

THE WRONG KIND OF BEAUTY

My mom doesn't try to conform to anyone else's image of perfection and that's maybe the greatest lesson I ever learned from her. Despite all the highlights and all the blunders along her journey, all the excuses she could have made to not succeed, or the temptation to quit, using the justification that she wasn't dealt the best hand, she refused to give up. She never allowed her failures or her successes to define her, she didn't allow others to define her, she stood tall, worked hard, and reminded all of us that beauty is a verb and not an adjective. She reminds us that being human, being *real*, is far more awesome than an artificial façade of plastic perfection. She reminds us that happiness, confidence, and joy will never be found externally, but authentic joy and self-worth will only ever be found within. Her message is one that we are all starving for because, if you haven't noticed, we're not doing very well right now.

Everywhere I look I see campaigns for wafer-thin models, another starlet heading back to rehab, and entertainment news celebrating opulence, wealth, fame, and a singular image of beauty as though it's our life's mission. I read the statistics of rampant eating disorders and bullying starting as young as elementary school. I watch my friends settle for people who blatantly disrespect them because they'd rather be in a relationship with someone (anyone) than be alone. I'm surrounded by girls who barely eat, or when they do they feel so guilty that the distracting thoughts prevent them from living a powerful life. I see consumption everywhere and temptation behind every corner for bigger and better.

I don't see a society filled with substance. I don't see a society full of integrity and contentment. I don't see a culture celebrating girls for what makes us truly beautiful, one that highlights our character, but rather, I see one that breaks us down for our physical "imperfections." I witness a sea of daily distractions that hold us down like shackles to our feet when we should be flying. Our narrow definition of beauty requires girls to pluck, dye, brush, shave, cut, bleach, wax, diet, shop, and endlessly compare; all of which leave very little time for us to really shine. What we haven't noticed is that we are forced into a lifelong beauty contest that we will never win, and didn't ask to enter in the first place.

I'm tired of it. And trust me, I'm not now and have never been above the lure of this competition. I too need to be reminded that my self-worth is not equal to whether or not I have a good hair day, or if I've been meticulously working out and looking thin. I have to work hard to remember that whether I'm five pounds heavier or my face is broken out that I am gorgeous because of who I am, not what I look like. The shell of my body houses the most precious thing, and like clams our real treasure is the pearly heart inside.

It's hard in today's society to ignore all the unrealistic expectations because they're everywhere you turn and everything from the ads on the street to conversations with our friends and family all reinforce it every day. We're fighting a battle to recognize daily our innate self-worth instead of allowing our confidence to reside in the approval of others, in our handbags, our job titles, our significant others, or our accomplishments.

For a long time I put pressure on myself to figure out this dilemma. I wanted to be able to identify the "problem" we all struggled with. Why don't we ever feel good enough or pretty enough? But I quickly realized it isn't about finding a "cure" for the epidemic of insecurity plaguing us today or a formula that will offer girls endless amounts of confidence. All I needed to do was start the conversation.

"You suppose you are the trouble but you are the cure. You suppose that you are the lock on the door but you are the key that opens it. It's too bad that you want to be someone else. You don't see your own face, your own beauty. Yet, no face is more beautiful than yours."

—RUMI

So I put up my white flag and waved it around violently for all to see. I quit. I gave up. I dropped out of the race to attain the image of perfection and asked myself, "Who signed me up in the first place?" Not me. I don't think any of us voluntarily sign up for it, but we somehow find ourselves sprinting along with every other girl we know, headed somewhere without knowing why or where. The crazy thing is, once I was honest with people in my life and stopped trying to pretend that I had it all figured out, they were free to do the same.

It was like we could all take a deep breath and say, "Okay, this is exhausting pretending to be something that we're not, pretending to have it all together." Then we were free to talk about things that really mattered. We were no longer competing in a stupid race we didn't want to run in the first place. Suddenly we were comrades, supportive sisters, and able to collaborate instead of compete. We were able to talk about all the things we wanted to do in the world, no longer threatened by one another. I shared my passions, my goals, and my ambitions and in turn so did they. And I realized just how small my conversations had been, how unoriginal they had become, until I threw in my towel and decided that I was going to play a different game. I was going to play the game of changing the world and finding other women who wanted to join *that* race.

I AM THAT GIRL hosted an event at the White House with a slew of influential women. With the number of gorgeous, confident, successful alpha females in the room I admit that I expected hints of cattiness or arrogance here and there. However, it was shockingly the opposite of what the stereotype would suggest.

Like an old Western standoff, the first few minutes were painfully silent. Then, one by one each woman set down the cumbersome façade of perfection, the heavy armor, and the Wonder Woman cape that we wear for the rest of the world. And that's when the magic occurred and the authenticity glittered on our faces as we began to candidly share our life's most personal battles—the good, the bad, the glamorous, and the downright ugly. Egos evaporated, pride melted, and we were left with our most beautiful characteristic, compassion.

Suddenly the Hollywood starlets, the powerhouse producers, and thought leaders of our generation found common ground that defied professional titles and couture nametags. Suddenly we were so much more than our impressive resumes; we were transformed into a group of girls patiently listening to each other's unique life stories, which were all dappled with the inevitable struggles and triumphs, love stories and heartbreaks, highlights and gaffes. I was left inspired by a group of women committed to collaborating instead of competing, and because of that dedication each of us walked out of the White House a better version of ourselves; picked up, dusted off, and ready to get back out on the battlefield.

So to hell with the stereotype of catty girls threatened by and lashing out at each other. While it may still be the reality for many, I believe that girls are ready for a new relationship with one another in which we support and encourage each other, where we challenge and inspire each other and stand in one another's corner instead of staring down our opponent in the middle of the ring. When girls choose to come together and join forces, the possibilities are endless, and yet conversely, if we continue to compete in an unproductive way the cancerous resentment will siphon out our fuel tanks and leave each of us stranded on the side of the road, going nowhere.

I know it is possible, girls empowering girls. I've seen it and it's breathtaking, magnifying every phenomenally powerful characteristic unique to us. I believe in a world in which girls feel worthy, where we have the audacity to dream big and have access to the tools and support to make those dreams a reality. I believe in a world where glass ceilings are shattered, where stereotypes are put to rest, where catty glances are exchanged for supportive smiles, and where girls are reminded everywhere that we are, in fact, on the same team. I believe in a world where compassion surpasses ego, a world where girls boldly challenge each other and use one another as resources instead of a means to an end.

I believe that in a single generation we can drastically change the future for girls, and that our daughters and granddaughters will have no concept of a time when we were anything other than each other's biggest fans. I believe that if you empower girls, you change the world. I dare you to dream that with me.

THE ENEMY IS US

The scariest, most terrifying aspect of the war we are in right now is that it is with ourselves, and it's difficult to defeat your enemy when you stare them in the face each morning in the bathroom mirror. We have been taught to be so self-critical, judgmental, and doubtful of everything we do and say. We are prisoners of our own minds, limited only by the extent of our own thoughts and looking everywhere but inside for permission and approval. It's easy to vilify the entertainment industry and media for its limited portrayals and objectification of women, we can point fingers in every direction, but I know if I'm being honest with myself, the harshest criticism I have ever heard comes from the tiny voice inside my own head, convincing me I'm not enough, I'll fail, or worse scaring me out of ever trying.

At the end of the day, we are the only ones responsible for our actions, and we need to stop looking outside ourselves for the change. Obviously there are massive influences on us, pressures and expectations, but to be a victim to them is our choice. Your greatest challenge lies in the depths of your own self-doubt, the you that binges on half a chocolate cake and then convinces you of the lie that you have no willpower, using the excuse you "couldn't" stop yourself. The real challenge is the you who lacks integrity and says you're going to do something and then doesn't hold yourself accountable. Your greatest bully is the you who looks in the mirror and immediately

> "You, who make angels stutter and mystics moan— congratulations for being here so well. It's not an easy gig, this thing called life. In fact, it's quite the ass-kicking experience. But oh, how you're living brilliantly anyway. Even when you think you've failed, the Universe stands in awe of you. Even when you forget who you are, blades of grass long to rub up against you. Even when you hide your gifts, the air aches to breathe you. In. Thank you for existing so perfectly."
>
> —SERA BEAK

tallies up your so-called physical flaws and begins the destructive commentary, "I wish my nose were a little more like this, my stomach a little more like that, my boobs a little bigger, my thighs a little smaller." The least attractive version of you is the one that gossips about other girls instead of encouraging them and uses words like *can't* and *impossible*. At the end of the day, we have to realize that more often than not, the real enemy is the voice inside our head telling us we don't matter, we're not enough, and we'll never measure up; it's *that* voice that we must learn to silence.

Defeating this enemy starts within each of us because if we cannot become the master of our own ships, the creator of our own thoughts, then we are but talking parrots repeating others' ideas and beliefs. Yes, our paradigm is greatly influenced by our culture, but I won't settle for being another comatose Barbie, to sit passively and allow this to go on any longer. We all just need new programming, a software update.

JESS WEINER (Author and Social Messaging Strategist): I've written a lot about my childhood and the requisite pain, excitement, and awe that come with those inevitable transitions when your girlhood dreams become adulthood realities.

Whether it was my beautiful transformation from a depressed, doubting, and diet-obsessed teenager into a sensitive, self-loving, and semi-sane adult, one thing remains abundantly clear, as I traveled through my twenties, and now round out my thirties, life totally gives you what you *need*—not always what you want.

What I thought I wanted in my twenties was attention. Attention meant approval. Approval meant love. And love meant I was worthy. I sought this attention by following every trend and fad, morphing myself to please others, and dare I admit, jumping into a few heart-wrenching love affairs. But at the end of the day, the attention never satisfied the deep hole within; I was looking for an approval I would eventually learn could never come from a compliment, a raise, or even a marriage proposal.

Into my thirties I felt I could hold my head higher, having weathered some storms, earning some stripes, and living through crushing disappointments. Now, my focus would be on balance. But on the way to seeking balance, I learned just how out of balance my life had become.

As an entrepreneur, I had made my career the primary focus of my life and now had to consider whether I had replaced seeking attention with "being busy." Girls and women get so much validation by their busyness. And I seemed to be in the running for a gold medal in this Olympic sport of overcompensation.

I loved my career. I have achieved incredible success that makes me truly proud. But something was missing. Had I bypassed the balance in order to serve my ambition? And did being busy actually make me feel more loved? Would I even have enough room in my life to let real love in when it called? True love. Not the kind of love you find in a sappy movie. The kind of love that forces you to dig deep, grow up, and actually create a balance between your work and play.

But before I could make that space for someone else, I needed to make it for myself. Because no matter who I ended up in a relationship with, I was always going to need to be *my own first true love*.

The first step to falling into loving balance with yourself is to order a cease-fire in the war you are waging with your childhood fears. The ones that keep you tethered to the past. The ones that still supply a heavy dose of shame around your worth. The ones that keep you mired in labels from long ago. If you want to skip down the path toward authenticity, then you must discover how to really be yourself.

Be bold enough to dream your own visions, to speak your own dreams, and to fortify your own confidence with a profound inner love. An inner love that isn't reliant upon attention or a jam-packed schedule, but one that comes from living a life filled with glorious honesty, rigorous self-examination, and gentle forgiveness.

This isn't easy. And you may not get to cross it off your to-do list tomorrow. But it's a relationship worth creating. And the good news is you can start on this relationship journey right now. Just like Dorothy in *The Wizard of Oz*, there really is no place like home. And there is no one just like you. Your true home is a balanced body, a searching mind, an authentic spirit, and a beautiful relationship with yourself.

When we can focus on becoming more of who we are, we may end up discovering that we are the ones we've been waiting for. And we are *so* worth the wait.

So stop blaming others for the obstacles in your life or beating yourself up for not living up to some ridiculous ideal. Be good to yourself, listen carefully, and pay attention to who you are. Yes, as Jess's story shows, it may take time and experience to develop your confidence and understanding of yourself. But why not try learning the lesson of self-love now? It's never too early or too late to come out of the trenches of a war you're waging on yourself. Be the first person and the last person every day who supports you and loves you for who you are. After all, why should anyone else do it if you don't?

FIGHT FOR SOMETHING
BIGGER THAN YOU

It is a luxury to worry about whether you look fat in those pants, if you're sporting the latest trends, or how to get your latest crush to notice you. I had never thought about this until I worked in Cambodia, dealing with girls who had nothing. I watched young girls fighting for their lives, at eight years old working twelve- to fourteen-hour days trying to help feed their families. I had never been so humbled in my life. I realized I had six different kinds of lotions for different body parts, more than thirty pairs of shoes, and enough clothes to wear a different outfit every day for a year. Not to mention a roof over my head, food to fill my belly, and a family who loves me and protects me.

These girls had none of that and yet one of the greatest lessons I've ever learned was from a beautiful five-year-old girl named Srey No. She taught me the art of appreciation. In the United States, we are so used to having so much, but the consequence of that consumer-driven mentality is our inability to appreciate it. We are taught that behind every corner there is something bigger and better. I remember the first time I bought Srey No a two-cent balloon. She had never seen one before and as I held her little body in my arms, and her right hand clung to that tiny string, her eyes lit up as she gazed at the floating magic ball. It was as if I were experiencing the phenomenon of balloons all over again, only through her eyes. This silly thing only cost two cents, but I realized that more than the actual balloon, she was enjoying feeling loved and was grateful to be in my arms. The balloon was the icing on the cake.

When I was in Cambodia working with these girls, I didn't stress over what outfit I was going to wear or if I'd eaten too many carbs that day, and I never once glanced in the mirror longer than the time it took me to brush my teeth. My worth to these girls had far less to do with my looks and

"How wonderful it is that nobody need wait a single moment before starting to improve the world."

—ANNE FRANK

so much more to do with my heart and how I was able to make them feel valued. I was consumed with something far greater than just trying to impress people, I was consumed with loving these girls, with teaching them basic hygiene, and encouraging them to read and write. My life was about something so much greater than just Alexis Whitney Jones.

Over the years, I've found that the easiest way to feel better about myself is to concern myself with someone or something bigger than me. When I step outside of my ego, my pride, and my desire to impress others, I find true contentment and the authentic confidence that makes me shine. When I chose to live an *others*-centered life as opposed to an *ego*-centered life, I began to feel the most fulfilled. That is not to say that my ego doesn't trip me up or that my pride doesn't stand in the way at times, but I certainly do my best each day to be thoughtful about others.

That life-altering experience in Cambodia shook me out of the trance I was in. I had bought into the glamorous stories of Hollywood's starlets and I believed that if my body was the right size, my shoes were the right colors, and my purse was the right brand then I too would belong in the world of glitz and glam. At one point, I thought I had it all and yet I still felt painfully lonely and insecure. After trips like Cambodia, I suddenly realized that all the fame, riches, and influence in the world could not make me feel complete or fulfilled the way I did when I was there. When we are myopically focused on ourselves, and I don't mean making yourself "first," I mean when you create a world where you are the "only sun in your universe," we board a direct flight to self-destruction. You need more than a single bottom line to measure whether you are successful or not, more than the right husband, perfect children, your dream job, or the perfect body. When we discover our unique passion and fight for it tooth and nail, when we are pursuing our purpose, pouring out our heart and serving others above just ourselves, we find the ingredients of real joy and wholeness.

BRITT DEBEIKES (Daughter, Sister, Advocate for Dreamers): I had caught him red-handed with another woman. The man who I loved and imagined building a future with broke my heart and shattered me in an instant.

I drove, first, to my parents' house and fell apart in my father's arms. He lifted me from the front seat of my car and carried me into the house where he and my mother spent the next two hours doing their best to calm my hysterical tears. Then, it was time for me to go home to my apartment and put myself to bed accepting that I would have to actually wake up tomorrow and start a new day.

As I pulled onto my street, my phone buzzed with two new text messages. Surely, my friends did not yet know of the terrible encounter and ensuing heartbreak that had occurred just hours earlier that evening. I reached for my phone and read, through the tears streaming down my face, a message from one of my best friends from college. She was newly engaged. The next message was from her new fiancé requesting my presence at a surprise engagement party he was throwing her the following night. Feeling empty and broken it was all I could do not to crawl into bed and simply turn off the phone.

That was just the beginning of the best year of my life.

My brother held back tears as he placed his arm around my shoulders and escorted me into the engagement party the next night. In the weeks that followed I was the recipient of an outpouring of love unlike anything else I had ever experienced in life. The number of people that came to my side, and the vastness of their love and loyalty, was mind blowing. I made a decision just weeks after that fateful night that I would dedicate the next six months to serving others and paying forward all of the selfless love that I had been so fortunate to receive.

My first order of business was to buy plane tickets to visit close friends all over the country because I had experienced, firsthand, the depth of emotional support that comes from physical human contact. It is the kind of connection that can simply not be replaced by an email or text message.

One of my longtime childhood friends had been living in Colorado for nearly ten years and in that time I had hopped on a plane only once to go see her. I had recently learned that her parents were in the midst of a terrible divorce, full of drama ripe for the hometown gossip chain. She kept it all close to the vest, rarely opening up to even her closest of friends, in hopes of keeping her family name off of the lips of the local women often found enjoying their Chardonnay lunches while talking about the lives of others.

I flew out to see her and spent a weekend indulging in all things fun and girly. We stayed up late drinking wine and listening to music, didn't take off our pajamas until noon while glued to a *Bachelor Pad* marathon, and spent the rest of the afternoon hiking with her dog through the Colorado mountain trails. On the last day we had a long lunch and she opened up to me about the struggle and pain associated with all the change that was slowly materializing within her family. I felt honored to have the opportunity to open up my ears and offer words of encouragement. She was carrying a heavy load on her shoulders, and I was anxious to try and share some of the weight.

There were countless other friends who I was determined to show my love and perhaps try and share in carrying some of the emotional weight burdening them as a result of changes or challenges in their lives. I wrote letters, sent cupcakes, and made homemade gifts of personal stationery with a note to encourage them to always be in touch with those whom they loved.

A particularly fond memory occurred one evening when I had the opportunity to present a book of letters to a dear friend who was a new mother. Close family and friends had written the letters to her son before he was born, and they expressed wishes of hopes and dreams for his life. We exchanged a tearful embrace before I was able to alleviate her of parenting duties for just a couple of hours so that she and her husband might enjoy a date night for the first time in weeks.

My relationships were developing in strength and complexity—the efforts of serving others were materializing into whole new chapters of existing friendships. With each passing month I could feel myself coming more alive.

My intention isn't to encourage you to serve others in order to achieve greater personal happiness. Rather, I hope to simply share with you the personal enlightenment that I experienced in shifting my mind-set from looking inward to looking outward. And then consider this a call to action.

Whether you help people in a far-off land or, like Britt, connect with and be there for your loved ones at home, seek out a way to give of yourself, not just to yourself. Particularly when you are feeling down, stuck, or directionless, sometimes the best way to awaken your spirit and your hope is to get out of your own head, your own routine, and fight for, give to, or focus on something meaningful outside yourself.

MY FINAL MESSAGE

I was told once that the two most important questions we will ever be asked are "Who did you love and who did you serve?" The idea is that the only things that really matter in life are the people you are surrounded by and the constitution you choose to follow. Are you surrounding yourself with negative influences or compassionate, creative, kind, challenging, humble, and socially conscious individuals? Are you self-serving, pursuing money, prestige, success, and external validation, or are you seeking to serve others, contribute instead of merely consume, pursue your passion and purpose instead of flying on autopilot?

Who will you choose to be in this lifetime? I want you to have the courage to answer that, to know and love yourself unconditionally, to believe in your own dreams and surpass your potential. I want you to have the life you dream of because you're willing to fight for it. I want you to find your happy or (as one of my dear friends, Seth Matlins, says) to "feel more better." I don't expect you to avoid life's messy, complicated, and scary storms, but rather in the midst of them have the confidence that your little boat will never sink. Waterlogged? Tossed around? Capsized even? Of course, but never sink. I just want you to feel comfortable and confident in your skin, to author your life according to your expectations, and delete the word *impossible* from your vocabulary.

I want you to remember above all else that on this crazy journey, you're not alone. There are so many of us, an entire generation and generations before and after, who've struggled and will struggle with the exact things you are right now. Our lives are not just about how we can change the world and leave our imprint on history, but more so about who we will choose to be on a daily basis throughout our adventure. Our lives are far simpler and far more complex than we'll ever know, and yet as I'm learning the whole point is that every day we wake up we get another shot. Yesterday has no impact on today and today has no indication of what tomorrow will look like. Because it's true what they say, we are not entitled to this lifetime, so learning to embrace the preciousness of it, of our relationships and of our experiences in the moment, is all we can ask of ourselves. I strongly believe that to live well is to simply appreciate what we have, when we have it.

This journey is a roller coaster of highs and lows and everything in between. We are meant to experience the magnificence, the disappointment, the inspiration, and the challenges in order to taste each flavor on the entire buffet line. Some things we won't necessarily like, but others we will marvel at their deliciousness. Regardless, we won't know until we try each and every one, so don't shy away from people, experiences, opportunities, success, or potential failures, heartbreaks, and disappointments. Through it all, the lessons we accrue, the shades of paint we collect on our palette, and the variety of foods we gather on our plate make our world more brilliant, more interesting, more diverse, and more scrumptious. Salty, sweet, bitter, spicy, and bland; we need them all. We *want* them all, for choice is the heartbeat of life.

And while I'm the greatest "dream advocate" out there, the greatest challenge is being your own dream advocate because you really can do whatever you want in this lifetime, and don't roll your eyes at me like I'm your mom telling you that your lame third grade finger painting should be hanging in museums everywhere. I mean it. If you are willing to sacrifice, work hard, maintain your integrity, and fight for it, it is possible to manifest your beauty-full dreams. But remember that whether your life is on display for two or two million, that regardless of what you accomplish, that you are truly magnificent. In a world obsessed with what you *do*, what cover of magazine your face graces, the amount of money in your bank account, the gorgeous body you adorn, I'm just here to remind you that you are inherently awesome.

Though I'm not your fairy godmother, capable of making all your wildest dreams come true, fixing all your problems, or magically transforming your life with a swish of my wand, I can offer you my unwavering belief in you. If you could see you through my eyes for even a few seconds, you would see how infinitely invaluable and how cherished you are. If you could see you through my eyes, you'd never spend another moment questioning your worth, questioning your beauty, or second-guessing your potential. Your fear would be replaced with love and your insecurities replaced with a peace and confidence transcending your chronic anxiety. The lies you've been told your entire life, the ones saying that you aren't enough, would be replaced with the fact that you are profoundly and utterly extraordinary. Your new truth would be, "I have enough, I do enough, I am enough."

With a strong, unapologetic sense of self you would find the freedom you've been searching for, the permission you've wanted to grant yourself for so long but maybe didn't know how. And in that space, without the help of Tinker Bell, you will have the ability to fly. You will witness the magic that we all have access to, the knowledge that you and everyone else we stumble upon truly are the secret weapons to all the hairy challenges threatening our world, our loved ones, and ourselves. Your civilian clothes will transform into the superhero costume you always knew existed. Knowing who you are, what you stand for, searching for your purpose, discovering it, and pursuing it creates an inspired life worthy of you waking up each day. Our dreams are only possible when we truly accept our awesomeness and let that girl inside us wave her badass flag.

So at the point of your flag-waving awesomeness, you will realize that, the thing you've been wondering about, brainstorming about, daydreaming about, is *actually* possible. Whether it's to start your own company, apply for your dream school, move to a foreign country to follow love, quit your job, start that workout regime you've talked about for years, sign up for that dance class, or just dedicate yourself to a ten-minute daily mediation, the only reason it won't happen is if you never take that big, fat leap of faith and try. So stop making excuses, believe in yourself, and know you're worth giving that "thing" of yours a real chance, not in a year, a month, a week; not when you have enough money, meet the right person, or when the right door opens. RIGHT. NOW. The world needs you to be awesome. So take a deep breath and go for it.

Also, let go of everything in the past, live today, right now for this moment regardless of the outcome. Throw caution to the wind, spread out your wings, and fly, my dear, because it was what you were meant to do. You were born into this world to find your unique voice, to love yourself, to love those around you, and even in the smallest way, to leave the world a little more beauty-full just because you were a part of it. You were meant to find your passion and to be enthusiastically contagious because you're lit up from the inside out. You were meant to dream and make those sparkly dreams come true so that at the end of a very long life, the tiny dash between your start date and end date on your tombstone would reflect a girl who gave life everything she had.

I need you, you need you, the world needs you, we all need you to be the most badass version of yourself, so find her and remind her to shine with all her might, every single day.

My only request,

Rock this world and be THAT GIRL!!

I AM THAT GIRL

There are few things that inspire me as much as the concept of building community. To me the term *community* always felt a bit more academic, as though it were referencing the Native American division of labor; the men hunting and gathering and the women "building community." The amount of books, articles, texts, statistics focus groups, and studies on the importance of *community* and *belonging* would make your head spin. I could certainly regurgitate the philosophy of why it's important to have a group of people who embrace you, with a barrage of stats on the confidence-damaging repercussions of not feeling a sense of community, but I'd rather just have a conversation and not lecture at you.

The reality is that it seems pretty obvious that life is better when you have friends to experience it with. How many movies back this notion up? It's always the best friend who saves the day, who nurses a broken heart back to love, and who somehow knows exactly what to say to cheer up an inconsolable friend. Looking back at the creation of I AM THAT GIRL, this was the unknowing guiding force behind it all. For a long time, I had a very eloquent and lengthy response when asked why I started I AM THAT GIRL.

The real and rather short answer is because I needed it. I needed a group of girls to help me make sense of my life and the world, yes, "a community where I felt I belonged."

My sophomore year of college after getting cast for *The Vagina Monologues*, I remember being in shock. Through this progressive play I learned about all the atrocities women and girls were facing all over the world—child marriage in Ethiopia, genital mutilation in Africa, and acid burning in Iran. Rather than screaming from a soapbox, telling all my friends that it's our duty as women to do something about this horrific reality, I just remember asking some of my girlfriends, "Did you know any of this stuff was going on, because I had no idea." I quickly followed up my inquiry with, "I mean, we have a lot of conversations about things that don't matter (clothes, shoes, boys, movies, gossip, etc.); what if once a week, we talked about things that did? Would you be interested? Would you come?" The first week, the few girls I initially chatted with showed up. A few weeks later that number had grown exponentially. These girls, like me, were starving for community.

Once a week, I'd put together a topic and a series of questions. Whether it was about global issues, social issues, something recently posted in the news, or something written up in the school newspaper, I used it as a conversation starter. The intention was to talk about the topic, I'd come up with a series of questions and we'd have a discussion. The reality was that even if we started out talking about what I'd prepared, we always ended up coming back to our personal lives. It was like nothing I'd ever seen. There was this huge group of girls who felt safe, who felt validated and accepted. It's as if all the girls who showed up gave one another permission to be real and to let go of the façade they carried for the rest of the world.

On top of it, there were guys who showed up in support of the girls in their lives. I realized that we were all normal kids, all with our challenges, our insecurities just like everyone else of course, but here we could talk about it and support one another. The sacred space provided that "community" that I'd read about in so many of my anthropology classes. It wasn't just athletes, sorority girls, frat boys, honors students, loners, or drama kids, it was all of them and together, bigger than any of our stereotypes, we were activists. We were all there because even if we saw the world differently, even if we had completely different contexts and operational manuals for life, we came together in the name of something bigger than ourselves. We came together as an inclusive, encouraging, empowering, and inspiring group of girls and guys who truly believed we could make the world better.

That's when it dawned on me, we can't be the only group of students like this, on a campus like this. There has to be more, so many more. My initial passion for empowering girls was blazing bright as I saw the change in girls when they no longer felt alone. More importantly, I saw the difference in myself when I felt like I belonged to something so special. It didn't make my personal struggles disappear, but it made them bearable. Something about building this kind of community gave me a sense of purpose like I'd never known. Why did I have to have a serious addiction, have lost a loved one in a tragic accident, or be struggling with cancer or some other serious disease to have a support group? Where could *all* girls, struggling with everyday things, go to be encouraged and surrounded by other girls just like her?

This phenomenon took me by surprise, and it dawned on me that I knew exactly what I wanted to do with my life. I was going to build that kind of community all over the world. I was going to name it I AM THAT GIRL. I would start local chapters just like this one. It would be a badass version of Girl Scouts meets book club with an activist twist. Because all I knew was that this kind of community was necessary, that I was a better human when I was surrounded by other girls who somehow made each other not feel so alone.

My journey to bring this crazy idea to fruition would carry me on to grad school, where I'd complete a two-year program specific to building I AM THAT GIRL. Every class I took, every project I completed was on the concept of I AM THAT GIRL, growing an idea, a teeny tiny seed, into what it is today. After grad school and my crazy stint on *Survivor*, I met my best friend at a lame party I was walking out of, and in that friendship I would learn my greatest lesson about community.

I remember it like it was yesterday because it's not often you stumble upon your soul sister, reunited from lifetimes and lifetimes of dancing and fighting side by side to make the world better. I was about to leave a birthday party; I was tired and it was already past my bedtime. As I was grabbing my purse and heading out this spunky, black curly-haired girl stopped me, "Alexis, right?" My response to this bubbly spunk-fest was a hesitant and exhausted, "Yeah." Her enthusiastic reply, "Oh perfect, I'm Emily! I've heard so much about you. Don't go anywhere, I'll be right back!" Two seconds later she pulled up a chair at a table and the rest is history.

She asked me what I did and I told her about I AM THAT GIRL. She lit up, asking question after question about it. I told her that my office was at the local coffee shop in Beverly Hills and she was welcome to join me any time. I was drowning under the work I needed to complete before the very public launch of I AM THAT GIRL, which I was debuting at the finale of *Survivor*. All my other girlfriends had been too busy to help out writing articles for the website, but sure enough, my new friend showed up the next day. Bright-eyed and bushy-tailed. She was happy to help, happy to write, happy to do anything really. Any hat, she'd wear it. We joke to this day how many different job titles she had the first year we worked together.

I soon realized our now shared dream was growing and we needed help. I put an intern ad online (in hopes of getting a few responses) and was shocked when we received over 300 applications! We interviewed and hired twenty-three new girls who proceeded to work out of my apartment. Then it just kept growing and growing and growing. Emily helped me build I AM THAT GIRL, and looking back on the past several years, I never could have done it without her. And we couldn't have done it without the support and unconditional love of our families, all our interns, our mentors, our advice-givers, even our naysayers because they were always just fuel for our fire.

It is crazy to look back at the initial question that sparked this global community of girls, "We have a lot of conversations about things that don't matter; what if once a week we had conversations about things that did. Would you be interested? Would you come?" The reality is that we do talk about things that matter because WE matter; our thoughts, ideas, fears, doubts, hopes, and dreams matter, and we should have a place, a group of girls, friends, community where we can share them. We should have a place where we can brainstorm how we collectively can make the world better. I AM THAT GIRL was an idea to create that, a place to remind girls every day (whether through our social media, our campaigns, our events, our healthy media, our local chapters, or any other way you engage with us) of your innate worth and provide you a community of girls to help *you* make sense of your life and of the world.

I AM THAT GIRL has grown bigger than anything I could have ever imagined. It has given Emily and me what we put into it tenfold. There have been skyscraping highs, there have been lonely, frustrating, heartbreaking lows. We've waltzed into the White House, visited local chapters in tiny towns, been highlighted in prestigious press, and shared our vision with homeless men outside Starbucks. We have struggled like any two girls with our egos and our pride, and also witnessed mind-blowing humility and grace. In the process of wanting to change the world *for* girls, I think it's us who have changed the most. I could write a novel just on my entrepreneurial adventure thus far, the past several years and the ups and downs of a "start-up," but for the purpose of this book, the life lesson I'll never forget that drives me and our mission forward is about the importance of community.

Having spent the past four years in the trenches with girls, Em and I joke that we have a PhD in GIRLS. Being the tenacious entrepreneur she is, Emily dove headfirst into the speaking world and started booking me to speak anywhere and everywhere that would listen. I've spoken in huge cities, to tiny one-horse towns, to the Girl Scouts, to Harvard, to the UN, to a Paul Mitchell East Coast school tour. From the NASA innovation summit, to New York Fashion Week, from the G8 Global Summit, to Fiji, to Canada, and to places in between, I've spoken all over the globe. Yet in the midst of us living the life of twenty-first-century gypsies, you saw two superheroes teaming up and doing what we each did so well. I used to laugh saying that Emily understands my crazy, visionary bursts of energy as well my inconsistency and exhaustion. She had faith in me when I didn't have faith in myself, breathed life to this dream of mine and made it her own. She held my feet firmly on the ground when my head spun so effortlessly in the clouds. Emily is the ultimate example of what the community of girls can look like and what's possible in that inspiring place. Even with two we could do so much better than just one. She is my sister, my friend, and the co-parent to our I AM THAT GIRL baby.

I AM THAT GIRL may have started with one girl, but it soon turned into two, and together Emily and I have turned it into well over 100,000 today and still growing. At the end of the day, community is the whole point of life. A trusted group of friends, a family (whether blood or chosen), makes this whole life adventure worth it. Whether we are struggling or soaring, it's always better when we have a buddy, a copilot, a best friend, a soul sister; Emily has always been that for me. While she and I are unique threads woven into the fabric of I AM THAT GIRL, the beautiful thing is that so is every single person who has been involved and who will one day be involved. WE are a name-less face-less organization, built for you, by you.

Learning how to be a cog in the wheel, to share the stage, to take turns at the microphone, to die to your ego, to include people, and to take off the queen bee crown is a challenge set before every girl. To be consciously selfless and thoughtful of others is something worth practicing every day. We live in a world trying to convince us that we're fine alone. We live in a world driven by convenience and taking time for others, investing in people, is not always convenient, but when we forget this is our priority to individually getting ahead, we forget the point. Emily has always had an enviable selflessness, her inability to exclude often made me uncomfortable and yet her community-building skills are like few I have ever witnessed. I still have so much to learn from her; I still have so many more thank-yous in store for her.

So whether you get plugged into I AM THAT GIRL's community and build your own local chapter in your neck of the woods or not, just promise me that you'll get plugged in *somewhere*. It's in our bones, our DNA, it's our greatest strength as girls, as the feminine species, to build a nest for people to feel safe and warm, loved and cherished. Our superpower is loving people until they are found, loving people back to life, loving people so their dreams come true, and loving them when they are soaring.

I believe the foundation of community has been broken because we've been convinced that we should be threatened by one other, convinced we are foes instead of friends. I AM THAT GIRL seeks to change that. Community has the ability to change the world because already two people can exponentially do more together than individually, so just imagine what tens, hundreds, thousands, and millions could do.

I AM THAT GIRL was never meant to *just* be a nonprofit building community both online and locally. The impetus behind my original idea was to remind girls everywhere of their innate worth. I wanted to encourage girls that they absolutely posses the power to pursue their purpose, to create magic, to chase down their passion-filled dreams, to ignite change, to inspire the world, and to shine so bright that people couldn't possibly take their eyes off them.

My only real goal with I AM THAT GIRL was to remind *you* that you're awesome and to JUST BE YOU. Because, my dear, if you haven't been told today, you are more than enough.

RESOURCES

CHAPTER 1: BE A PASSIONISTA

Eve Ensler, *The Vagina Monologues.* Paperback edition published by Villard, December 2007.

To check out Jackie Tohn's music and more visit www.jackietohn.com. I particularly love her song and video for "Got It In Me." Breezy, beautiful, and inspirational too!

CHAPTER 2: BE FIRST

Julie Shannan is the deputy director of an awesome organization called Girlstart that educates and empowers K–12 girls in science, technology, engineering, and math. Visit their website at www.girlstart.com to see what they're up to.

The Julia Roberts/Richard Gere movie *Runaway Bride* illustrates perfectly the dangers of living the life that others design for you (well, it's the Hollywood version of those dangers, but you get the point). I particularly love the scene in which Julia's character samples a counter full of eggs after she realizes she's so out of touch with herself that she doesn't even know what type of eggs she likes. It's a happily ever after rom-com to be sure, but there's a useful message at its heart. Enjoy!

Gina Rudan wrote a tremendous book in 2011 called *Practical Genius: The Real Smarts You Need to Get Your Talents and Passions Working for*

You. To see what else Gina has to say about how to fuel your genius, hop over to her website at www.practicalgenius.com.

Leon Neyfakh, "The Power of Lonely: What We Do Better Without Other People Around," *Boston Globe*, March 6, 2011.

I found Neyfakh's article through a March 23, 2011, post titled "The Hard Facts: The Benefits of Alone Time" on Rachel Bertsche's MWF Seeking BFF blog (www.mwfseekingbff.com). Rachel posts lots of interesting stuff there—check out Research Wednesdays!—and has written a great book by the same name. Thanks, Rachel.

CHAPTER 3: BE HARD-CORE

Gretchin Rubin, bestselling author of *The Happiness Project* and *Happier at Home*, recommends a strategy called "suffer for fifteen minutes" for tackling big projects. Follow this URL to find Gretchin's May 17, 2011, blog post and video: www.happiness-project.com/happiness_project/2011/05/sufferfor-fifteen-minutes.

CHAPTER 4: BE UNPOPULAR

Hop over to YouTube to check out Remi Nicole's music video for her song "What Is Your Dream": www.youtube.com/watch?v=JTkwSL1jWv8.

CHAPTER 5: BE BOLD

Sheryl Sandberg, "Why We Have Too Few Women Leaders," given at TED-Women, December 2010. Follow this URL to find Sheryl's excellent video on the TED.com website: www.ted.com/talks/sheryl_sandberg_why_we_have_too_few_women_leaders.html

Three of my favorite boys and good friends created a non-profit working to end the longest-running war in Uganda and to free the children soldiers under the rebel leader, Joseph Kony. Check them out at www.invisiblechildren.com.

Adam Braun is one of the most inspiring people I know, as is his life story. Check out Pencils of Promise at www.pencilsofpromise.org if you have a heart for kids and education.

For those of you passionate about third world countries and providing villages with clean drinking water, learn more about my friend Scott Harrison and Charity Water at www.charitywater.com.

Penny Abeywardena heads up the Girls and Women Program at the Clinton Global Initiative. Check out their site at www.clintonglobal initiative.org to learn more about the many initiatives the foundation has started and how you can get involved.

My friend and fellow sports nut Yogi Roth is always up to something fun and inspirational. Check out what he's up to now at www.yogiroth.com and read more about his thrilling life and career in his book, *From PA to LA*. Published in paperback by KMD in September 2010.

CHAPTER 6: BE RESILIENT

If you've never seen Pixar's 2003 short film *Boundin'* check it out. Created and performed by animator Bud Luckey, it's a great pick-me-up when you're feeling discouraged (when you "have a pink kink in your think") or just want to smile.

CHAPTER 7: BE A SPONGE

Nicholas D. Kristof and Sheryl WuDunn, *Half the Sky: Turning Oppression into Opportunity for Women Worldwide*. Published in paperback by Vintage in June 2010.

Seth Matlins, my mentor and friend, started the cool and inspirational website www.feelmorebetter.com with his wife Eva. They're "on a mission to make the world an easier place for women and girls to be happier." Pretty amazing stuff.

CHAPTER 8: BE OF SERVICE

Brené Brown, "The Power of Vulnerability," given at TedxHouston, June 2010. Follow this URL to find Brené's funny and inspiring video on the TED.com website: www.ted.com/talks/lang/en/brene_brown_on_vulner ability.html.

EVEN MORE

VIDEOS

Click on the I AM THAT GIRL YouTube channel (www.youtube.com/iamthatgirl) for tons of awesome, inspiring, entertaining, hysterical, and insightful videos. I've added a short list here of the videos that I particularly love.

A Pep Talk from Kid President to YOU:
www.youtube.com/watch?v=l-gQLqv9f4o

Jessica's "Daily Affirmation":
www.youtube.com/watch?v=qR3rKokZFkg

The Finish Line:
www.youtube.com/watch?v=OrTtDxd-4iY

Simon Sinek's TED talk called "How Great Leaders Inspire Action":
www.ted.com/talks/simon_sinek_how_great_leaders_inspire_action.html

Eve Ensler's TED talk called "Embrace Your Inner Girl":
www.ted.com/talks/eve_ensler_embrace_your_inner_girl.html

Aimee Mullins' TED talk called "It's Not Fair Having 12 Pairs of Legs":
www.ted.com/talks/aimee_mullins_prosthetic_aesthetics.html

Dove Evolution:
www.youtube.com/watch?v=iYhCnojf46U&list=PL3CA7E13F6BD2AB02&index=8

Nike Women, "Keep Up" with Sofia Boutella:
www.youtube.com/watch?v=gguOffpsImU&list=PL3CA7E13F6BD2AB02&index=13

Bethany Hamilton:
www.youtube.com/watch?v=MWeOjBCi3c4&feature=player_embedded

The Girl Who Silenced the World for 5 Minutes:
www.youtube.com/watch?v=TQmz6Rbpnuo&list=PL36C38C120DA9E059&index=19

"I Will Wait for You" by poet Janette…IKZ
www.youtube.com/watch?v=igCj3jsbcqs&list=PL36C38C120DA9E059&index=7

Flawz by Caitlin Crosby
www.youtube.com/watch?v=R_PpRpYME10

"Are you Happy Now?" Music video by Megan and Liz
www.youtube.com/watch?v=Lq3iagZzloU

The Girl Effect
www.youtube.com/watch?v=WIvmE4_KMNw

BOOKS

Some of my favorite books at the moment. The list is endless, but a few I'd recommend at this moment.

Eat, Pray, Love: One Woman's Search for Everything Across Italy, India, and Indonesia by Elizabeth Gilbert

Practical Genius: The Real Smarts You Need to Get Your Talents and Passions Working for You by Gina Rudan

What Do You Want to Do Before You Die? by The Buried Life, Ben Nemtin, Dave Lingwood, Duncan Penn, and Jonnie Penn

DOCUMENTARIES

I'm a huge fan of documentaries that are able to highlight a problem and give us hope that change is possible. Below are a few documentaries on body image, the current state of bullying, our educational system, the importance of what we're consuming, and the reality of living in a Facebook era.

The Bully Project	*Miss Representation*
Catfish	*Waiting for Superman*
Food Inc.	

ORGANIZATIONS

Below is a list of organizations that my friends founded and run. If you're looking to get involved in something, I'd strongly suggest googling these and taking some time to find a good fit. They are always looking for interns, ambassadors, donations, and support.

30 Project	Mama Hope
Charity Water	Movember
F Cancer	Pencils of Promise
Fallen Whistles	The Sold Project
FEED	The Somaly Mam Foundation
Friends of TOMS	Students of the World
Girl Talk	The Trevor Project
I AM THAT GIRL	The United Nations Foundation, Girl Up
Invisible Children	To Write Love on Her Arms
The Kind Campaign	

MORE INCREDIBLE STORIES FROM INCREDIBLE WOMEN

ON RADICAL SELF-LOVE BY FAY WOLF (Singer-Songwriter, Actor, Professional Organizer): I didn't always love myself. This is a common thing, I think. But here's what's worse: I didn't *know* I didn't love myself.

The summer I turned twenty, life was pretty darn swell. I was heading into my junior year at a top-notch acting school and was one of the few kids in my class not to be put on "warning," which felt like I was being deemed a great artist; I was starting to get the idea that people might actually find me physically attractive; my friends were the coolest (I'm still close with so many of them); and my classmates and I were about to spend an awesome semester in London.

And yet I started to crumble. For no reason. Or what looked a lot like no reason. I would find myself behind closed doors panicky and often numb, weepy about nothing in particular and wanting to punch walls (...and actually punching walls). A dear friend lent me a copy of *Prozac Nation*, and I decided I was depressed. And the thing is ... I *was*. After returning from London, I started a regimen of antidepressants. Ten years later, I stopped taking them.

They helped, they *definitely* helped. But after a decade, it felt like I was hiding something. From myself.

My eventual theory for why I'd felt shitty all the time despite everyday life being near-perfect? **Lack-of-Self-Worth *Buildup*.**

My solution for trying to cure it—without the meds? **The Pursuit of Self-Love.**

I secretly loathed and silently blamed so many parts of myself—*and I had no idea I was doing it.* I could write 5,000 words about how I uncovered this all-important gem of a solution (practicing meditation and beginning a now-second-skin esoteric journey has had a lot to do with it), but for the purposes of our time together, what's important is that I finally did.

It's a scary f-ing road being naked to what's really going on, and my dark days are shockingly darker without the pharmaceutical blankets. But more and more, I'm deeply happier because I believe I belong here. I deserve to be on this planet, in dark times and light. I *get* to be on this planet. I get to cultivate love and give it away. (Plus, people liking you is a lot more exciting when you like yourself.)

Even better news: We get to help each other through it all!

Teachers and soul-friends give me courage. Neighborhood saunters give me courage. Being nice to someone who's being an asshole gives me courage. (And sometimes that's a tough nut—I ain't perfect.) Dogs and precocious children give me courage. Contortionists give me courage. My older-than-me nephew gives me courage. My sad songs give me happy courage. And my unique truths (biracial, bisexual, half-Jewish, high metabolism, organized artist) give me some kind of crazy spin on all of it.

Yes, my depression is a longer story. Yes, it's different for everyone. Yes, there are chemicals in our brains that might make it better or worse. Yes, my diet played a part. Yes, sure, yes and okay yes. But it's been four years since I lifted off those blankets, and I know in my gut that it's my heart for the win. I have a need for this precious organ to be *aware,* to turn inward and upward and inside of itself and upside down and all around and reflect back the *deepest love* to the body that it's beating in.

Perhaps you do, too.

ON BEING A WORKING MOTHER BY ELIZABETH GORE (Resident Entrepreneur, the United Nations Foundation): I always knew I would be a working mother. The United Nations has been my career path for just short of a decade. I have had the opportunity to travel all over the world, meet amazing people, and participate in epic adventures. During one of those adventures— the Peace Corps in Bolivia—I met the love of my life, my husband Jimmy. It was then that I figured out that some adventures are better shared; in fact these days the only adventures I want to be on are the ones I can share. Little did I know that the greatest adventure I would ever have would be to become a mommy. A few years ago, I climbed Mt. Kilimanjaro to raise awareness for the global clean water crisis. When I reached 19,400 feet I decided it was time to have a baby. A couple of years later, here comes a seven-pound ball of extreme joy. My daughter has the joint adventurous spirit of both her parents. She is fourteen months old and has already been on over thirty flights with her parents. So, yes, I always knew I would be a working mother, but I didn't know my answer to the work/ life balance would be the following. When I am asked how I give time to both my daughter and my career, the answer is simple—it is not a debate; my daughter is number one. If my career has to suffer because of this, so be it. My job is to give mothers a voice globally as they fight malaria, abuse, and disparity, but all of us mothers want what is best for our kids, and the number one thing they need is to feel loved and secure with their folks. I am glad to say that my job is stronger than ever, but the adventures at home are just as awesome as those in Africa. I will continue to climb the global career ladder, but the best part of my life is walking in at the end of the day and hearing, "MAMA!!"

ON LEARNING TO TRUST YOURSELF BY TAWNEY BEVACQUA (Explorer): I was in love with him from the first moment I saw him, but felt very strongly that he should never find out. I just wanted him in my life and liked the thought of knowing IF it ever grew into something more, we were friends first. I was in my early twenties and learning heaps about who I was, what I wanted, and the power of choice. I was becoming a woman (a powerful and sometimes fragile seat to fill), I wanted happiness and stability, and I started to explore the idea that if I came across hurdles in my life, I have a choice to go over them or turn back. I learned about taking responsibility for any broken relationships in my life. A childhood friend, for example, got really wild and engaged in activities that I thought were dangerous and irresponsible. It was easy for me to say she has "changed" or she did this or that to upset me. But what if I didn't think of it that way? What if I saw her as the exact same person who was taking whatever path she needed to take to become the best *she* she could be? This idea created space for understanding, forgiveness, unconditional love, that is, going over the hurdle instead of turning back.

After a year of friendship, this guy found out about my little love-filled secret (which it turned out he had as well) and our dreamy relationship began. I use the word *dreamy* because while it was like a two-year-long honeymoon, the reality was there were holes that I tried to fill with love and innocence. Romantic relationships always present hurdles. We create stories or have old wounds that lead us to feelings of mistrust, insecurity, jealousy, etc. He wasn't your typical womanizer. He wasn't the go out, party, and hook up type. He was the introverted artist version of a womanizer. There were muses, email exchanges, and gifts he would receive in the mail so perfectly wrapped and sealed with hope. These relationships only existed in words. "There's nothing to worry about," I'd tell myself. I wanted to trust, I wanted to take responsibility for any feelings of jealously or concern, I wanted to JUMP OVER THE HURDLE!!!!!

His friends started to open up to me about how they felt like he was never really around for them, his closest friends didn't even know if they were really friends at all. He didn't have a great relationship with his family and wasn't great to my family. I started to understand that despite his fame and fortune there was something about his career that kept him from being the person he wanted to be. I wanted to forgive the choices he had made, I wanted to JUMP OVER THE HURDLE!!!!

There were moments when he'd put his heart in my hands and open up about his desires to be a great friend, son, and eventually husband and dad. I was there with open arms choosing to trust and support his path to being the best *he* he could be. I wanted to try loving unconditionally, and he was the perfect person.

So what's wrong with taking responsibility, forgiveness, and unconditional love? Nothing! Then what went wrong?

You know that feeling you have deep in your stomach that can sometimes feel like fear? That feeling is called intuition, and we women have it much stronger than most of us realize. I was ignoring my intuition, and my relationship eventually led to heartbreak. It was easy to blame him for breaking my heart, but the truth was I let it break and because of it I lost trust in myself.

After many tears my heart healed and I saw that I needed that relationship to truly understand my powerful intuition, our powerful intuition. If I could turn back time, I wouldn't take back any of the unconditional love. I was honoring my partner, but I wasn't honoring myself. I was brushing my feelings off, knowing I had a lot to learn about relationships. What I needed to learn was "that knowing" that's inside of all of us. I wasn't jumping the hurdles, I was cheating and walking around them. Decisions are driven by emotion so I don't let that "gut feeling" run the show, but I've learned not to ignore it either. All feelings are valid whether I'm creating them out of fear or I've manifested evidence to prove them. Whether they're "good" feelings or "bad" feelings they're MINE, all MINE.

Step 1. Taking responsibility for feelings, check.

Step 2. Communicate these feelings, no matter how silly they feel, in relationships that they might affect. Do not mask any feelings!

Step 2 is what I learned from that dreamy relationship. The stronger the love, the stronger the emotion; all those tears eventually shifted my mistrust in myself to a deep trust in myself. That trust has probably been the biggest turning point, or hurdle I guess I should say, in becoming the woman I am today.

Let the learning continue.

ON VULNERABILITY BY ELIZABETH KOTT (Fashion Entrepreneur and Founder of ClosetRich.com):

Dear Vulnerable Self,

I realize I owe you a bit of an explanation, as I am painfully aware of how long it has been since we last touched base. You might suspect I've been ignoring you … and you would be correct. You see, as a twenty-something running her own business and working constantly to achieve her goals, I just can't be seen associating with you, and your fear-acknowledging, emotional, self-assessing attributes.

I know you must be thinking, "How could she just pretend I DON'T exist? We have had a lifelong relationship!" And yes, I agree at times, we were close, at other times our relationship was nothing short of all-consuming and downright exhausting.

I'll always remember when you first became a part of my life—sixth grade—girls at school had me coming home every day in tears. Thankfully, you helped turn those tears into a valued lesson of empathy.

You followed me on to high school, where I begrudgingly accepted you as part of my life. You would always seem to pop up at times of anguish (loved ones lost, first love lost, friendships lost … virginity lost). All pinnacle moments of my adolescence that brought about the most necessary of lessons and solidification of ideals.

We hung out on and off in college—remember when I decided to take a semester off and transfer schools? You dominated THAT convo with mom and dad. Let's not forget it was you who led me toward my decision to study abroad … twice. It was the fear that you came with that led me to promise myself that fear would never dictate a decision in my life. Thus, I needed you, Vulnerability, to really push me to go away to those foreign places. You stayed with me in my travels, allowing me to grow and evolve with each uncharted step.

After college, you really wanted to remain close, but I just wasn't having it, I was far too busy starting my career—all-consumed with my other relationships to motivation, determination, hustle, and ego. With the help of these friends, I scored my dream job ... and subsequently lost it. This loss was the pivotal happening in my life that brought you back to me, changed our relationship from that of acquaintances to partners. Humbled, jobless, and lost, I found security and strength in you. Dear Vulnerability, you forced me to look at who I truly was without any exterior affiliations. In result, I was introduced to the coolest chick I know ... me. Thanks to the divine reacquaintance you facilitated, I was able to realize exactly what I didn't want and in turn exactly what I did want from my life.

Although you notoriously come about in congruence with life's curve balls, when I allow you to do your thing, you bring about an emotional clarity that is incomparable. So here I am, just a girl, writing an open letter in a badass book to one of the most valuable players in her life. Laying it on the table for all to see, that it's okay for me to be in touch with my vulnerabilities. In fact, Vulnerability, you are my friend.

With Strength,

Elizabeth S. Kott

ON LEARNING NOT TO FIT BY ROBIN JONES (Program Compliance Lead, Charity Water): When I was younger I was introduced to a type of people who didn't love their lives so much as to shrink from death. As international aid workers they spent their lives rushing into situations from which others were desperately trying to get out. That was something I wanted to identify with, and from age fourteen, I spent the next decade making decisions that would get me there.

But when I first got to the field in a professional sense at twenty-four, I quickly got disillusioned. Yes, some of these kinds of people existed, but a much larger proportion of them were slightly bitter expats who drove around in air-conditioned SUVs all day, burned out from their two-year assignments in regions plagued by corruption, governmental, social, and religious barriers.

Working in the development sector eventually landed me in New York City (from a hospital ship in West Africa to charity: water, etc.). In addition to the challenges above, very few things are stable or constant out here. People sprint in and out of your life, storefronts change ownership on a monthly basis, jobs that would be stable anywhere else are uncertain here due to the rapid pace and scale of this city. Ideas are thrown up and shot down with such rapidity that it's not even offensive. Seasons, fashions, music, people—the only constant seems to be constant change.

When you're living in New York City, you're in the pit. If you aren't comfortable with presenting yourself in a certain format, to a certain society, you are labeled as shy. And perhaps you are. Or perhaps the labels and formats and pitches are so intensely confining that it feels dishonest or betraying to your personality to play along. I keep showing up, I keep trying, but I often keep feeling alienated. And I can't be convinced that it's because I'm inferior in any way. For me my quietness comes from a place of not knowing you. How can I know you from a string of impressive facts and labels and other names that you might be associated with? I need to see the context of someone's life, their responses and interactions, the compounded observations from multiple conversations. I want to argue and discuss or alternately just say nothing but at that point understand where you're coming from due to a mere flicker of an eye or discreet nod of the head. And so I often just sit here quietly and observe or blend in. And yet I'm silently breaking to be known and to be heard and to be recognized in the same way.

It's so interesting, scary even, how people feed off of each other. Attitude breeds attitude, and perspective breeds perspective. Choose wisely who you surround yourself with. I need to be around people, real people. Real people balance you out. Remember this. As an introvert in this city I have to fight not to check out from people.

And furthermore, why do I keep getting surrounded by the spotlight, witty, polished, successful, influential people of this world? That's not me.

I've been racing around for so many years now that I think I've forgotten why I'm in this city, on this career path, in the first place. I take care of people. I'm drawn to it, it's in my makeup. I feel compelled, or felt compelled. Yes, there's an intellectual need I have that must be fulfilled as well—business, finance, theory, and writing. But at its heart, my strength in life is being compelled to take care of people, be it on a global scale, in my immediate circle, family, etc. My strength is in my character, in my heart. And this isn't something valued as a strength in this city. And so I've adapted and fit in here. I've allowed myself to not even recognize my strength. But people see through sometimes, typically seeing the characteristics that I find insulting—*sweet, quiet, shy*. But perhaps if I'd let go and let the full thing shine, these would make more sense. Let go, let go. Hills beyond hills. No need to fit neatly into the preset molds of this city, this culture, this field.

ACKNOWLEDGMENTS

Where do I begin? I've been so poured into by so many people, I'm afraid that I will leave someone out. So the following is but a few of the miracles who I've been gifted with in my lifetime.

Mom, Dad, and Jane—Thank you for raising me to actually believe that anything is possible. You gave me the greatest gift any parents could give, the courage to dream. I owe that to all of you.

Jess, Nathan, Josh, Zeke, and Scott—After being given such incredible parents it is icing on the cake to have you too, the best siblings a girl could ever ask for (including the wives who put up with you! Thank you Suz, Kell, and Amanda! Ha ha). Thank you for being my biggest fans.

BBB—Thank you for teaching me how to love again and how to be loved. You are my rock, and I couldn't and wouldn't want to do life without you. To all the endless adventures that await us … I love YOU with all MY heart. xo

Frannie, Blake, Emmy, and Illy—The four best friends a girl could ask for, you are the legs to my chair, and I couldn't function without a single one of you. From my childhood to my adult years, you have been the "family" I got to choose.

Dever, Ara, Seth, and Hance—You are the BOD of my LIFE. Thank you for the endless coffees, dinners, hangout sessions where you helped guide me to my best version.

Yogs, Erin, Robol, Bobby, Shan, Linds, KB, Susie, Tohn, Case, Soph, Jenny, Josie, Tam, Tawney, Jake, Ros, Prof. Smith, Dick, Slaby, Lauren, Fatter, Britt, Bec, Sara, Dan, E Gore, Adam, Wado, Mikey, and my whole Cali crew—If you are in fact judged by the company you keep, I am officially a badass. You enrich my life in ways you will never know.

The Summit Crew, all my homies at Summit Series, and all the amazing people I have met because of the awesome events bringing together great people, from Aspen to Eden—I love you guys.

Dr. Carlos—my second dad, thank you for pouring such unconditional love into me and teaching me that I am in fact "enough." You gave me my heart back and I will forever be grateful.

Momma G—I couldn't have written this book without the "Greener Cottage." Thanks for being my "home away from home," for treating me as your own, and for introducing me to all my loved ones in Sonoma.

Eve Ensler—Thank you for the initial spark that lit my fire. I do what I do because you lead the way.

I AM THAT GIRL—Thank you for being better than anything I could have ever imagined, to all the girls who helped build you (Kate, Morgan, all our chapter leaders, and all our interns!). I cannot imagine the number of girls you will inspire in the future, and I'm so grateful to be a part of something so much bigger than me.

All the women who contributed—You're my dearest friends. God, you rock my socks off and it just keeps getting better. Thanks for the ride.

Grandma and Granddaddy—I know you're always there with me, and I hope I've made you proud. I miss you both terribly.

Ashleigh—You continue to be a light unto my path, and I cannot wait to one day meet again, to lie on the warm rock wall of Barton Springs and giggle about life, about love, and about all the adventures we have left to do together.

Adrienne—Thank you for making this book make sense (Ha ha!), for your endless and beautiful edits, the passion you poured into this book, and all the future projects we have together.

Karen—Thank you for taking a leap of faith with me and giving my writing heart wings.

Me—You did it. I'm so proud of you girl, and I love you.

To all the women I've met along my adventure and to you, the readers—I love you all. There are no words to describe who you are and who you have been in my life. All I know is that I am who I am because you all dared to love me so fiercely, to support me and to love me so unconditionally. This book is dedicated to all of you for it has pieces of you sprinkled throughout its pages, just as I have sparkles of each of you in me.

SOME MORE ABOUT ME, ALEXIS JONES

I've worked in the entertainment industry for the past ten years (hosted a TV show on the Red Carpet for three years, worked at Fox Sports and ESPN, was a contestant on the CBS show *Survivor*, hosted an interview show called *The Society*, and was cast as a confidence coach for MTV's *MADE*. I completed my undergrad and master's degrees at the University of Southern California and founded I AM THAT GIRL, a nonprofit inspiring girls to think for themselves, to speak their truth, and to leave this world (even a little bit) better than when they found it.

But what you really need to know about me that you can't Google is I grew up in Austin with four older brothers and a baby sister. I am a hopeless romantic, bona fide adventure junky, a (self-proclaimed) food connoisseur; I love day-naps; and I am most passionate about reminding people how awesome they are. Italian is my favorite type of food, I cry at cheesy romantic comedies, and I was a professional hip-hop dancer in another lifetime. This book is hands down my greatest professional accomplishment.

In spite of all the pressure to "grow up," I am most proud of having maintained a childlike wonder for the magic that surrounds us all. My dad is the best man I know, and my mom is my hero. I live to dream, have yet to lose in air hockey, and am a terrible speller. I believe in the possibility that real change *is* possible, and it only takes everything you got. I also won the Showcase Showdown on the *Price Is Right*, have unfathomable parking karma, survived thirty-three days on a deserted island, and consider myself a professional hugger.

I AM THAT GIRL

If you'd like to get involved with I AM THAT GIRL or start a chapter in your town, please visit www.iamthatgirl.com for more information and other ways to join our mission and our movement.